PENGUIN BOOKS
THE BRITISH EMPIRICISTS

Stephen Priest· was born in Oxford in 1954. He studied philosophy at the University of Cambridge and is a lecturer in the Department of Philosophy at the University of Edinburgh. During 1977 he worked in the Press and Information Department of the Council of Europe, Strasbourg, and in 1986 was a Fellow in Philosophy and Public Affairs at the Salzburg Seminar in American Studies. He has held lectureships in philosophy at the universities of Manchester, Bradford and Leeds. Stephen Priest is the editor of *Hegel's Critique of Kant* (1987) and author of *Theories of the Mind*, forthcoming in Penguin.

D1120320

Stephen Priest

THE
BRITISH
EMPIRICISTS

HOBBES TO AYER

PENGUIN BOOKS

PENGUIN BOOKS

Published by the Penguin Group
27 Wrights Lane, London w8 5tz, England
Viking Penguin Inc., 40 West 23rd Street, New York, New York 10010, USA
Penguin Books Australia Ltd, Ringwood, Victoria, Australia
Penguin Books Canada Ltd, 2801 John Street, Markham, Ontario, Canada l3r 1b4
Penguin Books (NZ) Ltd, 182–190 Wairau Road, Auckland 10, New Zealand

Penguin Books Ltd, Registered Offices: Harmondsworth, Middlesex, England

First published 1990
1 3 5 7 9 10 8 6 4 2

Filmset in 10 on 12pt Baskerville

Made and printed in Great Britain by
Cox & Wyman Ltd, Reading

In memory of my father,
Arthur Priest MBE, MA (Oxon.)
(1921–1986)

CONTENTS

Contents

PREFACE

What exists? Is there anything beyond experience? If so, can we know it? What are minds? What are physical objects? Am I a physical object? Is there free will? Do numbers exist? If so, what are they? Are moral questions merely matters of subjective opinion or are some things right and some things wrong? Why should we obey the state? Are there limits to our knowledge – things we could *never* know? If so, can we know that?

Philosophy is about philosophical problems and nothing else. British empiricists have always understood this well and I have presented their ideas as attempts to solve problems about minds, language, physical objects, freedom, emotions, science, reason, numbers, causation, ethics, politics, and many other subjects.

Philosophical problems lie in the basement of commonsense and every intellectual inquiry. Often they go unnoticed for years or even centuries as some way of living or some pattern of explanation or criticism proceeds with unexamined assumptions. Then suddenly it is realized that the procedure requires people to be causally determined, or free; or it requires matter to exist, or minds; or it presupposes the existence of the past or remote events in space-time, or meaningful language, or a society, or the state, or the existence of God. Notions like these are taken for granted as the unquestioned tools and assumptions of other intellectual disciplines and commonsense. Philosophy calls them into question. Where other subjects and everyday life continue with more and more explanations, more and more information, more and more criticism, philosophy invites us to halt abruptly and ask what we are assuming. Other subjects build higher and ever more complex buildings. Philosophy takes us down to the basement to examine the foundations. There sometimes we find God, sometimes matter, sometimes societies, sometimes natural laws. Commonsense is one building among the others.

This book is an introduction to the approaches to philosophical problems of a group of philosophers with enough in common to be called 'the British Empiricists'. As we shall see, on some of the problems they agree, on others they disagree violently. I shall be well satisfied if the reader unearths some unquestioned philosophical assumptions from his or her own basement. We all have them.

The history of ideas is also a fundamentally important subject. There are few things more educative than the attempt to suspend one's own beliefs and imaginatively to enter the perceptions and values of alternative mentalities. As historians we do this all the better if we understand the social, political and economic climate in which a philosopher wrote, as well as the parental and educative influences on that philosopher. I have therefore opened each chapter with a short historical introduction to the empiricist concerned. Of course these sections should not be confused with philosophy; philosophical problem-solving being always and everywhere independent of biography. Because this is a philosophy book I have not entered into the interesting historical question of whether there is a clear distinction between rationalist and empiricist philosophers. There is clearly a distinction between rationalism and empiricism because rationalism is the view that the intellect is the best guide to the nature of reality, while empiricism is the view that experience is the best guide to the nature of reality.

I have had to omit some British empiricists, notably Jeremy Bentham and G. E. Moore, for reasons of space. I should also have liked to include Francis Bacon and Isaac Newton, even though they are natural scientists first and philosophers second. Newton is particularly important because so many assumptions in contemporary Anglo-American philosophy are Newtonian, and quite possibly false. However, I am convinced I have included the greatest of the British empiricists and I have tried to do some justice to their political theory as well as their philosophy.

I hope that it will be possible to use the book in two ways: firstly, to study a problem area, for instance the nature of matter, by reading the relevant sub-section within each chapter; secondly, to find out what one of the empiricists thought on a range of problems by reading a whole chapter. In the first method the reader studies, say, what Locke, Hume and Russell thought on causation. In the second method the reader studies, say, Mill on everything from language to politics. Both approaches are useful in philosophy. The first gives an appreciation of the peculiarly intractable nature of philosophical problems, which the serious student of the subject needs. The best way to this appreciation is to read radically different thoughts on the same topics: seemingly equally plausible arguments for mutually inconsistent conclusions. The second method enables us to appreciate how an attempt to solve one problem may help to solve another. What we think causation is, for example, will help to shape our views on freedom and determinism. Whether we believe that knowledge exists will govern our views on the possibility of moral knowledge. What we think physical objects are will influence our views on perception, and so on. Philosophical problems are conceptually and argumentatively interrelated in many complex ways.

I am most grateful to Professor Ted Honderich of University College, London and to Jonathan Riley of Penguin Books for their suggestion that I write this book. I thank my colleagues in the Department of Philosophy at the University of Edinburgh for providing a congenial and stimulating environment in which to think, talk and write and I also thank Professor Graham Bird for several discussions about empiricism. In so far as this book is an empirical object and not just a rational object, I am further indebted to Peggy Priest and Lynn Evans.

Department of Philosophy   Stephen Priest
David Hume Tower
University of Edinburgh
October 1989

ABBREVIATIONS

References after quotations in the text are to page numbers unless otherwise stated below.

D   David Hume, *Dialogues Concerning Natural Religion*, edited and introduced by Henry D. Aiken (Hafner Press, New York, 1975).

E   John Locke, *An Essay Concerning Human Understanding*, abridged and edited by A. S. Pringle-Pattison (Oxford University Press, Oxford, 1964). References are to book, chapter and paragraph.

E1   David Hume, 'An Enquiry Concerning Human Understanding', in L. A. Selby-Bigge and P. H. Nidditch (eds.), *Hume's Enquiries* (Oxford University Press, Oxford, 1975). References are to section and paragraph.

E2   David Hume, 'An Enquiry Concerning the Principles of Morals', in Selby-Bigge and Nidditch, op. cit. References are to section and paragraph.

HP   Bertrand Russell, *A History of Western Philosophy* (George Allen & Unwin, London, 1948).

IMP   Bertrand Russell, *Introduction to Mathematical Philosophy* (George Allen & Unwin, London, 1920).

IMT   Bertrand Russell, *An Inquiry into Meaning and Truth* (Penguin Books, Harmondsworth, 1973).

L   Thomas Hobbes, *Leviathan*, edited with an introduction by C. B. Macpherson (Penguin Books, Harmondsworth, 1985).

LA   David Pears (ed.), *Russell's Logical Atomism* (Collins, London, 1972).

LTL   A. J. Ayer, *Language, Truth and Logic* (2nd ed., Penguin Books, Harmondsworth, 1976).

NC   Bertrand Russell, *Why I am not a Christian* (George Allen & Unwin, London, 1977).

OL   John Stuart Mill, 'On Liberty', in John Stuart Mill, *Utilitarianism*, edited and introduced by Mary Warnock (Collins, London, 1973).

OP   Bertrand Russell, *An Outline of Philosophy* (George Allen & Unwin, London, 1970).

P   George Berkeley, *The Principles of Human Knowledge with Other Writings*, edited and introduced by G. J. Warnock (Collins, London, 1977).

PM   Bertrand Russell, *The Principles of Mathematics* (George Allen & Unwin, London, 1942).

PP   Bertrand Russell, *The Problems of Philosophy* (Oxford University Press, Oxford, 1952).

SL   John Stuart Mill, *A System of Logic, Ratiocinative and Inductive* (2 vols., Longmans, Green, London, 1879). References are to volume and page.

T   David Hume, *A Treatise of Human Nature*, edited by L. A. Selby-Bigge (Oxford University Press, Oxford, 1951). References are to book, part and section.

2T   'The Second Treatise of Government', in John Locke, *Two Treatises of Government*, edited and introduced by Peter Laslett (New American Library, New York, 1963).

U   John Stuart Mill, *Utilitarianism*, edited and introduced by Mary Warnock (Collins, London, 1973).

HOBBES

1 HOBBES IN HISTORY

Hobbes's philosophy is an expression of and an intervention in two seventeenth-century revolutions, one political, the other intellectual. The political revolution was the curtailing of absolute monarchy by rising professional and monied classes through the representative institutions of parliamentary democracy. The intellectual revolution was the abolition of the theocentric and Aristotelian world-picture of the Middle Ages by the new natural sciences with their reliance on experiment, and the rational exercise of the individual intellect. In the second of these revolutions Hobbes was with the revolutionaries; in the first, he was with the counter-revolutionaries.[1]

His scientific materialism contains the radical view that everything that exists is physical, and this is as opposed to the God and the soul of the medievals as it is to the mind–body dualism of his correspondent, Descartes.[2] Hobbes insisted that the observations and thoughts of the inquirer were to be relied upon always and everywhere, rather than the two great authorities of Western Christendom – Aristotle and the Pope. In this respect Hobbes, like Bacon, was a pioneer of scientific method.[3]

His political theory is motivated by a profound fear of anarchy and civil war; a fear that haunted most of Hobbes's thinking contemporaries. It is sometimes incorrectly maintained that Hobbes's insistence on a strong state as guarantor of the security of the citizen, at the expense of the latter's liberty, was not a consequence of anarchic political events in Hobbes's lifetime. The ground for this claim is that the views in *Leviathan* were formulated long before its publication in 1651, and even before the outbreak of the English Civil War in 1642.[4] In fact Hobbes had no need of the English experience of civil war to know and fear an anarchic condition of society without an effective state. 'Thirty Years War' implies a naïve classification of the series of revolts and conflicts which began in Europe before 1618 and ended long after 1648.[5] Nevertheless, propertied and educated Englishmen were as fearful of the destruction wrought by the continental conflicts as were their descendants a century and a half later during the years of the export of the French Revolution. Hobbes was no exception. *Leviathan* was written to answer a desperate need for security and it was because that need was perceived as so real after 1651 that the book proved immediately influential. Historians and philosophers who think of Hobbes as uninfluenced by anarchy and war take a narrow, England-centred view of the matter. Hobbes was a European with a European experience.

Even though Hobbes was a political conservative and a scientific materialist, it would be historically anachronistic, or out of tune with Hobbes's conception of his own project, to regard these two sides of his philosophy as utterly separable. Although *Leviathan* contains the separate chapters 'Of Man' and 'Of Commonwealth', Hobbes thought of his political theory as continuous with his materialism. His philosophical project was the production of a unified science, in which appropriate political institutions would be deduced from facts about human nature which, in turn, would be deduced from facts about the nature of the universe. His model for this – as with the rationalists Descartes and Spinoza – was geometry. Geometry had four impressive features for many seventeenth-century intellectuals. Its results were certain, *a priori*, deducible from a few first principles and informative, that is, non-trivial. It seemed to Hobbes to provide a paradigm of what knowledge should consist in. His tripartite science of the universe, persons and politics would be geometrical in its method. It is interesting to note that the adoption of a geometrical method is consistent with Hobbes's thoroughgoing materialism. If materialism is true then everything is physical, but if everything is physical that means everything is spatial, and geometry is the mathematics of space. It follows that if materialism is right, we ought in principle to be able to have geometrical knowledge of anything. Even things that seem *prima*

facie non-physical – like our own thoughts, or our political institutions – should be describable in sentences ultimately derived from
geometrical premises.

It would be historically anachronistic but true to call Hobbes a
'positivist'. The word is not a seventeenth-century one but it denotes
the view that every problem may be solved, in principle, using the
methods of the natural sciences. It follows from positivism that the
procedures of natural science may be appropriately extended to
explain persons and politics.

Hobbes himself did not draw our clear distinction between
philosophy and science. That distinction is Kantian, not seventeenth-century.[6] Rather, Hobbes's philosophy is the extension of
scientific method into the study of persons and politics.[7] Its scientific
and geometrical nature is clear in this passage:

By Philosophy, is understood the Knowledge acquired by Reasoning, from
the Manner of the Generation of any thing, to the Properties; or from the
Properties, to some possible Way of Generation of the same; to the end to
bee able to produce, as far as matter, and humane force permit, such
Effects, as humane life requireth. So the Geometrician, from the Construction of Figures, findeth out many Properties thereof; and from the Properties, new Ways of their Construction, by Reasoning.(L 682)

Who was Thomas Hobbes? Born in 1588, the year of the Spanish
Armada, he died in 1679, the nineteenth year of the reign of Charles
II. Thus Hobbes was a child in Elizabethan England, a teenager at
the time of the Gunpowder Plot (1604), in his fifties during the
English Civil War (1642–9), in his sixties during the Interregnum
(1649–60), seventy-two at the Restoration of the monarchy (1660)
and ninety-one when he died at the time of the Popish Plot (1679).
He lived during five regimes: those of Elizabeth I (1558–1603),
James I (1603–25), Charles I (1625–49), the Interregnum
(1649–60), and Charles II (1660–85).

Little is known of Hobbes's mother save that she was married to
the vicar of Westport, near Malmesbury in Gloucestershire. His
parents were poor so his early education was at his father's church,
but his wealthy uncle arranged for some private education at
Malmesbury school and later paid his fees at the then Magdalen
Hall, Oxford. Hobbes spent from his fourteenth to his nineteenth

year at Oxford. When he arrived he already had sufficient training
in the classics to have translated Euripides' *Medea* into Latin.
Oxford trained his mind in logic, and made him thoroughly
acquainted with the neo-Aristotelian philosophical orthodoxy. However, through his first employment, as private tutor to the son of the
scientist William Cavendish, Earl of Devonshire, he was exposed to
intellectual influences deeply subversive of that orthodoxy.

In 1610 Hobbes and young Cavendish travelled to France, where
they found Paris a ferment of political activity. Henry IV had just
been murdered by the insane Jesuit Ravaillac and many thought
that not just France but the whole of Europe would be plunged once
more into bloody, anarchic, politico-religious strife. Henry of
Navarre was revered as the monarch who had brought peace to the
Catholic–Huguenot conflict. He was himself a Huguenot. More
than this, Navarre had enforced militarily the rule of an absolute
monarchy over the warring French nobles who fought one another
as readily as they fought the central authorities. This political
turmoil would have had a profound impact on the sensitive 22-year-
old Hobbes. In the uneasily contained civil conflicts in France
Hobbes had already the model for the feared hand of every man
turned against every man of his later political theory.[8]

Hobbes and Cavendish travelled from Paris to Italy. There the
intellectual ferment matched the political ferment in France. Galileo
had just discovered the planet Neptune, not in a book of Aristotelian
cosmology but by the use of his own eyes and a piece of new
technology: a cylindrical tube with glass lenses which made distant
objects look larger.[9] Not only were the leading Italian intellectuals
engaged in something radically new to Hobbes, scientific practice,
the results of this scientific empiricism were available in books.
Hobbes read Kepler's pioneering work of 1607, *Astronomia Nova*.[10]

In the experience of Oxford, France and Italy the three main
components of Hobbes's philosophy were generated. Oxford gave
him his Aristotelian opponent, but also the rigour of mind to
challenge it.[11] France gave him respect for strong central authority
and the fear of political insecurity. Italy gave him scientific materialism. By his early twenties the main directions of Hobbes's thinking
were set.

On his return from Italy Cavendish introduced Hobbes to Francis

Bacon. [12] Bacon found in Hobbes a lively mind in tune with his own at a time when he was working on that masterpiece of seventeenth-century scientific empiricism, *Novum Organum* (1620). Hobbes nowhere acknowledges Bacon's influence, but the reasons for this are clear. Hobbes had already formulated the central themes of his philosophy before he met Bacon. In addition, Bacon and Hobbes were to be engaged in rather different projects. Bacon was what we should call a practising natural scientist rather than a philosopher. Bacon conducted experiments and used inductive methods. Hobbes was not a natural scientist in this sense. His philosophical project was to produce a unified science, which would exhibit the results of political studies as continuous with the study of human nature and the natural universe. To do this, a wholly inductive method would be inappropriate. We should not, then, conclude that Hobbes did not respect Bacon's work. On the contrary, we know from Aubrey that they spent many hours conversing on methodological matters, and Bacon liked Hobbes. [13]

During the 1620s Hobbes worked on the classics rather than philosophy and in 1628 published his translation of Thucydides. [14] His interests were politically motivated. The 1620s were a time of rapid deterioration in relations between king and Parliament that would issue in the Civil War of 1642–9. Hobbes would have viewed with apprehension the erosion of the royal prerogative by the growing powers of a representative assembly. Stability in France had, after all, been seen to be confirmed by the Estates General ceasing to meet after 1614. Thucydides was the classical author who maintained that the demise of Pericles and the rise of democracy accounted for the fall of Athens from political stability.

In 1628 old Cavendish died and Lady Cavendish sacked their son's tutor. Luckily Hobbes was able to find employment as tutor to the son of Sir Govase Clinton and, as in 1629, he took an earl's son to Europe. It was on this expedition that the famous incident occurred when Hobbes found Euclid's *Elements* open in a library in Geneva. Aubrey relates Hobbes's excitement at discovering necessary, informative conclusions flowing logically from self-evident premises. Whatever the reality of the incident, it was from this time that geometrical method became the model for Hobbes's ideal of a unified science of the universe, human nature, and politics. [15]

Hobbes's third visit to the Continent lasted from 1634 to 1637. This was most important for intellectual exchanges. He met Mersenne and Gassendi in Paris, and Galileo in Italy. The Cartesians not only respected empirical science but had the ideal of a unified geometrical philosophy. It may well be that Hobbes's idea of a single system of explanation predates 1634, but if so Hobbes's contacts, especially with Gassendi, would have confirmed it as his project.[16]

Hobbes returned to England in 1637, and soon afterwards rebellion broke out in Ireland and civil war in Scotland. Thinking, propertied people were aghast at the threat. In this climate Hobbes published *The Elements of Law* (1640). He had by then certainly decided upon the threefold structure of his system: 'Body', 'Man' and 'Citizen' – that is, the physical universe, human nature and politics. However, the need to write against growing political instability required that *The Elements of Law* be rushed into print with the section on 'Body' omitted.

In 1640 Hobbes fled to Paris. *The Elements of Law* would please neither royalists nor parliamentarians. It recommended strong government, not by divine right but to avoid anarchy. Nevertheless, Hobbes was tutor to the future Charles II in 1646–7, so it would be absurd to maintain that *The Elements of Law* offended those royalists who really mattered politically. However, it was during Hobbes's stay in Paris with Mersenne that he composed the famous *Objections* to Descartes's *Meditations*, and rewrote *The Elements of Law* as *De Cive* (1642), *De Corpore Politico* (1650) and *De Corpore* (1655). In 1648 Descartes and Hobbes met. Aubrey tells us that the meeting was amicable and founded on mutual respect, despite the acrimonious nature of some of the preceding correspondence. Hobbes thought Descartes hypocritical in publicly defending Catholic doctrines he privately thought false, and Descartes thought Hobbes's view of the state of nature too pessimistic. By this time Hobbes had already started work on *Leviathan*, which was published in 1651.

The aftermath of a revolution is a time of constitutional indecision. As in 1789–93 in France and in 1917 in Russia, in England in 1648–9 constitutional compromises had broken down. The king was executed and the monarchy abolished. Like Rousseau's *Social Contract* or Lenin's political tracts, Hobbes's *Leviathan* was read avidly as a set of political prescriptions for a possible new regime. Indeed, Hobbes's view that any stable, centralized authority was preferable to anarchy and civil war must have been welcomed by many who sought a return to political calm.[17] Clearly, however, royalists resented the absence of any defence of the doctrine of divine right and parliamentarians resented the absence of any insistence on representative institutions in Hobbes's 'commonwealth'.

At the Restoration in 1660 Hobbes found favour with his old pupil, now Charles II, and the king made him an allowance of £100 per year. Nevertheless his views were still regarded as disreputable by many and he was discouraged from publishing them, even by the king. His theory that God was a powerful physical object brought him a reputation as an atheist, and the Great Fire and Great Flood of London were blamed on him. However, it was Parliament which brought this charge, and it had been during the Interregnum that copies of *Leviathan* were publicly burned. Hobbes was always a royalist and royalists recognized that. Their fears concerned his potentially revolutionary and non-theistic justifications of monarchy, and his assumption as a pragmatic contingency that monarchy is the best form of government.

Hobbes lived out his remaining years peacefully enough, but his views remained contentious until the end. In 1668 he finished his own account of the events of 1640–60, called *Behemoth*. It could only be published in 1682, three years after his death.

2 MIND

Hobbes is both an empiricist and a materialist: that is, he not only maintains that all knowledge is acquired through sense-experience, but he also believes that everything that exists is physical – composed of matter.[18]

A clear statement of Hobbes's empiricism appears on the first page of *Leviathan*: 'there is no conception in a mans mind, which hath not at first, totally, or by parts, been begotten upon the organs of Sense' (L 85). Thoughts causally depend on sensation so there is no thought without sensation, and that is empiricism. Thoughts also depend upon physical objects logically because, *qua* thoughts, they are necessarily representations of them; 'they are every one a Representation or Apparance, of some quality, or other Accident of a body without us; which is commonly called an Object' (L 85).[19]

The relation between thought and object can be thought of as running in two directions, one representational and the other causal. The thought represents the object. The object causes the thought: '[the] Object worketh on the Eyes, Eares, and other parts of mans body; and by diversity of working, produceth diversity of Apparences' (L 85). This causal relation between thought and object is mediated by sensations. Physical objects cause sensations and sensations cause thoughts, but it still follows from this that physical objects cause thoughts because the causal relation is transitive: if *A* is a cause of *B* and *B* is a cause of *C*, then *A* is a cause of *C*.

It is important to note that Hobbes's account of the thought–sensation–object relation does not imply mind–body dualism. Hobbes thinks everything is material:

The World (. . . that is, the whole masse of all things that are) is Corporeall, that is to say, Body; and hath the dimensions of Magnitude, namely, Length, Bredth, and Depth; also every part of Body, is likewise Body, and hath the like dimensions; and consequently every part of the Universe, is Body, and that which is not Body, is no part of the Universe. (L 689)

Light, colour, sound, smell, taste, heat, cold, hardness and softness are in one respect in the perceived object, but in another respect in the perceiver. Nevertheless,

All which qualities called Sensible, are in the object that causeth them, but so many several motions of the matter, by which it presseth our organs diversly. Neither in us that are pressed, are they anything else, but divers motions; (for motion, produceth nothing but motion). (L 86)

Colours or sounds exist in us as a 'seeming' or a 'fancy' (L 86), so Hobbes makes a distinction between qualities as they appear to us and as they are in the objects.[20] His ground for this is the fact that illusions are possible – we may take an object to have a property it lacks or lack a property it has. That implies that 'the object is one thing, the image or fancy is another' (L 86), yet both are only matter in motion.

Hobbes's materialism seems to generate a problem. His remarks about motion suggest that the relation between sensations and matter in motion is identity. This makes him sound like a reductive materialist. He says sensations are not anything other than matter in motion. However, in a later passage he seems to imply that the relation between sensation and matter in motion is causal:

Sense in all cases, is nothing els but originall fancy, caused (as I have said) by the pressure, that is, by the motion, of externall things upon our Eyes, Eares, and other organs thereunto ordained. (L 86)

The difference is an important one. If *A* is identical with *B*, that would seem *prima facie* to preclude the possible truth of '*A* causes *B*', because if *A* causes *B* that presupposes that *A* is not (numerically) the same as *B*. There is then a *prima facie* tension between Hobbes's empiricism, which makes sensation causally dependent on physical objects in motion, and his materialism, which makes sensation identical with matter in motion. The tension is, however, easily dissolved in this way: that matter in motion which is sensation is causally dependent upon that matter in motion which is the physical objects we sense, but not identical with it. His materialism and his empiricism are thus mutually consistent.

Because all thought depends upon sensation and because of the way sensation depends upon physical objects, imagination and memory would be impossible without sensation of physical objects. Indeed, 'Imagination . . . is nothing but decaying sense' (L 88). Matter continues in motion unless impeded, and the motion of external objects causes motion in us, therefore 'after the object is removed, or the eye shut, we still retain an image of the thing seen, though more obscure than when we see it' (L 88). Over time, impressions become weak and obscure, rather as impressions of spatially distant objects are weaker and more obscure than impressions of those nearby.

Imagination and memory are the same faculty employed in two different ways, so that 'Imagination and Memory, are but one thing, which for divers considerations hath divers names'. Veridical memory is called 'simple Imagination', as for example when one

imagines a man or a horse as one has perceived them. Veridical
memory is defined as 'the imagining the whole object, as it was
presented to the sense'. Imagination, in contrast, is 'compounded'.
For instance, the image of a horse and a man are compounded in
imagining a centaur. Imagination that is distinct from memory is
called 'compounded imagination' (L 89), and its contents are
fictions of the mind because they do not represent objects in mind-
independent reality.

Dreaming, like remembering, is a kind of imagining: 'The imagin-
ations of them that sleep, are those we call Dreams' (L 90). The
account of dreaming in *Leviathan* is fundamentally anti-Cartesian.[21]
The content of dreams – what we dream – is derived from sensation,
but even though there is no sensation during sleep, dreams are
sufficiently clear 'that it is a hard matter, and by many thought
impossible to distinguish exactly between Sense and Dreaming'
(L 90), a clear reference to Hobbes's Cartesian contemporaries.
However, Hobbes points to three asymmetries between dreaming
and sensation which he considers sufficient to refute that Cartesian
scepticism which assimilates the two. Hobbes says that when
dreaming he thinks of different persons and things from those he
thinks of when awake, and that dreams are less coherent than
waking thoughts. Finally, 'because waking I often observe the
absurdity of Dreames, but never dream of the absurdities of my
waking Thoughts; I am well satisfied, that being awake, I know I
dreame not; though when I dreame, I think my selfe awake' (L 90).
What is required for the refutation of Descartes is what Hobbes
maintains: if a person is awake they may know that they are not
dreaming.

Hobbes's term for the everyday thinking that is not imagining is
'Consequence', or 'Trayne of Thoughts' (L 94), and he sometimes
calls it 'Mentall Discourse' to distinguish it from discourse in words
(L 94). Although mental discourse is not linguistic discourse it is
clear that there is a strong resemblance between the two: the
coherence of thinking is not best accounted for by the causal
relations between thoughts, any more than the coherence of speech
is best accounted for by the causal relations between words, and the
coherence exhibited by both is sufficiently similar to allow speech to
be the expression of thought (L 101).

There are two kinds of trains of thought, 'unguided' and 'regulated'. Unguided trains of thought are the result of association. The thought of A suggests the thought of B and so on, and one train of thought might be suggested by the memory of an analogous train. Regulated trains of thought are 'more constant'. They are in fact guided by desire and fear. Desire and fear give rise to means to end thinking; to fulfil the desire or obviate the fear. Indeed, desire or fear, trains of thought and actions form a mutually dependent triad in Hobbes's philosophy of the person. We fear or desire, we think how to act to obviate the fear or fulfil the desire, and we act according to our thoughts. None of the three makes sense in abstraction from the other two.

This completes Hobbes's theory of the workings of the mind, 'for besides Sense, and Thoughts, and the Trayne of thoughts, the mind of man has no other motion' (L 99). One question remains, however: What is the mind, ontologically speaking?

The mind is nothing over and above sensations and thoughts, and these are nothing over and above matter in motion. It is plain, then, that the most accurate characterization of the mind for Hobbes, ontologically, is 'matter in motion'.[22] It is a clear consequence that there exist no spiritual souls. Anything putatively spiritual is in fact material: 'Spirits . . . have dimensions, and are therefore really Bodies' (L 689). Indeed, 'the Existence of an Incorporeall Soule, Separated from the Body' (L 693) is founded on 'absurdities'. It is incoherent to suggest that something non-physical could burn in hell, feel pain, travel to heaven, or haunt churchyards.

Hobbes maintains that God and the soul are physical objects. The matter composing them is so refined that they are invisible physical objects. He thus effects a materialist transformation of the theistic world-picture he inherited from the Middle Ages.

3 LANGUAGE

For Hobbes, thought is prior to language because some thought could exist without language but no language could exist without

thought. Language is the vehicle for the expression and communication of thought: 'the generall use of Speech, is to transferre our
Mentall Discourse, into Verbal; or the Trayne of our Thoughts,
into a Trayne of Words' (L 101). This suggests that language is a
consequence of the causal chain which begins with the motion of
external objects. Objects cause sensations. Sensations cause
thoughts. Thoughts are expressed in language. However, in human
beings language transforms thinking. Mere imagination, the train
of images, is raised to the level of understanding by the use of
words, and this is what distinguishes humans from animals:

> That Understanding which is peculiar to man, is the Understanding not
> onely his will; but his conceptions and thoughts, by the sequell and
> contexture of the names of things into Affirmations, Negations, and other
> formes of Speech. (L 93–4)

So language makes possible propositional thought, the thought that
such-and-such is or is not the case, and animals allegedly lack this.[23]

Language exists in two forms: writing and speech. The main
function of writing is the recording of thoughts, so written language
is an extension of human memory. The main use of speech is
communication:

> . . . the first use of names, is to serve for Markes, or Notes of remembrance.
> Another is, when many use the same words, to signifie (by their connexion
> and order,) one to another, what they conceive, or think of each matter;
> and also what they desire, feare, or have any other passion for. And for this
> use they are called Signes. (L 101)

The function of speech breaks down into four sub-uses: registering
causal relations; teaching, or communicating knowledge; making
known wishes and so facilitating mutual aid; and allowing the
pleasure of the use of words for their own sake. To each of these
four uses there corresponds an abuse of language: the incorrect
recording of thoughts in language; the deceptive use of metaphorical
language; the misrepresentation of will; and the verbal abuse of
others. There exists in addition the philosophical abuse of language, especially by the Scholastic followers of Aristotle. Hobbes
anticipates a twentieth-century theme when he complains of 'the
frequency of insignificant Speech' (L 87) amongst certain
philosophers.[24]

Hobbes gives an account of the structure of language in which names, or as we should say, nouns, are fundamental.[25] Hobbes distinguishes proper names from common names. A proper name applies to only one thing, but a common name applies to many things. Thus 'Peter, John, This Man, this Tree' are proper (L 102), but 'Man, Horse, Tree' are common. Hobbes is a nominalist about universals. The problem of universals is the problem of what generality consists in, or what it is for there to be types or sorts of things. For Hobbes, generality does not exist over and above common names. It does not exist in non-linguistic reality: 'there being nothing in the world Universall but Names; for the things named, are every one of them Individuall and Singular' (L 102). Hobbes is not denying that there are similarities between objects. It is in virtue of such real similarities that a set of objects comes to be called by the same name: 'One Universall name is imposed on many things, for their similitude in some quality, or other accident' (L 103). But his allowing similarity is consistent with his nominalism.[26]

Common names differ in scope. The class of physical objects is larger than but includes the class of men, so 'the Name Body is of larger signification than the word Man, and comprehendeth it' (L 103). The scope of names depends on relations between physical objects, not on our ways of thinking about those physical objects.[27]

According to Hobbes, there are four, and only four, meaningful types of name and he uses this fourfold taxonomy as a philosophical weapon. Firstly there are 'names of Matter' (L 107), secondly there are abstract names, thirdly there are names for properties of our own bodies, and fourthly, there are names of names. These correspond to a physical object language, a predicate language, a sensation language and a meta-language. A name is a name of matter if, and only if, it both refers to a physical object and contributes to the understanding of what matter is. A name is abstract if, and only if, it is abstracted from some property of matter but functions substantively and not adjectivally; hence 'length' is a noun derived from the (relative) property of being long. The names for properties of our own bodies are more accurately called 'names of fancies' by Hobbes (L 107). A name is the name of a fancy if, and only if, it is the name of a sensation. Hence 'colour' and 'hearing' are names of fancies. Finally, a name is the name of a name if, and only if, it is the name of a part of language. Hence 'generall, universall, speciall, equivocall, are names of Names' (L 107).

The second meaningful use of language would seem to depend upon the first. Unless we could talk about physical objects we could not talk about their properties nor generate substantival modes of talking about properties, but those two functions of language would both seem to depend upon sensation: unless we sensed physical objects we would know nothing of them and so could not talk about them.[28] However, sensation depends upon physical objects and therefore it is clear that for Hobbes the existence of language ultimately depends upon the existence of matter. Clearly, a meta-language depends on a (first-order) language, so if the first-order language depends on matter then so does the meta-language because of the transitivity of 'depends on': if A depends on B and B depends on C, then A depends on C.

All and only meaningful names belong to one of the four categories. Crucially, Hobbes then asserts that 'All other Names, are but insignificant sounds' (L 108). In anticipation of certain verificationist arguments, Hobbes launches an attack on meaningless philosophy.

There are two sorts of meaningless term employed by philosophers: 'One, when they are new, and yet their meaning not explained by Definition; whereof there have been aboundance coyned by Schoole-men, and pusled Philosophers' (L 108). Hobbes is complaining about the invention of philosophical jargon and hints that if a word cannot be defined then it is meaningless. If we bear in mind the dependence of meaningful names on the perception of physical objects, then we can read Hobbes as criticizing certain metaphysical terms as meaningless. He cites 'entity', 'intentionality' and 'quiddity'.

The other sort of meaningless name is the result of conjoining two names the definitions of which are mutually inconsistent. If someone said 'a quadrangle is round' (L 108) they would have said something contradictory because the definition of 'quadrangle' excludes the notion of roundness, and vice versa. Hobbes thinks that 'incorporeal body' is internally inconsistent in the same way. The notion of a non-physical object is an incoherent one because the definitions of 'non-physical' and 'object' contradict one another. It is important to note that God and the soul are excluded by Hobbes's philosophy in so far as they are non-physical or spiritual substances. It is false that God and the soul exist in that putative sense because 'non-physical substance' is a meaningless name. Clearly, such meaningless names cannot possibly denote anything because it is logically impossible for a putative object to exist if its description is contradictory. Thus Hobbes's materialism gains additional support from his theory of meaning.

Hobbes has an impatience with the metaphysical abuse of language, which the later British empiricists inherit. The paradigms of meaningful discourse are commonsensical and scientific. It is to the Hobbesian ideas of rationality and science we should now turn.

4 REASON

Reasoning is a process of addition and subtraction for Hobbes, so all reason is to be understood on the model of arithmetic. Not only do arithmeticians add and subtract numbers and geometricians add and subtract lines and angles, but

the Logicians teach the same in Consequences of words; adding together two Names, to make an Affirmation; and two Affirmations, to make a Syllogisme; and many Syllogismes to make a Demonstration; and from the summe, or Conclusion of a Syllogisme, they subtract one Proposition, to find the other. (L 110).

Thus the whole of logic is a process of adding and subtracting names in different combinations.

Truth consists in the correct ordering of names in propositions, and falsity in an incorrect ordering. Thus 'a man is a living creature' is true because 'living creature' is one of the names added to make the name 'man' (another being 'rational'). The difficulty with Hobbes's theory that 'truth consisteth in the right ordering of names in our affirmations' (L 105) is that it either implies that all true statements are tautologies, which is false, or else 'right' in the definition appears to be question-begging: it means 'correct' or 'true'. In that case Hobbes needs an independent account of 'right ordering'. Despite these drawbacks in his theory of truth, Hobbes is entitled to maintain independently that 'True and False are attributes of Speech, not of Things' (L 105), and he is correct in his two suggestions that being grammatically well formed is a necessary condition of a sentence expressing a truth, and being tautologous is a sufficient condition of being true.

Hobbes not only makes reason logically depend on addition and subtraction but also makes the rest of arithmetic depend on these two functions. Multiplication and division are to be explained as sorts of addition and subtraction, so within the arithmetical model he omits them: 'In summe, in what matter soever there is place for addition and substraction, there also is place for Reason; and where these have no place, there Reason has nothing at all to do' (L 110–11). This makes it sound as though adding and subtracting are both necessary and sufficient for reason. Hobbes thinks that decision-making in politics and law may also be understood on the arithmetical model. In another passage, he suggests that the scope of 'Reason' is to be restricted to addition and subtraction in (non-mathematical) language: 'REASON, in this sense, is nothing but Reckoning (that is, Adding and Substracting) of the Consequences of generall names agreed upon, for the marking and signifying of our thoughts' (L 111).

In his account of reason Hobbes anticipates two important developments in modern logic. Hobbes is anti-psychologistic in that he rejects the thesis that the laws of logic are really the laws of thought, and he thinks of logic as a formal, indeed mathematical, enterprise. These broad themes are consistent with the vastly more sophisticated work of Frege and Russell.[29]

Hobbes makes an important distinction which approximates to that between invalidity and meaninglessness. Validity is a property of argument such that an argument is valid if, and only if, if the premises are true then the conclusion is true. An argument is invalid if, and only if, the falsity of the conclusion is consistent with the truth of the premises.[30] 'Error' is Hobbes's word for taking an invalid argument to be valid. Error is different from 'absurdity' which is 'senseless Speech' (L 113), for example the uttering of such phrases as 'a free Subject', 'a free Will' or 'Immateriall Substances'

(L 113). Although rationality is one of the defining characteristics of humanity for Hobbes, absurdity too is something to which only humans are prone. In his notion of absurdity Hobbes anticipates post-Kantian ideas of the misuse of reason.[31]

5 SCIENCE

Hobbes says that 'Science is the knowledge of Consequences, and dependance of one fact upon another' (L 115). Science includes, but is not exhausted by, knowledge of causal relations; so if *A* causes *B*, then that is a scientific fact, and the knowledge of that fact is a part of science. Science is not a mere inventory of facts about the universe. That would not in principle distinguish it from memory. Science is knowledge of dependencies between facts and those are logical as well as causal.

Hobbes's conception of science is essentially a combination of empirical and deductive methods. Science proceeds as follows, logically and chronologically: facts are known by observation (by 'sense') and retained by memory. Facts are named by 'Names', and 'Assertions' are generated which are true reportings of facts and the relations between them. Logical relations between assertions are then discovered by the use of 'Reason'. In this way 'we come to a knowledge of all the Consequences of names appertaining to the subject in hand; and that is it, men call Science' (L 115).[32]

Hobbes has thus characterized science in two ways: as knowledge of causes and effects, and as knowledge of the logical consequences of true assertions about facts. He does not think of these two as thoroughly independent, even though they are not identical. To know of causal relations is to know some assertions to be true, and when we know the logical relations between two assertions we may thereby know of some causal relation if the logically related assertions report such a causal relation. It is not only consistent with Hobbes's claim that science is knowledge of logical consequences that science contains predictions. He is arguably logically committed to the view that science predicts by the claim that science is knowledge of all the consequences of names of facts.

Science for Hobbes is an empirical and deductive method which gives us knowledge of facts and their relations, especially causal ones. Clearly, science is empirical for Hobbes because science would be impossible without knowledge of facts and knowledge of facts is impossible without empirical observation.[33]

6 FREEDOM

Hobbes makes a distinction between two kinds of motion: voluntary and involuntary. The vital processes of an organism, such as the circulation of the blood, respiration and digestion, count as involuntary because 'there needs no help of Imagination' (L 118). An action is voluntary if, and only if, it is caused by the making of a choice which, for Hobbes, is imaginative deliberation. Voluntary motion includes speaking and the movement of limbs. Hobbes might have pointed out (but does not) that breathing may be either voluntary or involuntary and so cuts across his taxonomy. I mean, I may breathe if I choose, or refrain from breathing (briefly); but if I do not choose to breathe, breathing continues in any case through causes other than my own choice. Voluntary actions are caused by the operations of the imagination: 'the Imagination is the first internall beginning of all Voluntary Motion' (L 118). If someone is walking, it makes sense to ask: Where? If they are speaking, it makes sense to ask: What? If they move their limbs, it makes sense to ask: Which way? Indeed, the thought of such options precedes and causes the voluntary action, and these thoughts are themselves motions. It is because thoughts are motions that they may cause actions. Actions are motions and only motions may cause motions. Also, if thoughts cause actions and actions are motions and if only motions may cause motions, then it follows that thoughts are motions. Hobbes's theory of the will is thus logically consistent with his materialism. We must not be misled into thinking that thoughts are not motions because they are invisible. There may be motion that is invisible because it is too minute to be perceptible.[34]

The thought that causes an action is a trying, an attempt: 'These small beginnings of Motion, within the body of Man, before they appear in walking, speaking, striking, and other visible actions, are commonly called ENDEAVOUR' (L 119). Endeavour may be described in two ways, depending on its relation to the object which causes it. Appetite is the endeavour to obtain something, the desire for it. Aversion is the endeavour to avoid something, the aversion to it. Hobbes assumes the object of an endeavour is always and everywhere identical with the cause of that endeavour and therefore he does not distinguish qualitatively or numerically between the intentional object and the cause of trying.

So, are we free? Hobbes has a particular account of what the will consists in which makes use of the appetite/aversion distinction. The oscillation of appetites and aversions and hopes and fears is called by Hobbes 'Deliberation' (L 127): 'it is called Deliberation; because it is a putting an end to the Liberty we had of doing, or omitting, according to our own Appetite, or Aversion' (L 127). So the liberty to do something partly consists in not having done it and partly in there existing the possibility of doing it. De-liberation is the process that ends this freedom by causing the action or preventing it. Appetites cause actions. Aversions cause omissions. Alternatively, deliberation may end in the thought that the action is impossible (and presumably if this thought is true there was no freedom to perform that action anyway).

So as long as there exists 'this alternate Succession of Appetites, Aversions, Hopes and Fears . . . wee retain the liberty of doing, or omitting' (L 127). By 'omitting', Hobbes means deliberately refraining from action. Arguably there is only freedom to act if there exists the possibility of refraining from acting and there is only freedom to refrain from acting if there is freedom to act. If there was not freedom not to act then there would be compulsion to act, and that is incompatible with freedom to act. If there was not freedom to act then there would be compulsion not to act, and that is incompatible with freedom not to act.

The will is simply the final thought in the succession of appetites or aversions before the action or its omission: 'in Deliberation, the last Appetite, or Aversion, immediately adhering to the action, or to the omission thereof, is that wee call the WILL' (L 127). Hobbes means an act of will, not the faculty of will, or the capacity to will. Our freedom thus consists in our being the causes of our own

actions and omissions, or at least our being amongst those causes.
A necessary condition of this freedom is the existence of the real
possibility of having acted when one omitted to act, or having
omitted to act when one acted.

Hobbes thinks the voluntary–involuntary distinction also applies
to (non-human) animals. He says, 'Beasts also Deliberate' and
'Beasts that have Deliberation, must necessarily also have Will'
(L 127). It follows that the will is not necessarily rational, because
animals are not rational yet have a will.

Hobbes's account of freedom contrasts sharply with that of the
Scholastics and in one respect with that of Descartes. The quasi-
Aristotelian definition of the will offered by the Scholastics was
'Rationall Appetite' (L 127). Hobbes rejects this definition because
it makes the irrational exercise of freedom a logical impossibility:
'then could there be no Voluntary Act against Reason' (L 127).
Hobbes maintains that people do act freely but irrationally, so the
Scholastic account is false and says instead, 'will . . . is the last
Appetite in Deliberating' (L 128).

Hobbes disagrees with Descartes over the status of animal action.
Descartes and Hobbes agree that non-human animals are merely
highly complex physical objects with no immaterial souls.[35] Hobbes,
however, maintains, while Descartes denies, that animals have a
will; in other words, animals' actions fall on the voluntary side of
the voluntary–involuntary distinction. A problem for Hobbes is that
in ascribing to animals a will he implicitly credits them with the
capacity to make environmental discriminations and even exercise
preferences, yet this requires a minimal rationality Hobbes wishes
to deny them. It may be that reason and the will are not so readily
separable as Hobbes supposes. After all, only a rational creature
may act irrationally.

7 EMOTION

Hobbes makes two important kinds of distinction between 'the
Passions', or as we would say, the emotions (L 118). He distinguishes them logically and exhibits the logical relations that

obtain between them, and he distinguishes them according to whether they are innate or learned through experience.

If someone desires something, in Hobbes's sense they 'love' it, or as we would say, like it. If someone has an aversion to something, then they 'hate', or as we would say, dislike it. There is therefore something identical between love and desire, and something identical between aversion and hate. Hobbes holds that 'by Desire, we always signifie the Absence of the Object; by Love, most commonly the Presence of the same' (L 119). He means that if someone desires a particular object, then it logically follows that the person does not possess that object. Desires *qua* desires are necessarily unfulfilled. However, if someone loves something in Hobbes's sense, then the thing loved is present to that person. Hobbes also thinks that 'by Aversion, we signifie the Absence; and by Hate, the Presence of the Object' (L 119).

It is clear that Hobbes maintains that desire and aversion, and love and hate, are the fundamental emotions. I mean that we could not, logically, be in any other emotional state unless we were capable of being in those states.[36]

Examples of innate desires are 'Appetite of food, Appetite of excretion, and exoneration'. The innate desires are few. The remaining desires are learned empirically, or 'proceed from Experience'. They are in fact 'Appetites of particular things' (L 120). It seems to follow that such desires cannot be innate because they are for empirical objects. Clearly, the objection might be made to Hobbes that food, for example, is empirical, yet on his account the desire for it is innate.

Hobbes has two reservations about his desire/aversion theory. Firstly, there may be many items towards which we feel neither desire nor aversion. To these we feel what Hobbes calls 'contempt'. However, Hobbes's seventeenth-century use of 'contempt' is much closer to our 'indifference' than to our 'contempt'. Secondly, because a human being is a complex physical object the parts of which are in continual motion, our emotions are constantly changing. Further, what causes our aversions and desires also changes, so that what causes a desire at one time might cause an aversion at another time. Despite these reservations, Hobbes thinks we cannot explain human behaviour without a theory of appetite and aversion.

Hobbes is both an empiricist and a materialist about emotion. There could be no emotion without the sense perception of external objects, and an emotion is nothing over and above a physical motion (of the heart). Indeed, external objects cause those motions called 'fancies' and they in turn cause the motions in the heart called 'passions'. Hobbes's materialist premise throughout is 'that which is really within us, is . . . onely Motion', and his empiricist premise is that any such internal motion is 'caused by the action of externall objects'. No matter what is received by the sense organs or occurs in internal experience, 'the reall effect there is nothing but Motion' (L 121).

Pleasure or delight is the appearance of appetite. Trouble of mind or displeasure is the appearance of aversion. All appetite is accompanied by some pleasure and all aversion by some displeasure. Pleasures and displeasures may arise either from the sense perception of objects or from the anticipation of some future event.

Hobbes offers us a rich set of definitions of connative concepts, each of which ultimately depends upon the appetite/aversion distinction. For example, 'Appetite with an opinion of attaining, is called HOPE', but 'the same, without such opinion, DESPAIRE'. Aversion with the expectation of being hurt is fear. Aversion with the hope of avoiding hurt is courage. Anger is 'sudden Courage' and confidence is 'constant Hope' (L 123). 'Desire of good to another' is called 'Benevolence' or 'Good Will' or 'Charity', and the desire for good for all humanity is called 'Good Nature' (L 123). The love of persons for society is 'Kindnesse' and the love of sense pleasure only is 'Natural Lust'.

There is one emotion which helps to demarcate humans from animals. This is curiosity. 'Curiosity' is defined by Hobbes as 'Desire, to know why, and how' and he says that it is not found in animals: it 'is in no living creature but Man'. Natural lust in animals is an obstacle to their possessing curiosity, which is a pleasure of the mind. In the human case, in contrast, the possibility exists of overcoming carnal pleasures and contributing to knowledge by the exercise of curiosity. This is a lasting and worthwhile pleasure which is more rewarding than any pleasure of the senses. Thus 'Man is distinguished, not onely by his Reason; but also by this singular Passion from other Animals' (L 124).

Hobbes has an interesting account of the language of emotion. There are four main grammatical forms of emotional language: indicative, subjunctive, imperative and interrogative. There is nothing peculiar to emotional language in this, but the forms are used to assert that some emotion is occurring, to assert that if some condition were fulfilled some emotion would occur, to urge and prevent emotion, and to inquire into emotion. According to Hobbes, the peculiarity of emotional language is that it is expressive of emotion. The use of such language is a sign of the presence of an emotion in the speaker even though such uses are not a logical guarantee of that presence: 'These formes of Speech, I say, are expressions, or voluntary significations of our Passions: but certain signes they be not' (L 129). The best guides to the accurate ascription of emotion to another are non-linguistic behavioural features, especially facial expressions, and the psychological context provided by our knowledge of the other's intentions.

Hobbes makes ethics depend upon the emotions, but I leave that until section 10 of the present chapter (page 44).

8 RELIGION

Hobbes distinguishes between religion, superstition, and true religion. This distinction logically depends upon the concepts of fear and imagination. Religion is fear of invisible power and superstition is fear of invisible power, the only difference being that religion is publicly endorsed and superstition publicly prohibited. If we imagine an invisible power and our imagination is accurate, then that is true religion. Hobbes is here making room for the logical possibility of God's existence. The notion of an invisible power, so long as it is physical, is not self-contradictory. The putative idea of an immaterial entity is self-contradictory and so incoherent. It logically follows that God as a spiritual entity does not exist. God for Hobbes may only exist on condition that He is a physical object or physical force.

The theory that God is a physical force is perhaps not atheism because atheism is the view that God does not exist, but if Hobbes maintains that God exists as a physical object or force then he does not thereby deny that God exists. More nearly atheistic is Hobbes's claim that religion's causes and effects operate only within the human sphere. Religion only pertains to the human: 'Seeing there are no signes, nor fruit of Religion, but in Man onely; there is no cause to doubt, but that the seed of Religion, is also onely in Man' (L 168).

In giving religion a purely human genesis and function Hobbes anticipates the later atheism of Feuerbach and Marx.[37] Because human beings are not wholly preoccupied with the pleasures of the senses they possess curiosity, and this is directed towards their own origins and the origins of the events they observe. Where no natural scientific, causal explanation is possible, people either rely on their imagination or are guided by authority in postulating an invisible, non-natural cause of events. 'Authority' and 'his own fancy' thus replace the desire to discover 'the true causes of things' (L 169). In this way religion is generated amongst human beings but not amongst other animals.

As we have noted, the experience of fear is essential to Hobbes's theory of human nature. People live in 'perpetuall feare' and man 'hath his heart all the day long, gnawed on by feare' (L 169). Humans fear in particular death and poverty. In the face of this fear, humanity postulates 'some Power, or Agent Invisible' as a source of comfort and security, and Hobbes cites with approval an old poetical remark that 'the Gods were at first created by humane Feare' (L 170).

Hobbes clearly thinks the concept of God a human invention, and that there is really no security-bestowing God. Rather the authority of the state is the only guarantee against human insecurity. Hobbes replaces God with the state. If Hobbes were a theist Leviathan would be redundant because God would guarantee human security.

The concept of God is modelled on the concept of the soul, and the idea of the soul is, as Nietzsche would suggest later, derived from dream experience. Like Nietzsche, Hobbes maintains that we would have no notion of God, the soul and ghosts if we did not dream or look in mirrors and were not thus acquainted with visually perceptible yet non-solid objects, that is, images.[38]

It is Hobbes's view that spiritual substances cannot even be coherently imagined because, as we have seen, 'immaterial substance' is contradictory and no one can imagine logical impossibilities: 'though men may put together words of contradictory signification, as Spirit, and Incorporeall; yet they can never have the imagination of any thing answering to them' (L 171). If the verbal definition of some name is contradictory, then what that name putatively denotes may not be conceived. According to Hobbes, it is precisely for this reason that theists claim the infinite omnipotent and eternal God is incomprehensible. They 'define his Nature by Spirit Incorporeall, and then confesse their definition to be unintelligible' (L 171). Hobbes's materialism, when taken to its logical conclusions, includes a thoroughgoing atheism. The concept of God is shorn of its traditional components of infinity, spirituality and benevolence in human affairs. With a certain irony Hobbes allows the one logical possibility which the theist is hardly likely to welcome. God is one physical object amongst others, albeit the largest and most powerful one.

9 NATURE

Hobbes's concept of nature exhibits the unity of his whole philosophy. Everything that exists is physical. There is not anything that is not, or is not composed of, physical objects in motion. There should ideally be one science which deals with the laws governing the non-human world, human beings and political society. Hobbes anticipates the modern idea of the unity of science in the views that the various special sciences should form a mutually consistent and mutually supporting whole, and that everything can be explained scientifically. It is not an exaggeration to say that Hobbes was the first positivist because he thought any problem – any meaningful problem – may in principle be solved by the methods of the natural sciences. He conceives of his theory of the person, and his political theory, as extending scientific methods beyond the natural realm. To do this consistently he believes he has to maintain a materialist theory of the person and politics. In his materialism, and in his ideal of a science of society, Hobbes anticipates two of the major tenets of Marxism, though Hobbes's and Marx's political theories are in many respects diametrically opposed.[39]

It is impossible to understand Hobbes's political theory without an understanding of his picture of 'the Natural Condition of Mankind' (L 183). This is his account of human beings as they would be if they did not live in political society. The sort of government Hobbes recommends is designed to prevent people lapsing into the unpleasantness of the state of nature.

It is Hobbes's view that human beings are sufficiently equally matched in physical and intellectual capacity to present the severest danger to each other. If one is stronger intellectually, the other is stronger physically. If one may mentally outwit and kill the other, the other may physically overcome and kill the former. It is important to note that mutual animosity is not an innate character-istic of human beings in Hobbes's philosophy, even though he is often misunderstood in this way. It is not an *a priori* fact about human beings that they seek to destroy one another, nor is it an inevitable, innate or essential component of human nature. Rather it is humanity in the state of nature; that is, in a particular situation which generates conflict. The particular contingency of that situ-ation which produces conflict is scarcity:

From this equality of ability, ariseth equality of hope in the attaining of our Ends. And therefore if any two men desire the same thing, which neverthelesse they cannot both enjoy, they become enemies ... (L 184)

It is thus wholly incorrect to ascribe to Hobbes the view that human beings are intrinsically evil or ill-disposed to one another. Human conflict is the result of competition over scarce goods. In particular, human beings 'endeavour to destroy, or subdue one an other' when there is competition over attaining an end essential to the preser-vation of each party yet which cannot be possessed by both. It is because of that that each tries to deprive the other of 'the fruit of his labour', 'his life' and 'liberty' (L 184).

People do not find pleasure in this situation of competition and actual and potential violence. On the contrary, each person desires from every other the same respect that he accords himself. Indeed, amongst the three 'causes of quarrell' the first is competition, and the other two are diffidence and glory. The goal of competition is gain, that of diffidence safety, and the quest for glory is the quest for reputation: something that depends upon competition.

This condition of endemic violence arising from the scarcity of life-preserving resources is called by Hobbes 'war'. The crucial claim of his political theory is that some strong authority is required to prevent humankind lapsing into a state of war. People prefer a strong state to the threat or actuality of destruction or slavery, and they are correct in this preference because the Leviathan is the only sure means to security:

. . . it is manifest, that during the time men live without a common Power to keep them all in awe, they are in that condition which is called Warre; and such a warre, as is of every man, against every man. (L 185)

In the state of war 'every man is Enemy to every man' (L 186). Hobbes does not mean that in the state of nature each person is always engaged in combat with another. War is a disposition to combat. It is a period of time during which each person is known to be a threat to every other, and this disposition may be realized in battle at any point during that time. The state of nature is thus a time of extreme insecurity and a disposition to violence. In the state of nature there can be no science, no arts, no industry, no agriculture, no building, no seafaring, no growth of knowledge, no society; and, 'which is worst of all, continuall feare, and danger of violent death; And the life of man, solitary, poore, nasty, brutish, and short' (L 186).

Hobbes cites as proof of the danger of any actual political society's possible lapse into the state of war the fact that we lock our doors, go accompanied or armed when we travel, and lock our chests even when at home. We do all this even though there are laws and 'publike Officers' to avenge any harm done to us. However, Hobbes emphasizes that although this shows we regard other people as a threat, it does not imply a pessimistic view of human nature. In reply to the question whether either the person who secures himself, or he, Hobbes, 'accuse mankind by his actions', Hobbes says 'neither of us accuse mans nature in it' (L 187). Man's inhumanity to man is a product of the possibility of lapsing into the state of nature, and not a necessary part of human nature. Indeed, it does not make sense to talk about good and evil outside a framework of law, and law is a product of political society.

10 ETHICS

Ethics logically depend upon emotion for Hobbes. This is because that which is good is the object of a man's desire or appetite, and that which is evil is the object of a man's aversion or hatred. It follows that the distinction between good and evil could not exist in the absence of the distinction between human desires and aversions.

Several theses follow from this idea of ethics. Ethics are a uniquely human affair. It does not make sense to talk about good and evil as having their sources in God, nor as obtaining in the world of non-human animals. Hobbes's view of ethics is therefore thoroughly anthropocentric.

Nor are morals absolute. Because it is the case that different people at different times, and the same person at different times, find different things objects of desire and aversion it logically follows that what is good and what is evil is subject to a similar historical and geographical fluctuation.

Morals are relative because they are relative to a person and, more specifically, relative to that person's connative state: 'these words of Good, Evill, and Contemptible, are ever used with relation to the person that useth them' (L 120). So to say that such-and-such is good or evil is really to make an autobiographical claim – a covert report on the object of the speaker's emotions in relation to those emotions.[40] Indeed, the reason why morals are not absolute is that no object is intrinsically good or evil but only counts as such when the object of a human emotion. It follows that there is no consensus among human beings about what is moral or immoral because the variety of morals is as great and as changing as the variety of emotional attitudes to objects: 'There being nothing simply and absolutely so: nor any common Rule of Good and Evill, to be taken from the nature of the objects themselves'. Any such putative rule derives 'from the Person of the man' (L 120).

Finally, it clearly follows that morals are subjective rather than objective, for two reasons. Firstly, they are not properties of things, persons and deeds which exist independently of emotions. Secondly, even though it makes sense to talk of the truth or falsity of value judgements, when thus construed as truth-valued they only make sense as reports of the subject's emotions.

Within his emotivist, relativist and subjectivist framework
Hobbes distinguishes three kinds of good and evil. There is the
intention, or 'Promise' (L 121), to do good or evil. There are good
and evil effects, and there are good and evil means. The concept of
promise or intention includes people's mental states as possible
objects of ethical appraisal. The concept of ethical effects denotes
the consequences of actions, and the concept of ethical means
admits actions themselves as objects of ethical appraisal. Hobbes
not only has an emotivist theory of ethics but the elements for a
deontological and a consequentialist theory also. In these respects
he anticipates the central tenets of some modern theories of ethics.[41]

11 POLITICS

Hobbes's political theory is a set of prescriptions for the creation of
a human society that will escape the state of nature. It would be a
severe misreading of Hobbes to suggest that *Leviathan* depicts a
chronological progression from one historically real state to another,
the state of nature to commonwealth. Nevertheless, Hobbes no
doubt had in mind actual feared societies without a state upon
which to model his own hypothetical state of nature. These range
from the warring social groups in Europe during the Thirty Years
War to the Indian communities reported to exist in newly settled
North America.

Hobbes's recommended state is one which will enforce most
closely a set of rules or precepts he calls 'Natural Laws'. He lists
nineteen of these in Chapters 14 and 15 of *Leviathan* and we need to
be clear on these because they are requirements which must be met
by any society which will escape the state of nature. I paraphrase
them as follows:

1. No person should resort to war until all peaceful means are
exhausted, and all persons should seek to establish peace. (L 190)

2. Each person should be content with as much liberty for himself
as he would allow others against him. (L 190)

3. People should keep to their agreements and act on them.
(L 201)

4. Any person receiving some good should not cause the other to regret giving that good. (L 209)

5. Each person should try to accommodate himself to every other person. (L 209)

6. Each person should pardon offences against him, where pardon is desired. (L 210)

7. In revenge, each person should consider future consequences, not past wrongs. (L 210)

8. No person, by action, word or expression, should declare hostility to another. (L 211)

9. Each person should acknowledge every other as his equal by nature. (L 211)

10. No person should require for himself any right he is not happy to allow every other person. (L 211)

11. If a person judges more than one person, he should judge them equally. (L 212)

12. Goods should be enjoyed equally in common. (L 212)

13. If goods cannot be divided equally, they should be distributed by lot. (L 213)

14. Lots may be arbitrary or natural, that is, in favour of the first possessor. (L 213)

15. Any person mediating for peace should be allowed safe conduct. (L 213)

16. Controversies between persons should be submitted to an arbitrator. (L 213)

17. No person may arbitrate in his own case. (L 213)

18. Arbitrators must be impartial. (L 214)

19. If a dispute between two persons cannot be settled in favour of either, it must be decided in favour of a third (or fourth, etc.). (L 214)

Hobbes's natural laws are not natural in the sense in which what obtains in the state of nature is natural. Rather, they are the rules to which any secure society must conform. They are natural in that they are pre-political in the sense of being preconditions for any adequate political society, and not for historically changing contingencies. The study of them is what Hobbes calls 'Morall Philosophy' (L 215–16). It is the holding to these laws which ensures security, the avoidance of anarchic war, so in principle any kind of empirical political institution which would sustain them is politically acceptable. There is no well-founded justification for any political institution except its power to enforce the natural law, and the sort of institution which enforces the natural law most effectively is the most legitimate form of government. The divine right of the monarch to rule and the democratic aspirations of the populace are thus equally spurious legitimations of the institutions of state.

The crucial concept in Hobbes's political theory is the concept of the person and Hobbes devotes Chapter 16 of *Leviathan* (which immediately follows the chapters discussing the natural laws) to the explanation of what a person is.

There are two kinds of person: natural and artificial. When the words and actions of a person are his own, that person is natural. When the words and actions of a person are another person's, that person is artificial. Crucially for Hobbes, the state is an artificial person. Natural persons relinquish their right to govern themselves and consent to being governed by an artificial person: the Leviathan. In this way, persons abdicate the state of nature and become citizens of the commonwealth.

There are in fact two contracts implicit in the justification of Leviathan. There is the contract between natural persons which is their mutual agreement to sacrifice individual self-government and accept government by Leviathan. Then there is the contract between Leviathan and the citizens whereby Leviathan guarantees their security. Here is the contract between natural persons:

I Authorise and give up my Right of Governing my selfe, to this Man, or to this Assembly of men, on this condition, that thou give up thy Right to him, and Authorise all his Actions in like manner. (L 227)

Hobbes's name for persons thus united in civil society is 'commonwealth' or 'civitas'. In the commonwealth they are protected from one another and from enemies abroad and have the security to work, feed themselves and live contentedly. It is an important part of Hobbes's political theory that the worst tyrannies of Leviathan are unlikely to be worse than the anarchy of the state of nature, so rebellion against Leviathan is only justified if he fails in his duty to protect his citizens.

Twelve rights of Leviathan result from the contract establishing him. I paraphrase these as follows:

1. The subjects cannot change the form of government. (L 229)
2. No subject may be freed from subjection. (L 230)
3. No subject may protest against the sovereign. (L 231)
4. No subject may accuse the sovereign of injustice. (L 232)
5. No subject may punish the sovereign for his actions. (L 232)
6. Only the sovereign may decide what is necessary for the peace and defence of his subjects, and what they should be taught. (L 233)
7. Only the sovereign may make rules for owning property. (L 234)
8. Only the sovereign may decide controversies. (L 234)
9. Only the sovereign may make war or peace. (L 234)
10. Only the sovereign may choose councillors and ministers (in war and peace). (L 235)
11. Only the sovereign may make laws, reward and punish. (L 235)
12. Only the sovereign may control the armed forces, and all social rankings. (L 236)

Through the covenant the subjects have bestowed these rights on the sovereign, but because Leviathan is an artificial person, the citizens are the only true agents in society. Therefore, the enforcement of these rules on the subjects by Leviathan is really their enforcement on the subjects by the subjects themselves: 'every Subject is by this Institution Author of all the Actions, and Judgments of the Soveraigne Instituted' (L 232). It follows that the sovereign can do the subject no real injustice because all *prima facie* acts of the sovereign are acts of the subject himself.

In the institution of sovereign authority there exists a choice between three kinds of government: monarchy, democracy and aristocracy. The only appropriate criterion to employ in making the choice between these is 'Aptitude to produce the Peace, and Security of the People' (L 241). Particularly irrelevant is the popularity of the kind of government. Indeed, a tyranny is merely an unpopular monarchy, an oligarchy an unpopular aristocracy, and an anarchy an unpopular democracy. The only overriding concern is to avoid true anarchy – society without the state – because this is the state of nature, the state of war.

In Hobbes's view the most appropriate kind of government for the enforcement of the natural law is monarchy: 'in Monarchy, the private interest is the same with the publique' and 'where the publique and private interest are most closely united, there is the publique most advanced' (L 241). Monarchy has the unity of one person, and may readily take counsel from a group. An assembly may split and disagree, but the unity of a monarch may even be continued through progeny. Clearly, however, Hobbes's preference for monarchy is utterly pragmatic and rests on no theological premises. The monarch is sovereign through a contract between the people. If the sovereign fails to protect the subjects, they no longer owe him allegiance: 'The Obligation of the Subjects to the Soveraign, is understood to last as long, and no longer, than the power lasteth, by which he is able to protect them' (L 272).

Hobbes's political theory, which seems to sacrifice so much of the liberty of the subject to the rights of the sovereign, contains this revolutionary tenet. Sovereigns are not sovereigns by divine right. Sovereigns are sovereigns through a contract of the people, and if the sovereign does not rule in their real interests he no longer has authority over them.[42]

LOCKE

1 LOCKE IN HISTORY

Locke's philosophy, like that of Hobbes, is both a result of and a contribution to the political and intellectual revolutions of the seventeenth century. Locke lived later than Hobbes, so his philosophy is part of the later phases of those revolutions. His political theory is a justification of the Whig and Protestant protest against the Catholic and anti-parliamentarian tendencies of the Stuart kings Charles II and James II, which culminated in the Glorious Revolution of 1688. His philosophy is an empiricist epistemology. Newton's natural philosophy made redundant the quest for a holistic quasi-geometrical depiction of reality as a whole, but generated a new question: What could be known? Anticipating by a century two of the central themes of Kant's *Critique of Pure Reason*, Locke tried to define the limits of human knowledge and to describe the place of the knowing, rational, self-conscious individual in the Newtonian universe. In politics, Locke is arguably the inventor of liberalism; his writings had an enormous impact on eighteenth-century intellectuals and contributed to the intellectual origins of the American Revolution of 1776 and the French Revolution of 1789. In philosophy, he developed the anti-metaphysical empiricism of Hobbes, but (with dubious consistency) rejected materialism for a mind–body dualism of the kind endorsed by Descartes.[1]

John Locke was born in 1632 at Wrington, Somerset, ten years before the outbreak of the English Civil War, and died in 1704, the year of Blenheim. He was thus a teenager during the later years of the Civil War, in his twenties during the Interregnum of 1649–60, and twenty-eight at the Restoration of the monarchy. He was in his thirties and forties during the golden years of Charles II, and fifty-three in 1685, the year of the latter's death, the accession of James II, and the abortive Monmouth Rebellion. As a writer Locke matured late. He was in his mid-fifties when *An Essay Concerning Human Understanding* was published in 1689 and *Two Treatises of Government* in 1690. Locke's twilight years were passed under the Protestant rule of William and Mary and he died at the age of seventy in the second year of the reign of Queen Anne, the last Stuart monarch and a Protestant.[2]

Locke was educated at Westminster School and Christ Church, Oxford. Like Hobbes, he was disaffected with Oxford's prevailing Aristotelianism and did not confine his studies to philosophy. His reading ranged over Greek, rhetoric and medicine. In 1659 he was elected a Student of Christ Church (that is, a Fellow of the college), and rose to become lecturer, Reader, and then Censor. During this period he read and taught in all the subject areas he had studied as an undergraduate.

A crucial episode in Locke's career occurred in 1666 when he made the acquaintance of Lord Ashley, later the Earl of Shaftesbury, Lord Chancellor and one of the most notorious yet influential trimmers in British politics. Locke became Ashley's personal doctor and adopted his political views as his own. Indeed, Locke's endorsement of religious toleration for all except Roman Catholics, his insistence that rights to life, liberty and property are natural, and his repugnance at the absolutist tendencies of monarchy may be correctly understood as a systematization and legitimization of the interests of the capitalist and Protestant middle classes which had emerged as the socio-economic victors of both the Civil War and the Restoration settlement. Locke tied his own political fortunes to those of Ashley.[3]

The political affinity between the two resulted in Locke's appointment as Ashley's political secretary. Locke held this post when Ashley became Earl of Shaftesbury and Lord Chancellor in 1672. When Shaftesbury fell from royal favour in 1673 because of his urging the Test Act as a safeguard against Catholics occupying positions of military and political authority, Locke lost his position with Shaftesbury and returned to Christ Church.

Locke spent the years from 1674 to 1679 in France, and it was during two stays in Paris that he thoroughly familiarized himself with Cartesian philosophy. He shared its anti-Scholastic ambitions, its mind–body dualism, its respect for scientific method and, ironically, some of its tacit Scholastic assumptions.

When Locke returned to England in 1679 Shaftesbury had been restored to favour, so Locke resumed his duties as his political secretary. Until his death in 1683 Shaftesbury plotted the overthrow of Charles II by the Protestant Duke of Monmouth, the king's illegitimate son. It seems probable that Locke was closely implicated in this plot. Locke was now Shaftesbury's political confidant, and when Shaftesbury died, he felt sufficiently threatened to flee to the Netherlands. While he was away the king removed him from the studentship at Christ Church, and when Monmouth's rebellion actually broke out in 1685, the first year of the reign of James II, the British government tried to extradite Locke from the Nether-lands and he had to go into hiding. It was during his stay in the Netherlands that *An Essay Concerning Human Understanding* was written.

In November 1688 William of Orange landed in England and James II fled to France, abandoning his throne to the Protestant Dutchman and his wife Mary. Locke, I think, both knew of beforehand and actively supported that bloodless British *coup d'état* which became known as the Glorious Revolution of 1688. We know that Locke was in close contact with other Protestant and Whig exiles in the Netherlands, that he was introduced to William of Orange shortly before the 1688 coup, and soon after it was offered the post of Ambassador to Brandenburg Prussia. Although Locke gratefully refused the offer, it was most likely a reward. Locke became instead a minor civil servant in the new administration.

Philosophical publications followed swiftly: *A Letter on Toleration* was published in 1689, *An Essay Concerning Human Understanding* in the same year, and *Two Treatises of Government* in 1690. (The date of publication of the *Essay* is frequently given incorrectly as 1690 because that date appears on the frontispiece. We know now that it was published the previous year, in the immediate aftermath of the coup.) Clearly, the new administration produced a political climate which motivated Locke to publish.

In his remaining years Locke held the post of a Commissioner of Trade, and worked on new editions of the *Essay* until his death in 1704.

Locke's humanism, his respect for science, his distrust of religious superstition and his liberal politics were immensely influential on the French Enlightenment. Also the natural rights to life, liberty and property were later to be incorporated into the preamble to the first United States constitution. The 1776 Declaration of Independence of that country is thoroughly Lockean:

> We hold these truths to be self-evident, that all men are created equal, that they are endowed by their creator with certain unalienable rights, that among these are life, liberty and the pursuit of happiness. That to secure these rights, governments are instituted among men, deriving their just powers from the consent of the governed – That whenever any form of government becomes destructive of these ends, it is the right of the people to alter or abolish it, and to institute new government.[4]

The Americans in 1776, like the English in 1688, rebelled when their natural rights, as characterized by Locke, were threatened. Through the writings of the French Enlightenment, and through the publication of the *Two Treatises* in France, a similar influence is apparent on the quest for a constitutional settlement in France after 1789. It is no exaggeration to assert that what is common in the political theories of the English, American and French revolutions is essentially Lockean. Locke's political theory makes explicit the ethos of the individualist, capitalist, property-owning parliamentary democracies of the contemporary world. Locke's political theory is the blueprint for the West.

2 INNATE IDEAS

Empiricism is the doctrine that all knowledge is acquired through experience. Innate knowledge is knowledge we are born with and so did not acquire through experience. It follows that empiricism logically implies that no knowledge is innate.

In the *Essay* Locke adopts two main strategies to persuade us that there is no innate knowledge. In Book I he seeks to refute a set of arguments for innate knowledge by demonstrating that none of them is sound. He devotes Book II to an empiricist epistemology designed to make the postulation of innate ideas redundant. In addition, Locke argues, God would not have equipped us with sense organs highly appropriate to the acquisition of knowledge if that knowledge were innate. In this section I shall confine my attention to Locke's attack on innate ideas, and in the next I shall examine his empiricist epistemology.[5]

Locke distinguishes two sorts of putatively innate idea: 'speculative principles' and 'practical principles' (E 1.2.2). Speculative principles include fundamental axioms of logic, such as ' "What is is" and "It is impossible for the same thing to be and not be" ' (E 1.2.4). Such principles were first formulated reasonably precisely by Aristotle and have important functions in the foundations of modern logic. Practical principles, in contrast, are moral principles, such as the rule that one ought in general to keep promises, or that one ought to act justly rather than unjustly (E 1.3.2). Locke argues that neither kind of principle is innate.

(a) Speculative Principles

The Argument from General Assent

This is the suggestion that from the fact that some speculative and practical principles are agreed by all humankind it follows that those principles are innate. If, for example, it is universally assented to that 'What is is', it must be the case that 'What is is' is a principle people are born knowing, not one they have learned.

Locke seizes on the argument's two main deficiencies. He denies the premise that there exist some principles assented to by all humans, and he denies that it follows from any such universal assent – even if it obtained – that such principles are innate.

There are two reasons why the argument is invalid. Firstly, from the fact that something is universally agreed it does not logically follow that it is true. It is, in principle, possible for everyone to be mistaken. So from the fact that something is universally believed it does not follow that it is known, but if it does not follow that it is known it cannot follow that it is known innately.

The second reason why the argument is invalid is that even if something were universally known it would not logically follow that it is known innately. This is because there might be some other explanation of some universal knowledge than that knowledge being innate. At most, universal assent to some principle is logically consistent with that principle being innate; it does not logically imply it.

Locke denies the premise of the argument because he thinks it is empirically false that there are any principles every person agrees to. For example, if the principles were innate they would be known to children. They are not known to children, therefore they are not innate (E 1.2.5). It is Locke's view that most of humankind is wholly unacquainted with the logical axioms which are alleged to be innate, and if most people do not know them then clearly those people do not know them innately. Nor does it follow that a principle is believed because it is not denied. The empirical onus is on the proponent of innate ideas to show that some ideas are innate. If Locke's criticisms of the argument are sound, then he is entitled to his conclusion that 'universal consent proves nothing innate' (E 1.2.3).

The Argument from Unconscious Knowledge

If someone knows something unconsciously, then they know it but they do not know that they know it. It does not follow that if some knowledge is unconscious it is innate, but a defender of innate ideas, thinks Locke, may try to defend the premise of the Argument from Universal Assent by arguing that it is still the case that humankind believe certain principles, even if they do not affirm them, because they subscribe to them unconsciously. They do know them, but they do not assent to them because they do not know that they know them.

It is interesting to note that although Locke does not use the term 'unconscious', he has a clear conception of a doctrine of the unconscious mind two centuries before Freud. Those historians of ideas who maintain that the concept of the unconscious was originally invented by Freud or his immediate literary or psychological predecessors are therefore mistaken.

In Locke's view it is a false assumption that there are any unconscious thoughts: 'No proposition can be said to be in the mind which it never yet knew, which it was never yet conscious of' (E 1.2.5). This is partly a consequence of Locke's empiricism. If someone thinks some proposition – thinks the thought that something is the case – then they acquired that thought through experience. But experience is necessarily conscious, so that thought must have been had consciously. Locke also subscribes to the Cartesian view that it is contradictory, or nearly so, to suppose that there are unconscious thoughts: 'it seeming to me a near contradiction to say, that there are truths imprinted on the soul which it perceives or understands not' (E 1.2.5). Thus thought for Locke, as for Descartes, is necessarily conscious thought. If you think, then you know that you are thinking; and if you think, you know what you are thinking.

If the notion of unconscious belief is contradictory, there are no unconscious beliefs; if there are no unconscious beliefs, there cannot be any unconscious innate beliefs. Therefore it cannot be the case that any portion of humankind holds their innate beliefs unconsciously. If Locke is right, we believe consciously or not at all and the Argument from Unconscious Knowledge offers no support to the Argument from General Assent.

The Argument from Capacity

Suppose the proponent of innate ideas revises his position to make it more tenable. He no longer maintains that innate knowledge is consciously or unconsciously thought, but that some knowledge being innate to a person consists in that person's capacity to acquire that knowledge. We have, then, on this account, not occurrent innate knowledge but an ability or a disposition to acquire knowledge. The ability is therefore innate, and so is the 'knowing' it facilitates.

Locke's reply is that such a position collapses the distinction between 'learned' and 'innate'. All knowledge someone acquires in this way will count as innate: if someone acquires some knowledge it logically follows they have the ability to acquire it. To suggest it is therefore innate is, according to Locke, 'a very improper way of speaking' (E 1.2.5), suggesting, perhaps, that it does not make sense to imply that what is learned is innate.

Locke has an even more damaging reply. A person no doubt has the capacity to know things he does not know – say, he simply does not acquire those particular items of knowledge during his lifetime. It follows that some innate knowledge consists of truths that are not known. Something can be part of my innate knowledge even if I do not know it, if knowing innately is a capacity to know. That view leads to the contradiction that I both know and do not know something, and therefore it is false.

The Argument from the Use of Reason

On this account non-rational beings, including children and idiots, both know and assent to certain principles when they come to the use of reason. This, allegedly, shows that they were known all along and were therefore innate.

Locke has three objections to this proposition: 'If reason discovered them, that would not prove them innate' (E 1.2.8); 'It is false that reason discovers them' (E 1.2.9), and coming to know these principles does not coincide in time with becoming rational. On the first of these, Locke urges the important distinction between 'innate' and '*a priori*'. If some claim is decidable *a priori*, this means that its truth or falsity may be established independently of sense perception. For example, if I told you there was a triangular object in the next room, you could decide *a priori* that there was a three-sided object in that room on the assumption that what I said was true. The point is that you did not decide this by observation (you used rational reflection in this case). You did not have to inspect the contents of the room. But clearly, no one would claim that your knowledge in this instance was innate. You were not born with the knowledge of the triangular object. This is what Locke has in mind when he says that the fact that certain principles may be discovered by reason does not prove them to be innate.

In any case, according to Locke it is impossible that any knowledge should be both innate and discoverable by reason. The one logically precludes the other, because reason is the faculty of deducing what we do not know from what we do know (E 1.2.9), but if we already know some truths innately we cannot deduce them, because that would imply we do not know them until we deduce them. The claim that reason deduces innate principles therefore contains a contradiction, and it logically follows from that that it is false. Besides, it is implausible to suppose that logical axioms depend upon reason for their truth. They are primitive and self-evident.

Finally, it is empirically false, according to Locke, that children assent to speculative principles when they reach the age of reason. Locke readily grants that people do not assent to logical axioms until they are rational, but then adds wryly, 'nor then either' (E 1.2.12).

The Argument from Instant Assent

Locke considers next the view that innate truths have the characteristic of being 'assented to as soon as proposed' (E 1.2.17). Here the proponent of innate knowledge confuses innateness with self-evidence. Tautological propositions, such as $1 + 2 = 3$, $2 + 2 = 4$, 'White is not black' and 'A square is not a circle' (E 1.2.17), are self-evident because if they are understood then they are known – the perception of their truth is a condition of their being understood. But it does not follow from their self-evidence that they are innate.

Also, some allegedly innate principles are, or contain, empirical concepts, 'ideas of colours, sounds, tastes, figure'; but no proposition may be known innately if it presupposes empirical concepts because the latter are acquired only through experience and to deny that we obtain, for example, colour concepts empirically is 'opposite to reason and experience' (E 1.2.17).

The Argument from General and Universal Principles

Even if particular tautological propositions are not innate, it does not follow that the logical axioms they presuppose are not innate.

$1 + 2 = 3$, for example, presupposes the axiom of identity, so even if $1 + 2 = 3$ is learned, the axiom of identity is plausibly unlearned but known and so innate.

Locke's reply is that knowledge of logical axioms is not presupposed by knowledge of particular tautologies. To see this we need a distinction between epistemological and logical presupposition. Sentences of elementary arithmetic logically presuppose the axioms of logic: those axioms have to be true for those sentences of arithmetic to be true. But sentences of elementary arithmetic do not epistemologically presuppose the axioms of logic: those axioms do not have to be known for those sentences of arithmetic to be known. Indeed, Locke thinks it empirically false that the axioms of logic are known to most people and if they are not known then clearly they are not known innately.

The reason why certain truths are self-evident to a person is not that they are innate to him, but that 'the consideration of the nature of the things contained in those words would not suffer him to think otherwise' (E 1.2.21). They are analytic truths: propositions which are true by definition, or true in virtue of the meanings of their constituent terms.

The Argument from Implicit Knowledge

If logical principles are not explicitly known, that would still seem to allow the possibility of their being implicitly known. Perhaps if someone has implicit knowledge, that knowledge is innate.

But what does 'implicit' mean here? Locke is able to attach no sense to the term in this context unless it means that 'the mind is capable of understanding and assenting firmly to such propositions' (E 1.2.25). Then this suggestion is vulnerable to the same objections as the Argument from Capacity.

(b) Practical Principles

In Chapter 3 of Book I of the *Essay*, Locke turns from speculative principles to decide whether there are any innate practical, or moral, principles. He decides there is none.

Faith and Justice and the Argument from Universal Assent

If the Argument from General Assent is applied to the moral sphere, two *prima facie* plausible candidates for principles to which there exists universal assent are faith and justice; 'justice, and keeping of contracts, is that which most men seem to agree in'. However, it is simply empirically false in Locke's opinion that there are any universally agreed moral principles: 'whether there be any such moral principles wherein all men do agree, I appeal to any who have been but moderately conversant in the history of mankind, and looked abroad beyond the smoke of their own chimneys' (E 1.3.2). So again Locke denies the premise of the Argument from Universal Assent, and, it will be recalled, he thinks the argument in any case invalid. If there is no universal assent over speculative principles, 'it is much more visible concerning practical principles, that they come short of an universal reception' (E 1.3.3).

The Argument from Thought

Even if people depart from moral principles in practice, or fail to live up to them, perhaps they still adhere to them in thought – that is, they know that they ought to adhere to them in practice: 'the tacit assent of their minds agrees to what their practice contradicts' (E 1.3.3).

For Locke, this is implausible on two counts. The best guide to a person's thought is his actions and, in any case, 'it is very strange and unreasonable to suppose innate practical principles that terminate only in contemplation' (E 1.3.3). After all, practical maxims are rules for guiding actions.

In addition, it is always legitimate to ask for a reason for subscribing to a moral principle, but innate principles are allegedly self-evident. But if reasons may be produced for principles, then those principles cannot be self-evident and so cannot be innate. On top of that there is not even general agreement about the reasons for subscribing to a principle like 'one should do as he would be done unto' (E 1.3.4). A Christian will reply that God requires this of us but a 'Hobbist' will reply that the public requires it and the Leviathan will punish transgression from it (E 1.3.5).

Locke is a historical and cultural relativist about moral values. He thinks there exists a 'great variety of opinions concerning moral rules' (E 1.3.6) and gives these examples:

> Are there not places where, at a certain age, they kill or expose their parents without any remorse at all? In a part of Asia, the sick, when their case comes to be thought desperate, are carried out and laid on the earth before they are dead, and left there, exposed to wind and weather, to perish without assistance or pity . . . The virtues whereby the Tououpinambos believed they merited paradise were revenge, and eating abundance of their enemies. The saints who are canonised amongst the Turks, lead lives one cannot with modesty relate. (E 1.3.7)

Such a variety of beliefs and practices is inconsistent with the doctrine that moral principles are adhered to universally, and if it is true that if a principle is innate then it is adhered to universally, Locke has shown that no such principle is innate.

3 SENSATION AND REFLECTION

If knowledge is not innate, then how is knowledge possible? Locke's sustained reply, which absorbs the whole of Book II of the *Essay*, is: 'Through experience.' It is here, if anywhere, that Locke's empiricism is positively argued for.

There are two, and only two, sources of knowledge according to Locke: 'All ideas come from sensation or reflection' (E 11.1.2). This gives rise to three questions: 'What is an idea?', 'What is sensation?', and 'What is reflection?' I shall treat each of these in turn.

Ideas

Locke says: 'idea is the object of thinking' (E 11.1.1). This may strike the reader as a strange definition, because the object of thinking is what thinking is about, but if, for example, I am thinking about you

that does not make you one of my ideas – even if my thinking of you
consists in my having an idea of you. The solution is twofold.
Firstly, Locke's conception of an idea is much broader than ours. It
includes not only our notions of a mental image and a concept, but
also our notion of an experience. An idea for Locke is any mental
content whatsoever. It is the medium of thought and what our
minds are stored with. This broad notion of an idea needs to be
borne in mind not only in what follows, but also in reading the
philosophy of Berkeley who shares it with Locke. Secondly, Locke
thinks that only ideas are perceived directly – not physical objects.
The mind perceives or has ideas and these ideas represent the
physical objects which cause them. These two exegetical points
explain away the *prima facie* strangeness of Locke's calling ideas the
'object of thinking', and his giving as examples of ideas 'whiteness,
hardness, sweetness, thinking, motion, man, army, drunkenness'
(E II.I.I).

Sensation

Because there are no innate ideas, the mind at birth is like 'white
paper, void of all characters, without any ideas' (E II.I.2). There
can be no knowledge, no ideas in the mind, without experience.
Sensation is the fundamental kind of experience for Locke and he
means by it perception using one or more of the five senses. Through
the senses we are caused by physical objects passively to receive all
the ideas we have of the external world:

> Our senses, conversant about particular sensible objects, do convey into
> the mind several distinct perceptions of things, according to the various
> ways wherein those objects do affect them, and thus we come by those ideas
> we have of yellow, white, heat, cold, soft, hard, bitter, sweet, and all those
> which we call sensible qualities. (E II.I.3)

This, then, is Locke's definition of 'sensation'. A quality is a
property or characteristic of something, and a sensible quality is
one which may be detected by one or more of the five senses. For
example, two sensible qualities of a physical object are its shape
and its colour. Ideas of sensible qualities are acquired by sensation

and these ideas are caused by some of those qualities: 'External objects furnish the mind with the ideas of sensible qualities' (E II.1.5).

Reflection

Once the mind is stored with ideas through sensation, it has the capacity consciously to consider or reflect upon those ideas. This introspective or self-conscious activity is called by Locke 'reflection'. It is, as he puts it, 'the perception of the operations of our own minds within us' (E II.1.4). Reflection is clearly impossible without sensation having taken place; nevertheless, acts of reflection upon the ideas of sensation produce a new sort of idea – ideas of reflection – and these could never be acquired through sensation alone. The ideas of reflection include 'perception, thinking, doubting, believing, reasoning, knowing, willing, and all the different actings of our own minds'. Rather as the ideas of sensation are caused by physical objects, the ideas of reflection are caused by the ideas of sensation. Reflection is rather like another sense: 'This source of ideas every man has wholly in himself: and though it be not sense, as having nothing to do with external objects, yet it is very like it, and might properly enough be called internal sense' (E II.1.4).

Reflection and Sensation

Locke presents us with a series of arguments for the conclusion that 'external material things as objects of sensation, and the operations of our own minds within as the objects of reflection are . . . the only originals from whence all our ideas take their beginnings' (E II.1.4). Locke's empiricism fundamentally consists in the view that 'all our ideas are from one or the other of these' (E II.1.5).

Locke invites us to reflect on our own ideas to decide whether any of them is not either an idea of an object of the senses, or else an idea of the mind's own reflections. He thinks we will conclude that all our ideas are either of sensation or reflection.

There is a strength and a weakness in this appeal to introspection. The strength is that if one considers one's own mental contents they do all seem to be about either objects one has perceived or one's own mental processes. According to Locke, even if we think of imaginary objects the materials for such thinking are derived from sensation – however radically we may recombine them in reflection. The weakness of the appeal is that although all our ideas introspectively seem to be of either sensation or reflection, it does not logically follow that they are. It is logically consistent with the findings of introspection that ideas should be innate, God-given, the result of brain-in-a-vat experiments, or have no origin at all.

The central problem for Locke's empiricist epistemology is this. All knowledge comes from sensation or reflection, but how do we know this? Sensation and reflection offer us no proof that all knowledge comes from sensation or reflection. Experience cannot teach us that all knowledge comes from experience. The problem of empiricism is that there can be no empirical proof of empiricism.

Ideas and Experience

One essential component of Locke's empiricism is notably inconsistent with a central development of twentieth-century analytical philosophy: Wittgenstein's Private Language Argument.[6] Locke holds there can be no idea of a sensible quality without sensation of that quality because the sensation of that quality causes the idea of that quality. In other words, the sensation of some quality we may call Q is both necessary and sufficient for the acquisition of the idea of Q. Here is Locke on the necessary condition:

> If a child were kept in a place where he never saw any other but black and white till he were a man, he would have no more idea of scarlet and green, than he that from his childhood never tasted an oyster or a pineapple has of those particular relishes. (E II.1.6)

Wittgenstein claims that the ability to use a concept in a rule-governed way as a member of a linguistic community is sufficient for the understanding of that concept – even in the case of a putatively experiential concept like 'pain'.[7] The experience of pain is neither necessary nor sufficient for understanding 'pain'. Locke, on the contrary, maintains that the experience is both necessary and sufficient for the acquisition of the idea, and hence (as he argues in Book II of the *Essay*) for being acquainted with the meaning of the word. On the Lockean view, meaning is something psychological and private; on the Wittgensteinian view, something rule-governed and public.

It seems to me that both the Wittgensteinian and the Lockean accounts of mental concepts are incomplete. Locke underestimates the social presuppositions of meaning. Wittgenstein underestimates the subjective, experiential presuppositions of the use of ordinary psychological concepts. A synthesis is clearly required.[8]

Simple and Complex Ideas

As we have seen (pp. 61–2 above), ideas for Locke are the objects of thinking, or the contents of our thoughts and experiences. There are two sorts of idea: 'some of them are simple, and some complex' (E II.2.1). We need to decide now exactly what this distinction between simple and complex ideas amounts to.[9]

Simple ideas may be acquired by either sensation or reflection and, like all ideas, by no other route, but they have this special characteristic: they are ideas that are not composed of ideas. As Locke puts it, a simple idea is 'in itself uncompounded' and 'contains in it nothing but one uniform appearance or conception in the mind, and is not distinguishable into different ideas' (E II.2.1). Simple ideas cannot be invented by any act of human imagination, and the will has no control over their existence or nature, so 'the mind can neither make nor destroy them' (E II.2.2). The powers of the imagination are limited to the combining and recombining of simple ideas, rather as the configuration of the physical universe is confined to the combining and recombining of matter and does not involve the creation of extra matter *ex nihilo*. Simple ideas are epistemologically primitive in Locke's philosophy in the sense that if we were not acquainted with simple ideas we could have no knowledge of anything else. They are 'the materials of all our knowledge' (E II.2.2).

Locke thinks our imagination is further constrained by the type of simple ideas we are acquainted with. For example, if I have not tasted a certain taste I cannot imagine (correctly) what that taste is like. Similarly, it is impossible to imagine a smell one has never smelled, or for a blind person to have ideas of colours, or a deaf person of sounds. Locke's empiricism logically implies that the thinking of a simple idea requires the empirical acquisition of that idea.[10]

Is Locke's epistemology of the imagination correct? In what sense is it impossible for a congenitally blind person to imagine the colour red? Is this a contingent or a logical impossibility? What is the connection between an idea's being simple – uncompounded – and its being unthinkable without its acquisition in sensation?

Locke does not have answers to these questions, but he does admit two logical possibilities about simple ideas. We humans could have had fewer senses than the five we do have, and we could have had, or other creatures could have, additional senses to our five. In the first case fewer sorts of simple ideas would be received in sensation, so our imagination would be more constrained than it is. In the second case extra sorts of simple ideas would be received in sensation, so our imagination would be less constrained than it is. In either case, Locke's empiricist principle that thought is constrained by sensation is maintained.

Locke devises a fourfold taxonomy for simple ideas according to their origin, that is, according to the various causal routes by which we acquire them. There are the simple ideas acquired by one sense only, that is by one, and only one, of our five senses. There are the simple ideas acquired by more than one sense. There are the simple ideas acquired by reflection only, and finally, those acquired by both sensation and reflection.

The ideas Locke lists as received by only one sense are colours through the eyes, sounds through the ears, smells through the nose, tastes through the palate and solidity through touch. If this classification appears trivial to the reader, we may raise the interesting epistemological question of whether it is in principle impossible to, for example, hear colours or see sounds.

Locke holds that there are three physiological prerequisites for the reception of each kind of simple idea through each sense. These are: the appropriate sense organs, the brain (which Locke calls 'the mind's presence room' (E II.3.1), and the rest of the nervous system. The well-functioning of these parts of the body is a causally necessary condition for the receiving of simple ideas.

Locke says that 'the ideas we get from more than one sense are of space or extension, figure, rest and motion' (E II.5). 'Extension' was sometimes used in the seventeenth century to mean 'space', but could also mean 'size', and a clear distinction was not always drawn between our concepts of space and size in the use of 'extension'. 'Figure' means 'shape'. Clearly, these ideas are received by more than one sense because they are acquired by both sight and touch. You may detect the size and shape of an object, and tell whether it is moving either by touching it or by looking at it.

The simple ideas obtained only by reflection are of two sorts: 'perception or thinking, and volition or willing' (E II.6.2). Locke uses 'perception' in different senses in the *Essay*. Sometimes he uses it to mean 'sense perception', sometimes – as here – to mean 'thinking', sometimes to mean 'introspection' and sometimes, broadly, to mean 'being conscious' or 'being aware'. Thinking and volition are the operations of the two principal Lockean mental faculties: the understanding and the will. These two faculties are powers or abilities, in Locke's view. They are nothing over and above our capacity to think and to will: 'the power of thinking is called the understanding, and the power of volition is called the will' (E II.6.2). Simple ideas of reflection are gained only by reflection on the operations of these two faculties.

Simple ideas acquired by both sensation and reflection include 'pleasure or delight, and its opposite pain or uneasiness; power, existence, unity' (E II.7.1). According to Locke, pleasure and pain may be produced by any idea, and if there were no pleasure or pain 'we should have no reason to prefer one thought or action to another' (E II.7.3). Without such motivation life would be 'a lazy, lethargic dream' (E II.7.3). It is interesting to note that Locke counts existence as a simple idea, because that concept has proved notoriously difficult to analyse in the history of philosophy. The idea of unity is that deployed in thinking of 'whatever we . . .

consider as one thing' (E II.7.7), so if we think of something as a whole rather than some parts, or as a set rather than some elements, we thereby employ the simple idea of unity.

The final two simple ideas of sensation and reflection Locke lists are power and succession. Power is the ability to cause effects. For example, when we think or move we have the power to do this, and when physical objects interact causally they exhibit power. The idea of succession is the idea of *A* preceding *B* in time, or *B* succeeding *A* in time. It is possible to acquire the idea of succession by sense perception,

yet [it] is more constantly offered us by what passes in our own minds . . . for if we look immediately into ourselves, and reflect on what is observable there, we shall find our ideas always, whilst we are awake or have any thought, passing in train, one going and another coming without intermission. (E II.7.9)

In criticism of Locke's theory of simple ideas it might be objected that he underestimates the degree of psychological preconception required even to see a colour as red. Perhaps there is nothing simple given to consciousness, in the sense that whatever is given is given in a particular way and at least partially determined – made what it is – by the constitution of the subject. Locke rules this out when he says that 'the mind is wholly passive in the reception of all its simple ideas' (E II.12.1). He needs an argument to show that at least some experience is without content-determining preconceptions. Also, it seems to be the case that concepts like 'red' and 'exists' are semantically primitive, as are many terms denoting simple experiential contents. Locke has no explanation of why ostensive but not verbal definitions are possible for these parts of our vocabulary. Such objections are not necessarily fatal to Locke's empiricist epistemology, but any neo-Lockean needs to meet them.

Only a person acquainted with simple ideas may have complex ideas. This is because complex ideas are combinations of simple ideas which result from imaginative activity: 'When the understanding is once stored with these simple ideas, it has the power to repeat, compare, and unite them, even to an almost infinite variety, and so make at pleasure new complex ideas' (E II.2.2). It logically follows from this account that complex ideas are 'made by the mind out of simple ones' (E II.12.1).

So while a simple idea is not composed of ideas, a complex idea is precisely such a combination of ideas. While the mind is passive in the reception of simple ideas, the mind is active in the creation of complex ideas. In addition, the mind has a measure of control over the existence and nature of complex ideas that is wholly lacking in regard to simple ideas; they are subject to the will.

Locke thinks that complex ideas are the result of one of three kinds of imaginative operation which may be performed on simple ideas. He calls it 'combining'. The other two kinds of operation produce ideas of relations and general ideas. The operation that produces complex ideas is 'combining several simple ideas into some compound one'. As Locke puts it, 'thus all complex ideas are made' (E II.12.1). However, 'ideas of relations' are produced by 'bringing two ideas, whether simple or complex, together, and setting them one by another so as to take a view of them at once without uniting them into one' (E II.12.2). So the idea of a relation is produced by the mental juxtaposition of two ideas and their being grasped by a single mental act. Even though this is not the mental combining of more than one idea into one new idea, ideas of relations are complex ideas. Finally, 'general ideas' are produced by 'abstraction', which is 'separating them [ideas] from all other ideas that accompany them in their real existence' (E II.12.2). A general idea is an idea which is of or about more than one thing. (See below, p. 71–2.)

Despite these three kinds of mental operation, the imagination remains constrained by its simple ideas. It is powerless to invent simple ideas, even though it may combine and recombine those it has into new complex ideas at will. Locke offers us the following definition of 'complex idea': 'Ideas thus made up of several simple ones put together I call "complex"' (E II.12.2). He provides these examples: 'beauty, gratitude, a man, an army, the universe' (E II.12.2). If we ask what it consists in for simple ideas to be combined into a complex one, then Locke's answer is that the mind may consider several simple ideas as one complex idea – whether or not such a complex idea depicts anything physical; 'it can, by its own power, put together those ideas it has, and make new complex ones which it never received so united' (E II.12.2).

Locke thinks there are three kinds of complex idea: 'modes', 'substances' and 'relations' (E II.12.3ff.). A mode is an idea which depends upon at least one other idea, and may not subsist by itself. In particular a mode depends upon a substance, so that 'the ideas signified by the words triangle, gratitude, murder, etc.' are modes. Locke makes a distinction between two kinds of mode. Some modes are simple (even though a mode is a complex idea). A mode is simple if its component ideas are qualitatively similar, as in the case of a dozen or a score, but a mode is mixed, not simple, if its component ideas are qualitatively dissimilar, as in the case of beauty which (according to Locke) contains the ideas of shape and colour.

Whereas modes depend upon other ideas – ultimately, substances, 'ideas of substances are such combinations of simple ideas as are taken to represent distinct particular things subsisting by themselves', for example the ideas of 'lead' and 'man' are ideas of substances. There are two kinds of idea of substance. The first is a 'single' substance, for instance the idea of a man or a sheep. Here the idea of a substance is the idea of one, and only one, individual. The second idea of substance is that of 'several of those put together' or 'collective substance', such as 'an army of men, or flock of sheep' (E II.12.6).

The third and final category of complex idea is that of relation. This is the idea that results from the comparison of one idea with another. However abstract and seemingly remote from the objects of sensation they may seem, every idea has its origin in either sensation or reflection, and, we should recall, sensation is necessary for reflection. No matter how complex the operations of juxtaposition and abstraction performed, 'even large and abstract ideas are derived from sensation or reflection' (E II.12.8). Thus Locke is a thorough empiricist about even our most imaginative and seemingly non-empirical thinking.

The question that needs to be raised here is: Is all our thinking empirical? Is it true that our mathematical thinking, even perhaps our thinking about God and the soul, depend in the last resort upon sense perception? A Platonist would argue the reverse, that empirical uses of mathematics – for example, counting physical objects – depend upon an innate acquaintance with pure, non-empirical, mathematical objects, and all our knowledge of empirical appearances depends on a prior acquaintance with non-empirical reality. The metaphysical choice between Locke and Plato is still open.

Abstract Ideas

Abstract general ideas are ideas that represent more than one thing of a particular sort. They are acquired by abstraction, which is a process whereby 'the mind makes the particular ideas, received from particular objects, to become general'. Abstraction is the consideration of an idea without attention to 'all other existences and the circumstances of real existence, as time, place, or any other concomitant ideas' (E II.11.9). In this way the idea of a particular thing becomes the representative of all the things of the same kind as that thing. As we shall see, general or abstract ideas have an important role in Locke's theory of meaning – his explanation of how language works. General ideas are the meanings of general terms (see p. 96–7 below), and in this they are what are called 'universals'. The problem of universals in philosophy is the problem of what generality consists in: What are *sorts*? What are *kinds*? Locke's solution is that generality consists in the existence of general ideas. Here is his account of the general ideas applied to the idea of the colour white:

. . . the same colour being observed today in chalk or snow, which the mind yesterday received from milk, it considers that appearance alone, makes it a representative of all that kind; and having given it the name whiteness, it by that sound signifies the same quality wheresoever to be imagined or met with; and thus universals, whether ideas or terms, are made. (E II.11.9)

The capacity for abstraction is the most important difference between people and animals, according to Locke. His word for non-human animals is 'brutes', so, as he puts it, 'Brutes abstract not' (E II.11.10), and 'the having of general ideas is that which puts a perfect distinction between man and brutes'. Locke's argument for this conclusion is this: animals are not language-users. As general ideas are the meanings of general terms, if animals are not users of general terms they are not users of general ideas. The problem with this is that Locke has failed to show that general ideas are *only* the meanings of general terms. Logically room is left for animals to engage in the psychological process of abstraction and so to acquire general ideas even if they are *not* language-users. When Locke says that 'they [brutes] have not the faculty of abstracting or making general ideas, since they have no use of words or any other general signs', 'since' must be taken in a weak inductive sense and not in a strictly logical sense.

Animals cannot think in generalities, but humans can. Locke thinks that only individual or particular things exist, and that generality belongs only to thought. Mind-independently and non-linguistically, what is is a plurality of particulars: 'general and universal belong not to the real existence of things; but are the inventions and creatures of the understanding' (E III.3.11). Locke is not thereby denying that there exist real similarities between the particular things that exist independently of minds and language. In his view the acquisition of general ideas depends upon the perception of such similarities. However, the classification of things into sorts or types depends upon human thought, so the existence of such sorts or types is essentially mental: 'abstract ideas are the essences of genera and species' (E III.3.12). The essence of something is what that thing is, so the classification by sort or type is something mental. It logically follows that if there were no abstract ideas there would be no sorts or types of things, even though similarities would remain between particular things. This is the careful path Locke treads between conceptualism, the view that the universal is conceptual, and realism, the view that there exist types and sorts of things irrespectively of how we classify them linguistically. Locke says of essences, sorts and species: 'They are the workmanship of the understanding, but have their foundation in the similitude of things' (E III.3.12).

Ideas, then, for Locke are simple, complex or abstract. Ideas are mental and experiential contents, but they also represent physical objects in the external world which cause them. This gives rise to new questions. How accurate are such representations? What is a physical object? Is perceiving a kind of mental representing? To these questions and Locke's answers to them we should now turn.

4 PHYSICAL OBJECTS

Locke, like his French near contemporary Descartes, is a mind–body dualist; that is, he thinks there exist two, and only two, sorts of substance: mental or spiritual substance, called 'mind', and physical or material substance, called 'body'. (The seventeenth-century use of 'body' is much broader than ours. It means 'matter' or 'physical object'.) In the next section I shall examine Locke's concept of mind and here his concept of a physical object. This is best explained via two notions: the distinction between primary and secondary qualities and the idea of substance, but first 'idea' and 'quality' need distinguishing.

Ideas and Qualities

A quality is a property or a characteristic of something, so being red or being cuboid are amongst an object's qualities. Ideas are in the mind but qualities are in physical objects or, as Locke puts it, 'in bodies' (E II.8.7). Locke has an important supplementary definition of 'quality'. A quality of a physical object is a power or disposition of the object to produce ideas in us. Locke uses this definition as a criterion to distinguish qualities from ideas:

Whatsoever the mind perceives in itself, or is the immediate object of perception, thought or understanding, that I call idea; and the power to produce any idea in our mind, I call quality of the subject wherein that power is. (E II.8.8)

This concept of an idea needs to be borne clearly in mind in what follows. Locke thinks that certain qualities are not just powers to produce ideas in us but actually resemble our ideas of them, while other qualities of the object only exist in the object as powers to produce ideas in us. In the latter case our ideas do not resemble anything in the object. Ideas of the first kind are called by Locke ideas of 'primary qualities'; ideas of the second sort are called ideas of 'secondary qualities'.[11]

Primary Qualities

The primary qualities of a physical object are its 'solidity, extension, figure, motion or rest, and number' (E II.8.9). An object is solid in so far as it cannot be penetrated by another object. The 'extension' of an object is its size, and its 'figure' is its shape. These primary qualities of a physical object are intrinsic to that object, so that an object is in motion or at rest whether it is being perceived or not, and if there exist some physical objects then there exists a certain number of them, quite irrespective of whether those objects are being perceived or not. We may think of the primary qualities of a physical object as the objective properties of that physical object, if we mean that they belong to the object just as they are, whether the object is perceived or not.

Locke says the primary qualities are 'utterly inseparable from the body' (E II.8.9). He means by this not just that they are intrinsic properties of the object and resemble our ideas of them, but also, and more strongly, that possessing primary qualities is both necessary and sufficient for being a physical object. Consider any individual, call it x. If x possesses the primary qualities, it logically follows that x is a physical object. That means that possessing primary qualities is a sufficient condition for being a physical object. Consider any individual, call it x. If x does not possess the primary qualities, it logically follows that x is not a physical object. That means possessing the primary qualities is a necessary condition for being a physical object. We see now the essential outline of Locke's answer to the question: What is a physical object? An object counts as physical if, and only if, it possesses primary qualities. Another way of putting the point is to say that primary qualities are essential to a physical object, or part of the 'real essence' of body.[12]

However a physical object may change, and however the primary qualities of that object may change, it may never lack primary qualities. For example, if you take a grain of wheat and divide it repeatedly, then each part, although smaller than the original whole, retains all its primary qualities (E II.8.9).

Locke thinks that our ideas represent physical objects, and physical objects cause our ideas. As in Hobbes's epistemology, the relation between ideas and physical objects is two-way: in one direction it is representational and in the other direction it is causal.[13] The next question therefore is 'how bodies produce ideas in us'. Locke's solution is: 'primary qualities produce their ideas' (E II.8.11). Our ideas of both primary qualities and secondary qualities are produced by the action of imperceptible physical particles on the sense organs. These are emitted by physical objects, and are themselves physical objects because – although very small, like the divided parts of the grain of wheat – they possess primary qualities. They operate on our sense organs by impulse, that is, by motion and physical contact. For example, in the case of the visual perception of some physical object, 'it is evident some singly perceptible bodies must come from them to the eyes, and thereby convey to the brain some motion which produces these ideas which we have of them in us' (E II.8.11). All ideas – ideas of primary as well as secondary qualities – ultimately depend upon the operation of physical particles which have primary qualities.

It is worth remarking that Locke faces as great a problem as Descartes in accounting for the nature of causal interaction between mental and physical. Physical particles cause a motion in the brain. That is comprehensible, but that motion in the brain then causes something qualitatively dissimilar to occur: an idea, and that causal connection is far from clear. How does matter in motion – which is only matter in motion, however minute or complex – produce an image or an experience? Even if it is clear what it means for an idea to represent a quality (which may be doubted) it is not clear what it means for a quality to cause an idea.

The idea of a primary quality resembles that primary quality, whereas the idea of a secondary quality, as we shall see, resembles nothing in the object. As Locke puts it: 'ideas of primary qualities are resemblances; of secondary not' and 'the ideas of primary qualities of bodies are resemblances of them' (E II.8.15). It follows that our ideas (including our experiences) of shape, size, motion, solidity and number are like shape, size, motion, stability and number as those qualities really are, in the object. The patterns of primary qualities 'do really exist in the bodies themselves' (E II.8.15) and our ideas of them represent them as they are.

Secondary Qualities

The secondary qualities of a physical object are its colour, sound, taste and smell. Our ideas or experiences of these qualities resemble nothing actually intrinsic to the object: 'the ideas produced in us by these secondary qualities have no resemblance of them at all' (E II.8.15), so what we normally think of as the colour of an object is not an objective property of that object according to Locke, rather it is an idea produced in us by our causal interaction with the object's primary qualities. If we raise the question in what sense secondary qualities are properties of physical objects at all, Locke's reply is that secondary qualities 'in truth are nothing in the objects themselves, but powers to produce various sensations in us by their primary qualities' (E II.8.10). So colours, sounds, tastes and smells may be correctly thought of as properties of physical objects, but only as dispositional properties. An object is coloured, for example, in so far as it possesses the capacity to cause certain ideas in us: sensations we should commonsensically classify as the colours red, blue, etc. It is not misleading to think of secondary qualities as objective, or mind-independent, so long as we remember that they only inhere in objects as powers, dispositions or capacities to cause ideas in us. Much of what we pre-philosophically count as colour, taste, sound and smell Locke assimilates to our idea, or experience, of these phenomena.[14]

Ideas of secondary qualities are produced in us by the same sort of causal route as ideas of primary qualities, 'by the operation of insensible particles on our senses' (E II.8.13). Notice that the problem of psycho-physical causal interaction within the framework of mind–body dualism arises again here: how may physical causes have mental effects? How may insensible physical particles cause ideas? Locke's only gesture towards a solution is the suggestion that

God has no difficulty in maintaining causal relations between radically heterogeneous events (E II.8.13).

Secondary qualities depend upon primary qualities for their existence because a secondary quality is a capacity to produce ideas in us and this capacity only exists by virtue of the primary qualities of an object. It follows that there could be no idea of secondary qualities without the existence of primary qualities. Locke says of colours, tastes, smells and sounds:

> Whatever reality we by mistake attribute to them, [they] are nothing in the objects themselves, but powers to produce various sensations in us, and depend on those primary qualities, viz., bulk, figure, texture, and motion of parts. (E II.8.13)

Possession of primary qualities is, as we have seen, both necessary and sufficient for being a physical object. What of secondary qualities? Certainly, that x possesses secondary qualities is not a necessary condition of x's being a physical object. It is logically possible that there should exist physical objects with no secondary qualities – no powers to produce experiences of sounds, colours, and so on in us. However, might not possessing secondary qualities be sufficient for being a physical object? This is debatable, but I think not. It is logically possible that something should produce ideas of colours, sounds, etc. in us yet not be a physical object. As we shall see, Bishop Berkeley exploits this logical possibility in his idealist version of empiricism (see below, pp. 108 ff.). However, it could be argued that it makes no sense to conceptually separate a disposition from its physical ground. Locke sometimes argues that the disposition, which itself is a secondary quality, really consists of a configuration of primary qualities. This would identify a secondary quality with a disposition, and then identify that disposition with some primary quality. Clearly, this is ultimately to identify a secondary quality with a primary quality because, logically, if A is identical with B and if B is identical with C, then A must be identical with C. Here is a passage where Locke identifies secondary qualities with primary qualities:

> They are, in the bodies we denominate from them, only a power to produce those sensations in us; and what is sweet, blue, or warm in idea, is but the certain bulk, figure, and motion of the insensible parts in the bodies themselves, which we call so. (E II.8.15)

Nevertheless, Locke does not successfully reduce secondary qualities to primary qualities, because no disposition may be wholly reduced to its ground. No power is just what makes that power possible.[15]

In drawing the primary–secondary quality distinction, Locke is drawing a subjective–objective distinction consistent with the science of his day. Galileo, Descartes, Boyle and Newton all thought the physical universe intrinsically colourless, tasteless, odourless and silent.[16] Indeed, the mind-independent physical universe was thought to consist in the movement of silent, bulky objects possessing only shape, size and solidity, and only causal interaction with conscious beings produced the appearance of colour, sound, taste and smell. Interestingly, this has led to the view that what is mind-independent is more real than what is mind-dependent. We owe our opinion that matter is more real than mind to the seventeenth-century scientific revolution. For example, here is Locke on the reality of primary qualities:

> The particular bulk, number, figure and motion of the parts of fire or snow are really in them, whether anyone's senses perceived them or no; and therefore they may be called real qualities, because they really exist in those bodies. (E II.8.17)

However, in the case of secondary qualities:

> Take away the sensation of them; let not the eyes see light or colours, nor the ears hear sounds; let the palate not taste, nor the nose smell; and all colours, tastes, odours, and sounds, as they are such particular ideas, vanish and cease, and are reduced to their causes, i.e. bulk, figure, and motion of parts. (E II.8.17)

The most conspicuous theme of the philosophy of mind since the seventeenth century, and perhaps of philosophy since then *tout court*, is the dogma that to explain the mental is to explain the mental away. Locke is partly responsible for that.[17]

Substance

The qualities of an object are its properties – but what exactly are these properties properties of? We say that something has the qualities of being square, blue, or big, but what exactly has these particular qualities? This is a difficult question in philosophy, and to answer it many philosophers have postulated a substance as being that which bears properties – or what properties are properties of. The properties of a physical object are on this account properties of a material substance.[18] There is a parallel question about what mental properties are properties of, and a mind, soul, or mental substance is sometimes postulated to answer that question. However, I postpone discussion of mental substance until the next section (pp. 81–2 below).

Locke introduces the concept of substance in the context of his theory of perception. He believes that perceiving an object consists in mentally representing it: perceiving an idea which represents it. It follows that we are never directly acquainted with physical objects themselves, but only with our ideas of them. So, 'not imagining how these simple ideas can subsist by themselves, we accustom ourselves to suppose some substratum wherein they do subsist, and from which they do result, which therefore we call substance' (E II.23.1). A substance is therefore postulated as the cause of our ideas. It is clear that Locke is only reporting a mental habit, albeit one fundamental to our ordinary ways of thinking. He is not thereby committed to the view that substance really exists, even though he believes physical objects really (mind-independently) exist.

Locke says that our idea of substance is extremely vague. It is that which bears or supports the properties of a physical object, but little else may be said about it: if someone examines his own idea of substance, he finds 'only a supposition of he knows not what support of such qualities which are capable of producing simple ideas in us' (E II.23.2). Locke is evidently dissatisfied with such a vague concept, yet is unable to offer a satisfactory account of what the properties of a physical object are properties of. He comes close to anticipating Ayer's view that the properties of a physical object are properties of each other (see LTL 57) when he says: 'if anyone should be asked, what is the subject wherein colour or weight inheres, he would have nothing to say, but the solid extended parts' (E II.23.2), although later he says it is inconceivable that qualities should inhere 'in one another' (E II.23.4).

Locke is on the brink of claiming that 'substance' is meaningless when he cites it as one of those cases 'where we use words without having clear and distinct ideas' (E II.23.2). After all, the meaning of a word is an idea for Locke, so if the idea is not clear then the meaning of the word is not clear (see pp. 99 ff., below). However, Locke does not say that 'substance' is meaningless:

the idea . . . to which we give the name substance, being nothing but the supposed, but unknown, support of those qualities we find existing, which we imagine cannot subsist *sine re substante*, 'without something to support them.' (E II.23.2)

Substantia is translated by Locke as 'standing under, or upholding' but this is a 'confused idea', even though 'when we speak of any sort of substance, we say it is a thing having such or such qualities' (E II.23.3). Locke's considered view is that the idea of substance is confused but hard to dispense with as it is so fundamental to our conceptual scheme.

It should be borne in mind, therefore, that when Berkeley makes Locke the target for his attack on material substance – the idea that there is a kind of material stuff called 'matter' that the universe is made of – Locke himself has severe reservations about this idea (see pp. 108–16 below).

Locke regards the problem of substance as unsolved. Only two options seem available, and both are unacceptable. We cannot imagine that there should be just properties, without something for them to inhere in, or be properties of. Nor can we imagine that properties should be properties of each other, so 'we suppose them existing in, and supported by, some common subject; which support we denote by the name substance, though it be certain we have no clear or distinct idea of that thing we suppose a support' (E II.23.4).

There is therefore a fundamental lack of clarity in Locke's concept of a physical object. Despite the fact that physical objects possess primary qualities necessarily and secondary qualities contingently, he cannot say what 'matter' is. However, Locke is not alone in this. At the time of writing there is still no satisfactory analysis of 'matter', even though the ruling paradigms in philosophy are materialist and physicalist. Perhaps unwittingly Locke leaves us a message here by his failure. The concept of matter is as obscure, and perhaps as bogus, as the concept of mind.[19]

5 MINDS

Locke, as we have seen, is a mind–body dualist. He thinks both minds and physical objects exist – no physical object is a mind and no mind is a physical object. But what are minds? Is Locke's concept of mind any clearer than his concept of matter? In this section I shall attempt to answer these questions.

Locke certainly thinks an unclarity exists about minds or mental substances which parallels the unclarity about matter. Because we believe that 'the operations of the mind, viz., thinking, reasoning, fearing etc.,' do not occur on their own account, nor are they straightforwardly characteristics of a physical object, 'we are apt to think these the actions of some other substance, which we call spirit' (E II.23.5). When Locke says 'we have as clear a notion of the substance of spirit as we have of body' (E II.23.5), he is either being tactful in deference to the commonsense of his time or else being supremely ironic. He finds the concepts of mind and matter equally unclear, mainly because they are ideas of substances.

I have been calling Locke a mind–body dualist, and that is the most apposite characterization of his philosophy of mind. However, it is evident that he regards 'mind' and 'matter' as unclear concepts. He also believes we have no knowledge of their true natures and that such knowledge may always escape us. Perhaps it is in principle impossible. On Locke's representational epistemology we are never directly perceptually acquainted with physical objects or minds, only with ideas. The title of Locke's book is *An Essay Concerning Human Understanding*, and one of his principal aims is precisely the delineation of the limits to human understanding. In trying to understand mind and matter we are coming up against those boundaries. The project of defining the limits to our understanding anticipates by a century that of Immanuel Kant in his *Critique of Pure Reason*. His criticisms of the ideas of mental and material substance are the first step on the road to Russell's neutral monism, which is premised on the claim that materialism and idealism are both false. (See 'Russell', section 6, below.)

Locke's attitude to Cartesian mind–body dualism is rather ambivalent.[20] He accepts that 'we are able to frame the complex idea of an immaterial spirit' (E II.23.15) despite the unclarity of the idea of substance, because we can join together in thought the ideas of thinking and willing. He also thinks it more probable that mental substance exists than that material substance exists. Even though he explicitly rejects the supposedly Cartesian view that the soul always thinks, he accepts that there exists psycho-physical causal interaction. We have seen that for Locke those mental items called 'ideas' have physical causes (p. 75 above). He also maintains that 'everyone finds in himself, that his soul can think, will, and operate on the body' (E II.23.20). It logically follows from the conjunction of those two claims that mind may affect matter and matter mind. However, when he argues that the soul is capable of motion he ascribes a physical characteristic to it and thus blurs the clean mental–physical distinction of the Cartesians (E II.23.19–21). Nevertheless, his definition of 'mind' or 'soul' 'as an immaterial spirit . . . a substance that thinks' is thoroughly Cartesian.[21]

Locke is a mind–body dualist who perceives some of the deepest problems inherent in that position. However, the unclarities he detects in 'mind' and 'matter' also threaten the cogency of idealism and materialism, the most usually favoured alternatives to dualism. Interestingly, mind and matter suffer from the same obscurity – the obscurity of being substances. Even though the idea of a substance – a kind of ultimate material, of which the world is made – is as deeply rooted in Western commonsense since the seventeenth century as it is in competing ontologies of the mind, it is perhaps just that assumption which will have to be relinquished by any cogent metaphysics for the twenty-first century.

6 PERSONAL IDENTITY

The problem of personal identity is stating what the identity of a person over time consists in. Consider a person at a time, t_1, and consider a person at a later time, t_2. The problem is to state the logically necessary and sufficient conditions for the person at t_2 being numerically identical with the person at t_1 – the same person in the sense of the same one. Under what conditions is the earlier person the later person (and the later person the earlier person)?[22]

Two traditional solutions to this problem are, firstly, the claim that the later person is the earlier person if, and only if, the later person has the same soul as the earlier person; and, secondly, the later person is the earlier person if, and only if, the spatio-temporal continuity of the human body which existed at t_1 reaches t_2 unbroken. Locke's account of personal identity contrasts with both of these, but elements of the second are to be found in his discussion of types of identity other than that of the person. I shall discuss these before turning to personal identity specifically.

Identity

The contrast between identity and diversity, or numerical sameness and difference, arises 'when considering anything as existing at any determined time and place, we compare it with itself existing at another time' (E ii.27.1). It is not as though we could not take something to be numerically identical with the very thing we are perceiving while we are perceiving it, whatever it is, but we may take one thing for another if we perceive it at different times, whether or not it is in the same place at those times.

Locke introduces several principles of identity essential to his account. It is impossible 'that two things of the same kind should exist in the same place at the same time' (E ii.27.1). If we raise the question whether something is the same thing or a different thing from some other thing, then this must always concern some spatio-temporal thing. Locke also maintains that 'one thing cannot have two beginnings of existence, nor two things one beginning' (E ii.27.1), because that would violate the principle that two things cannot exist in the same place at the same time. It logically follows that if two things, x and y, have numerically distinct beginnings, then x is not y, and if two putatively distinct objects, x and y, turn out to have the same beginning, then x is numerically identical with y. An objection to these Lockean criteria is that they logically preclude the possibilities of fission and fusion. If two numerically distinct objects, x and y, fuse, the resultant single object arguably had two numerically distinct origins. If a single object bifurcates into numerically distinct objects, x and y, then arguably x and y, although numerically distinct, had a single origin.

According to Locke, we have ideas of three, and only three, substances: 'God', 'finite intelligences' and 'bodies' (E II.27.2). There is no problem about God's identity because God is 'without beginning, eternal, unalterable, and everywhere' (E II.27.2). Both finite spirits and physical objects have spatio-temporal location so there is the question of the nature of their identity; but there is also a solution. Any soul and any physical object is necessarily identical with some spatio-temporal occupant. Any substance of one of those two kinds necessarily excludes occupancy of the same space–time region by a substance of the same sort. However, two qualitatively different substances may occupy the same space–time region. Hence a soul and a physical object may occupy the same place at the same time. However, the identity of each consists in its unbroken spatio-temporal continuity.

Finally, Locke maintains that everything is identical with itself. For example, an atom is 'the same with itself' (E II.27.3). Whatever something is, it is just that thing and not anything else. It is 'what it is and nothing else'. In other words, each thing is self-identical.

The Identity of Vegetables

In the case of inanimate physical objects, the addition or subtraction of one atom implies that 'it is no longer the same mass, or the same body' (E II.27.3). However, the identity of living creatures is unaffected by the addition or subtraction of matter so their identity cannot consist in the spatio-temporal location of what they are made of. There exists, then, a difference between 'an oak' and 'a mass of matter' (E II.27.4) even if the oak is composed of the mass of matter. It is not identical with what it is made of. Being a mass of matter is not logically sufficient for being the oak that comprises it, even if it is logically necessary. What is the residual difference?

Locke distinguishes the mass of matter from the oak as follows: 'the one is only the cohesion of particles of matter anyhow united, the other such a disposition of them as constitutes the parts of an oak' (E II.27.4). A mass of matter is a mass of matter however its constituent parts are mutually related, but a mass of matter counts as an oak if, and only if, its constituent particles are mutually related so as to constitute the structure of an oak. To have the structure of an oak is to be oak-shaped, include oak leaves, and perform the function of an oak including internal distribution of nourishment. This arrangement of parts constitutes what Locke calls one 'vegetable life', and being a certain vegetable life is logically constitutive of being a particular kind of object – an animate one: 'it continues to be the same plant so long as it partakes of the same life' (E II.27.4). The identity of the living object consists in the identity of its structure. No matter how the constituent particles of the object may change numerically, the continued identity of the living object is logically guaranteed through the continued qualitative structural identity of the object.

Note that Locke only discusses life in structural terms. He rejects the view that being alive consists in the presence of some special element within the living organism, a soul or vital spark. On the contrary, being alive for Locke consists in having a structure appropriate for the exercise of certain functions. Being alive and having a soul he considers two quite separate matters, although, clearly, human beings are both alive and have souls.

The Identity of Animals

Locke extends his functional and structural account of plant identity to non-human animals – 'brutes' (E II.27.5). An animal's identity is like that of a watch. Its being the sort of thing it is logically depends upon the organization of its parts into a structure with a function. The only significant difference between an animal and a watch is that the motion of an animal originates within it but that of the watch originates without:

> An animal is a living organized body and the same animal is the same continued life communicated to different particles of matter, as they happen successively to be united to that organized living body. (E II.27.8)

The Identity of Man

Locke makes a conceptual distinction between being a person and being a man (or, as we should say, a human being). The functional and structural account is used by Locke to explain what the identity of a man consists in – what the identity of a human being as a certain kind of living organism consists in. He says that 'the identity of the same man consists . . . in nothing but a participation of the same continued life by constantly fleeting particles of matter, in succession vitally united to the same organized body' (E II.27.6). Being numerically the same life consists in the spatio-temporal continuity of the 'organized body', however the constituent parts may be replaced. This criterion enables 'an embryo, one of years, mad, and sober' to be 'the same man' (E II.27.6), whereas it precludes 'Socrates, Pilate, St Austin, and Caesar Borgia' being the same man. The criterion is designed to retain the numerical identity of the human being through qualitative changes of that human being, but it excludes the numerical identity of numerically distinct men even if they are qualitatively similar. In particular, Locke rejects the theory that the identity of the human being consists in the identity of the soul, because that would allow human beings existing at different times and with different personalities to be numerically identical.

What is it to be human? Interestingly, Locke thinks it essential to being human to have a body of human shape. This overrides the traditional Aristotelian view of man as a 'rational animal' on the following grounds. If, Locke maintains, we encountered an irrational being shaped like a man we would call it an 'irrational man', but if we encountered a rational being shaped like a cat or a parrot we would call it a 'rational cat' or a 'rational parrot'.

Personal Identity

Locke defines 'person' as 'a thinking intelligent being, that has reason and reflection, and can consider itself as itself, the same thinking thing, in different times and places' (E II.27.9). Therefore if a particular being is a person, it is rational and self-conscious in such a way as to be aware of its numerical identity over time and space. It does this 'by that consciousness which is inseparable from thinking' (E II.27.9). Locke holds that if a being is conscious then it is self-conscious, 'it being impossible for anyone to perceive without perceiving that he does perceive' (E II.27.9). It follows that if a person is in a mental state they know they are in that state: 'when we see, hear, smell, taste, feel, meditate, or will anything, we know that we do so' (E II.27.9). This rather Cartesian incorrigibility thesis is most questionable, but it is required as a premise for Locke's account of what a person is.[23]

When Locke maintains that 'consciousness makes personal identity' (E II.27.10), he means by 'consciousness' self-consciousness. It is his view that there are no unconscious mental states, and it is the awareness of one's mental state as one's own that makes one the person who one is to oneself: 'consciousness always accompanies thinking and it is that that makes every one to be what he calls self' (E II.27.9). Because I am conscious of myself I may distinguish myself from other thinking beings and have a concept of myself. Locke says, 'in this alone consists personal identity', meaning by personal identity 'the sameness of a rational being' (E II.27.9). Being the same person consists in being conscious of being the same person. The identity of the person over time consists in the consciousness of the identity of the person over time:

> As far as this consciousness can be extended backwards to any past action or thought, so far reaches the identity of that person; it is the same self now it was then; and it is by the same self with this present one that now reflects on it, that that action was done. (E II.27.9)

The objection to this theory is that because a person at $t2$ remembers a person perform an action at $t1$ it does not logically follow that the person at $t2$ is the person at $t1$, and because a person at $t2$ is unable to remember a person at $t1$ perform an action, it does not logically follow that the person at $t2$ is not the person at $t1$. Remembering a person is therefore neither necessary nor sufficient for being that person.[24]

Perhaps there are no necessary and sufficient conditions for the identity of a person over time. Perhaps the whole problem is in some way thoroughly misconceived. There do seem to be severe objections to the idealist and materialist alternatives to Locke's memory criterion. The spatio-temporal continuity of the body over time is neither logically necessary nor sufficient for personal identity. It is not necessary because if it were broken there would not seem to be good grounds for holding that the person existing after the break is not numerically identical with the person existing before the break, if qualitatively similar. It is not sufficient because it is logically possible that numerically distinct subjective conscious points of view on the world should occupy the same body at different times.[25]

Nor is the identity of the soul over time necessary or sufficient for personal identity. If reincarnation is logically possible then it is logically possible for your soul to be numerically identical with that of, say, Napoleon; yet you and Napoleon are numerically distinct persons.[26] It is not necessary, if being the same person consists in being anything other than the same soul. If being the same structure, or the same brain, or having the same functions over time is sufficient for personal identity, then being the same soul is not necessary.[27]

Our thinking about personal identity takes place within the framework of dualist, idealist and materialist ontological alternatives. It would require our abdicating this framework to solve the problem.

7   SPACE AND TIME

The problem of identity arises only for spatio-temporal beings, but what are space and time? Locke treats space and time separately in the *Essay*.

Space

The concept of space is acquired through two, and only two, senses: 'we get the idea of space both by our sight and touch' (E II.13.2) so for Locke the concept of space is clearly an empirical concept.

Space contains various 'modifications' which are best understood as components of the concept of space. For example, distance is the length of space between any two objects (E II.13.3); capacity is a region of space considered in length, breadth and thickness. Immensity is the notion of size derived from imaginatively multiplying distances (E II.13.4). 'Figure' (shape) is a relation between parts of occupants of space detected only by either sight or touch (E II.13.5). Place is a relative idea, which depends upon sameness of distance between two points. Thus A is in the same place at $t2$ as it was at $t1$ if, and only if, the distance between A and some second object B has not changed. In Locke's example, the pieces on a chess board might be in the same places *vis-à-vis* one another even if the board has moved – changed place; yet the board remains in the same place, if it has not moved from the cabin of a ship, even if the ship constantly changes place. The ship itself is in the same place if it remains the same distance from the land, even though the cabin moves. Thus any physical object is only in the same place or in a different place in relation to other physical objects. Place is a 'modification of distance' (E II.13.9), and 'our idea of place is nothing else but . . . a relative position of anything' (E II.13.10).

Locke is keen to distinguish between the concepts of size and matter and therefore argues that 'extension and body [are] not the same'. Matter is 'something that is solid and extended', so being extended is a property of matter, not what matter is, whereas extension or size is the amount of space occupied by matter. Nor should solidity be confused with extension, or motion with space, even though 'solidity cannot exist without extension' and 'motion can neither be, nor be conceived to be without space' (E II.13.11). Because A depends upon B for its existence, and because the conceivability of A depends upon the conceivability of B, it does not logically follow that A is B. On the contrary, dependence precludes identity: 'many ideas require others as necessary to their existence or conception, which yet are very distinct ideas' (E II.13.11).

Space, for Locke, is not identical with the set of all physical objects, nor even identical with the set of all physical objects including the spatial relations between them. Space is what physical objects occupy. He calls space, in this sense, 'pure space'. His conclusion, 'space is not body' (E II.13.11), depends on the premise that the idea of space includes no idea of solidity but the idea of matter does, so space and matter cannot be the same. His reasoning rests on the principle that if A and B are numerically identical, it logically follows that A and B share all and only each other's properties.[28]

An important property of space is that it is unique. There is only one space. This is because putatively numerically distinct spaces will turn out to be spatially related, and so not distinct spaces but parts of one and the same space: 'the parts of pure space are inseparable from one another' and 'the continuity cannot be separated, neither really nor mentally' (E II.13.13).

Locke also thinks that motion is not a property of space. Although it makes sense to talk of the physical objects located in space as in motion, it makes no sense to talk of space itself as in motion because 'the parts of pure space are immovable, which follows from their inseparability' (E II.13.14). Motion is only a change in distance between two things, but that may only happen between separable things. Space is not separable, so space does not move. This, for Locke, is another essential difference between space and matter.

Locke's philosophy of space is essentially Newtonian, and directed against Descartes's thesis that there is no vacuum.[29] A problem for Locke – as for Newton – is this. Space is not identical with the set of all physical objects and the spatial relations between them, but is rather what those objects occupy. But if space is 'pure space', what distinguishes pure space from nothing at all? What is the difference between physical objects occupying space and occupying nothing? If 'space existing without matter' (E II.13.22) were possible, some account is needed of the nature of such space. If a physical object were to be annihilated, what would the space it formerly occupied be? Locke and Newton have no satisfactory answers to these questions, and it may be that Leibniz is right that space is nothing over and above the set of all the physical objects including the spatial relations between them.[30] Other than that, it may be that space is nothing: void.

Time

Locke's concept of time is best understood through his concept of
duration and 'duration is fleeting extension' (E II.14.1). Locke
means that duration is like extension – a kind of size – analogous to
spatial extension but derived from 'the fleeting and perpetually
perishing parts of succession' (E II.14.1). Duration is an empirical
concept derived from observing one sort of event perennially
followed by another. Ultimately, duration is acquired 'from reflection on the train of our ideas' (E II.14.2). Reflection cannot but
reveal to a person 'a train of ideas which constantly succeed one
another in his understanding so long as he is awake' (E II.14.3), and
this makes possible the idea of succession, that is, the idea of before
and after. Duration is the 'distance between any part of that
succession' (E II.14.3). Locke does not say what such a distance
consists in, and his account therefore faces two dangers. Firstly, he
tries to explain duration by spatial metaphors: distance and extension, and does not thereby say what it is for two events to be
temporally rather than spatially separated. Secondly, if the 'distance' between two events is the time that elapses between those
two events, then there is a clear danger of circularity. The term
'time' is invoked in the explanation of what time is.

Locke does not solve these problems. Nevertheless, it is plain that
duration is an idea of reflection for Locke because on his account
the only consciousness we have of duration is the consciousness of
our own ideas: 'When that succession of ideas ceases, our perception
of duration ceases with it' (E II.14.4). It follows that 'men derive
their ideas of duration from their reflection on the train of the ideas
they observe to succeed one another in their own understandings'
(E II.14.4). It is only because we are conscious of the duration of
our own ideas that we may ascribe temporal properties to objects
existing independently of our ideas. Given that this is Locke's view,
an interesting philosophical problem arises. If the only time order
with which any of us is directly acquainted is the temporal order in
which our own experiences take place, how is it possible for each of
us to form the conception of an objective, mind-independent, time
order in which the events of the physical universe occur? After all,

the succession of our experiences is not the same succession as that of mind-independent physical events.

It seems to me that solving this problem requires giving up the assumption that physical objects are not perceived directly. Locke would have to relinquish the view that perceiving objects is being acquainted with representations of them and adopt either direct realism – physical objects are perceived as they would be if they were not being perceived – or phenomenalism, the view that physical objects are logical constructions out of sense perceptions (see pp. 237–8 below). On either of these theories of perception room is left for perception of an objective time order.

Time, for Locke, is duration measured in units of days, weeks, years, historical epochs (and presumably smaller units); so 'time is duration set out by measures' (E II.14.17). The question we must answer is: What is it for time to elapse between two events? or, indeed, what is it for something to last? The answers to these questions would give sense to 'duration'.

Locke's account of time is fundamentally at variance with that of Aristotle.[31] Aristotle thought the concept of time depended upon motion, but according to Locke, 'the idea of succession [is] not from motion' (E II.14.6). Time logically depends only on duration, and duration, whatever it is, does not logically depend on motion; therefore time does not depend on motion.

In Locke's theory, the idea of time as a whole – all time, or eternity – has an empirical origin. The ability imaginatively to add units of duration in principle *ad infinitum* facilitates the thought of duration without ideas or objects, and so of eternity – infinite duration. Thus logical room seems to be left for an absolute time: a time which does not depend on the existence of anything else for its own existence, and in which physical objects are located. As with object-independent space, the problem is this: What distinguishes a time which is something over and above temporal things from nothing at all? Suppose there were no temporal things, would there be the time when they were, left over, or nothing at all? Perhaps time is nothing over and above the set of all temporal things and the temporal relations between them. Other than that it may be that time is nothing at all.

8 NUMBERS

What are numbers? How is it possible to possess the concept of number? As numbers are arguably among the most abstract of objects, these are *prima facie* difficult questions for an empiricist to answer. Locke thinks the idea of number logically and epistemologically depends upon the idea of unity or one, and that is a thoroughly empirical concept in his view. By 'logical dependence' here I mean it would be contradictory to maintain that the idea of number exists without the existence of the idea of unity or one. By 'epistemological dependence' I mean it is impossible to know what a number is unless it is known what unity or one is. If the concept of number depends on the idea of unity or one, and if the idea of unity or one is empirical, then it follows that the concept of number is empirical, just so long as we grant this premise: if a concept depends on an empirical concept, then it is an empirical concept. If we allow that premise we are allowing a broad sense of 'empirical', such that for a concept to be empirical the having of some experience was a necessary condition of the concept's acquisition. The reason why Locke thinks the idea of unity or one so thoroughly empirical is that there is no experience that does not cause us to have it. In other words, it is perpetually sustained in us by experience while we experience: 'every object our senses are employed about, every idea in our understandings, every thought in our minds, brings this idea along with it' (E II.16.1). It follows that the idea of unity or one is acquired by both sensation and reflection.

The idea of one or unity is the idea of that which has no parts, or is uncomposed; 'it has no shadow of variety of composition in it' (E II.16.1). It is the most general and universal of concepts because it applies to every item there is, whatever sorts of items exist.

Locke argues that the acquisition of the ideas of any other numbers depends upon acquiring the concept of one. The concept of one is psychologically inescapable because it accompanies all our experiences. It is not a psychological option for us not to acquire it, given that we have at least one experience. Numbers larger than one are intellectually constructed out of one by adding; thus adding one and one constructs the concept of two, adding twelve ones generates the concept of twelve, etc.

This account faces several difficulties. It is not clear what adding is, over and above simply thinking 'one', thinking 'one' again, and so on. Unless Locke has an independent account of what adding is, it is not certain that whoever adds ones to 'make', say, twelve does not already possess the concept of twelve. Locke's account would then clearly beg the question. Also, it might be doubted whether we do acquire our number concepts by adding ones. It might be that Locke has confused the logical truth that any whole number may be analysed into a set of ones with the dubious psychological claim that we learn numbers other than one by adding ones. Consider very large numbers.

'One' is a simple idea and any number larger than one is a complex idea. But counting depends upon more than acquaintance with ideas; it depends upon words. A counting being must, for example, not only possess the simple idea of 'one' and the complex idea of 'two' but also the name for one, 'one', and the name for two, 'two', and so on. Locke hints that the ability to count, and hence to learn numbers other than one, partly consists in the ability to give the name 'two' to two tokens of the simple idea of 'one'. The procedure would seem to consist in thinking the simple idea of 'one' once, then thinking the simple idea of 'one' a second time, and then giving one label to both these episodes: 'two'. Because of this, and similarly for other numbers, 'without such names or marks we can hardly well make use of numbers in reckoning' (E II.16.5).[32]

Locke may well be right that only language-users can count. However, he has no answer to this question: What are numbers? Is it the case that numbers do not exist over and above the numbers of things that there are? Or are numbers non-spatial, non-temporal items that exist independently of minds and physical objects? In counting, do we discover numbers or invent them? If we discover them, where do we discover them? If we invent them, where do we keep them? Suppose a number is an idea. What have we said about an idea when we have said that it is a number?

9 LANGUAGE

One way of posing the central question in the philosophy of language is to ask: What makes black marks on a piece of paper, or sounds emitted from someone's mouth, into words and sentences – in short, into language? The page in front of you now is covered with black squiggles on a white background. How can a distribution of ink molecules be meaningful language? If I spoke to you, what would make those sounds into meaningful language? What is it for a piece of the world to be language?

Locke's answer to this question is that sounds are 'signs of internal conceptions' which 'stand as marks for the ideas within [the] mind' (E III.1.1). The meaning of a word is an idea. Ideas make sounds and marks into signs.

Clearly, it does not of itself solve any problems in the theory of meaning to say that words are signs or that language signifies. The notion of a word being a sign or of language signifying is every bit as obscure as that of a word being meaningful. However, Locke thinks that words stand for ideas, and this makes it sound as though words go proxy for ideas and experiences. He also suggests that words refer to ideas, but he does not give an account of what it consists in for a word to refer to an idea. He does not say what exactly is the relation between a word and an idea if the word refers to the idea. The relation called 'reference' is as shadowy as signification and meaning.

Central to Locke's theory of meaning is the claim that 'words in their immediate and primary signification stand for nothing but the ideas in the mind of him that useth them' (E III.2.1). Depending on how we read this, Locke is either an ideational or a referential theorist about meaning. On the ideational construal, the idea is the meaning of the word. The image, to paraphrase Wittgenstein, is what gives life to the sounds or marks. On the referential construal, we remember that for Locke 'ideas' denotes not only images but any experiential content. Then meanings are the items referred to within our experience.

On either construal, words have what Locke calls 'a secret reference to two other things'. These are 'the ideas in the minds also of other men with whom they communicate' and 'the reality of things' (E III.2.I). These references are 'secret' because on Locke's theory we are not directly acquainted with other minds or the physical objects which our own ideas represent.

Meaning is prior to communication for Locke. My words are meaningful to me if, and only if, they refer to some ideas of mine. Your ideas are meaningful to you if, and only if, they refer to some ideas of yours. You and I communicate if, and only if, either your speech or writing causes me to have an idea qualitatively similar to the idea to which your word refers, or my speech or writing causes you to have an idea qualitatively similar to the idea to which my word refers.

Locke is committed to three theses which are targets of Wittgenstein's attacks on traditional notions of meaning in his *Philosophical Investigations*: meaning depends on reference; meaning is something psychological; meaning depends on the possibility of private ostensive definition. Wittgenstein's later philosophy turns Locke's theory of meaning on its head. Wittgenstein argues that even the intelligibility to oneself of one's own experience depends upon being a public language-user, that is, depends upon the communicability of that experience to other language-users by following the rules of a common language. Wittgenstein wishes to banish 'meaning' from philosophical discussion of language but it is not too misleading to make the following statement: for Locke, meaning is prior to the possibility of communication; but for Wittgenstein, the possibility of communication is prior to meaning.[33]

Locke accepts that not all words refer to ideas. Grammatical connectives (such as 'not', 'and' and 'if') contribute to sentence structure but do not denote any ideas or physical objects (E III.7). However, the largest section of Book III of the *Essay*, 'Of Words', is devoted to the meaning of general terms: words which refer to more than one thing. Most words in any language are of this kind, and there is a problem for a thoroughgoing empiricist about how a word may be known to denote all the objects in a given class, given that we have experience of, at most, a sub-set of that class.

Locke's solution is to argue that 'words become general by being made the signs of general ideas' (E III.3.6). An idea is made general by abstracting it from all spatio-temporal contexts, so that an idea, call it 'the idea of *x*', is made general by mentally disregarding any thoughts or facts of the form 'x is at place p' or 'x is at time t'. In this way the idea of x is able to represent any x, not only some specific x. The idea of x may represent an x at any time in any place, whichever x that x is. So far, this account is not vulnerable to the objections Berkeley will bring against it.[34] However, abstraction also proceeds in this way: to make the general idea of man, for example, 'leave out of the complex idea . . . of Peter and James, Mary and Jane, that which is peculiar to each, and retain only what is common to them all' (E III.3.8).[35] As we have seen (pp. 71-3 above), for Locke 'general natures are nothing but abstract ideas' (E III.3.9).

Generality, then, only exists in language because general terms refer to abstract general ideas and generality only exists in those ideas, not in what they represent. Only particulars exist independently of minds.

Locke's theory of meaning may be vulnerable to Wittgenstein's objections. More likely, though, Wittgenstein and Locke each have only half a theory of meaning, Locke emphasizing the subjective, private and individualistic components of meaning, and Wittgenstein emphasizing objective, public and rule-governed linguistic uses.

Locke's theory of meaning has a surprising affinity to two recent developments. In so far as he holds that meanings are or depend on mental states, and because he thinks of those mental states as representations, he may find sympathy with modern cognitive psychology. In so far as our sentences could not mean what they do without the 'secret reference' to mind-independent physical objects, his view is consistent with the idea that much thought and language is *de re* (concerning the thing). The idea is that you and I cannot be thinking the same thought if, in fact, what you are thinking about – the object you are thinking about – is numerically distinct from what I am thinking about. It may be that there is a tension between internalist cognitive science and the externalist doctrines of *de re* thought and meaning. If so, that tension is prefigured in Locke.[36]

10 CAUSATION

What exactly does it mean to say that some event, C, causes some event, E? According to Locke, there are four possible answers to this question, and they correspond to four kinds of causation: creation, generation, making, and alteration.

In creation, 'the thing is wholly made new, so that no part did ever exist before' (E II.26.2). It follows that C creates E if, and only if, at some time, t_1, E and no part of E exists, but at some later time, t_2, C makes E (and so all parts of E) exist. Locke does not explain what it consists in to bring something into being, so an unanalysed notion of causation is presupposed in this account of creation *ex nihilo*. He does give this example, however: 'as when a new particle of matter doth begin to exist' (E II.26.2). The idea of creation of matter *ex nihilo* is strikingly modern in terms of physics and at variance with the Newtonian orthodoxy Locke elsewhere espouses.

In generation, 'a thing is made up of particles which did all of them before exist, but that very thing, so constituted of pre-existing particles, had not any existence before' (E II.26.2). It follows that C generates E if, and only if, at some time, t_1, the prospective parts of E, but not E itself, exist, but at some later time, t_2, C makes E out of E's prospective parts. Again, an unanalysed notion of causation is presupposed in 'generation'. Locke tends to reserve 'generation' for natural effects of imperceptible causes where cause and effect could be counted as parts of one and the same natural process. Eggs, roses and cherries are results of generation.

In making, C is not part of the same process as E: 'the cause is extrinsical, and the effect produced by a sensible separation or juxtaposition of discernible parts'. Therefore, C makes E if, and only if, C separates or juxtaposes the parts of E and this process is observable. 'Such are all artificial things' (E II.26.2), according to Locke. Artifacts are made.

In the alteration of objects, a 'new sensible quality or simple idea is produced in them, which was not there before' (E II.26.2). So C alters E if, and only if, C causes E to have a property, P, at t_2 and there was an earlier time, t_1, when E lacked P. A picture or a man may be altered.

Again, in the last two accounts of causal relations 'cause' or something nearly synonymous is logically presupposed. Locke therefore has a fourfold taxonomy of causation but no more primitive analysis.

We acquire the concept of causation empirically when we observe 'both qualities and substances begin to exist', and observe the 'application and operation of some other being'. Locke also says an effect 'receives' its existence from a cause (E 11.26.1).

The problem is that the concept of a causal power is not straightforwardly empirical. Although we are empirically acquainted with those events we believe to be causally related, we do not seem to be thus acquainted with the causal connection itself. It is left to Hume to develop a more subtle empirical approach to causation based on this sceptical idea.[37]

11 GOD

The idea of God is not innate because there are no innate ideas. However, we are capable of knowing that God exists with the same certainty we have that mathematical propositions are true.

Locke's proof of the existence of God is nearly as Cartesian as his mind–body dualism. His argument has two parts. He first seeks to prove that something has always existed. He then seeks to prove this is God. The first premise is that each person is certain of their own existence: 'Man knows that he himself is', so something exists now. Locke argues from this that something has always existed: 'from eternity there has been something; since what was not from eternity had a beginning; and what had a beginning must be produced by something else' (E IV.10.3). Everything has a cause, so there was no first event or else that putative event would have had no cause. Therefore there was always something. Given universal causation, if something exists then something always existed. What always existed is the cause of what subsequently exists.

What has always existed must be God, because the divine attributes of eternity, omnipotence and omniscience are implied in always being and in being the cause of what is. The eternal being must be intelligent because it is impossible that intelligence should result from the random operation of what is not intelligent. The eternal being is omnipotent because it is the source of all that happens. It follows that 'there is an eternal, most powerful, and most knowing being' (E IV.10.6).

Nor is it possible that God should be physical.[38] God has knowledge and therefore mental processes. But it is impossible that thought should be or result from matter. One particle of matter cannot think, nor can many particles of matter think jointly, however complex their arrangement. They are, after all, just particles of matter. Thought and particles of matter are so qualitatively dissimilar that thinking matter would be an absurdity (E IV.10.14–15).

Locke's defence of the existence of God is brief but forcefully argued. It stands in need of refutation by modern atheists and materialists.

12 POLITICS

I shall concentrate on the second of the *Two Treatises of Government* because while the first contains Locke's negative critique of any absolute monarchy founded on divine right, the second is a theory of the conditions under which government is justified at all.[39]

Like Hobbes, Locke argues that government is needed to avoid an undesirable state of nature. Locke, however, distinguishes the state of nature from the state of war and perhaps has Hobbes in mind when he says that some have mistakenly assimilated the two (2T 19). Both the state of nature and the state of war function only as heuristic devices in Locke's political theory. They are hypothetical conditions with which to contrast political society, although it is clear that Locke thought actual and historical analogies existed for those conditions.[40]

In the state of nature people are in 'a State of perfect Freedom' (2T 4) with regard to their actions, lives and property. What each does is not constrained by the wishes of any other. The state of nature is 'a State also of Equality' (2T 4), where the power one person has over another is equally distributed among persons. Life in Locke's state of nature is not nearly so dire as in that of Hobbes. Locke's state of nature is not a state of civil war; it is, rather, inconvenient. People in the state of nature have fundamental, God-given natural rights to 'the Preservation of the Life, Liberty, Health [and] Goods' (2T 6) but there exists no government to ensure their preservation. Instead, punishment for the denial of these rights is in the hands of the people. Each person has the natural right to punish any other who denies him his rights: 'Execution of the Law of Nature is in that State, put into every Man's hands' (2T 7). Locke's objection to this arrangement is that it is inconvenient. Even if, as Locke allows, several persons may be allies in the punishment of one transgressor of the natural law, rights are not thereby guaranteed in practice, nor are they necessarily enforced in an orderly way. So 'Civil Government is the proper Remedy for the Inconveniences of the State of Nature'. This obviates the inconveniences of 'Men being judges in their own cases'. However, the reader is urged to recognize that even an absolute monarch is only a human being, and if he abuses or fails to protect the natural rights of the people he may legitimately be overthrown (2T 13).

The state of nature is 'Men living together according to reason, without a common superiour on Earth' (2T 19) but it is in perpetual danger of lapsing into the state of war, that is, the abdication of reason and the actuality or the intention of violence by one person on another. Where there exists no sovereign authority to prevent such conflict, 'Force, or a declared design of force upon the Person of another, where there is no common superiour on Earth to appeal to for relief, is the State of War' (2T 19). Absence of government is both necessary and sufficient for a society to be in a state of nature. Absence of government is necessary but not sufficient for a society to be in a state of war. Absence of effective government and the intention or actuality of violence are each singularly necessary and both jointly sufficient for a society to be in a state of war. In this respect Locke's vision of society without the state differs from that of Hobbes, for whom absence of government is both necessary and sufficient for the state of war, because the state of nature is a state of war.

For Hobbes it is the actuality, but for Locke it is the threat of war that legitimizes the state. For Locke, 'to avoid this state of war . . .

is one great reason of Men's putting themselves into Society, and quitting the State of Nature' (2T 21), and it is precisely in society with the state that there exists 'a Power on Earth' to arbitrate in disputes, protect life, liberty and property, and administer punishment. Persons are naturally free and it is to protect, not to curtail, this freedom that the state should exist. Freedom is not as Locke's contemporary, the apologist for absolute monarchy Sir Robert Filmer, supposed: 'anarchic licence, but to live with one's natural rights protected and not abused by government'.[41]

A state of war may obtain not only between one person and another because of the absence of authority in the state of nature, but also between government and citizen, if that government seeks to destroy rather than protect the natural rights of the citizen. Hence, crucially, all legitimate government is government by the consent of the governed:

The Liberty of Man, in Society, is to be under no other Legislative Power, but that established by consent, in the Common-wealth, nor under the Dominion of any Will, or Restraint of any Law, but what the Legislative shall enact, according to the trust put in it. (2T 324)

Government without consent is slavery, and every citizen has the right to rebel against slavery.

Conspicuous amongst the natural rights to be preserved and not abused by government is the individual's right to private property. Locke's account of the right to property is a legitimization of the capitalist belief that a person has the right to own and keep that which he was the first to discover, inherit, or produce, but it is also – interestingly – an anticipation of the Marxist doctrine of surplus value.[42] Locke's paradigm of ownership is a person's relation to their own body. By extension, the labour of one's body is one's own, and by extension again, the products of one's labour are one's own. So 'whatsoever he then removes out of the State that Nature hath provided, and left it in, he hath mixed his Labour with, and joyned to it something that is his own, and thereby makes it his Property' (2T 27). *Prima facie*, no person has a right to anything produced by another because the second person, but not the first, has laboured in its production. However, Locke has a rather socialist reservation about this right. One only has a right to what one has produced or discovered 'where there is enough, and as good left in common for others' (2T 27). By implication, the interests of the community as a whole must override the individual's right to private property. This aspect of Locke's philosophy has been little noticed by political theorists.

If the government fails to guarantee life, liberty, or property, then it may be resisted. Locke quotes a contemporary, Burley, approvingly for holding 'that it is lawful for the people, in some cases to resist their king' (2T 232) and argues as follows:

Whosoever uses force without Right, as everyone does in Society, who does it without Law, puts himself into a State of War with those, against whom he so uses it, and in that state all former Ties are cancelled, all other rights cease, and everyone has a Right to defend himself, and to resist the Aggressor. (2T 232)

The very last paragraph of the *Second Treatise* reiterates the principle that legitimate government is always by the consent of the governed, and once government is against the natural rights of the citizen that legitimacy is forfeited. Many thought that legitimacy forfeited by James II in 1688, George III in 1776 and Louis XVI in 1789.[43]

BERKELEY

1 BERKELEY IN HISTORY

The central thesis of Berkeley's philosophy is that matter does not exist. Ever since he propounded it, it has been much maligned and much misunderstood. It has been objected that his idealism is inconsistent with both science and commonsense, yet Berkeley positively insists it is consistent with both. In what follows I hope to show not only that idealism was a perfectly reasonable philosophy for Berkeley to formulate in his historical context, but that it is quite possibly true.[1]

Berkeley's idealism is both a continuation of and a reaction against the philosophy of the seventeenth century. It is a reaction against the scientific materialism which implied that the universe is ultimately constituted by imperceptible material atoms in motion. It is a continuation of empiricism; indeed, it is a pushing of empiricism to some of its logical conclusions. Empiricism is the theory that all knowledge is acquired through experience. Idealism, to put it simplistically, is the theory that only the contents of experience may be known with certainty to exist. This is a simplistic interpretation because Berkeley also contends that the subjects of knowledge and experience – God and the soul – may also be known with certainty to exist, even though they are not empirical objects. Berkeley's primary philosophical motivation was theological. He wished to arrest the growth of atheism which seemed to draw sustenance from the scientific materialism of the previous hundred years. However, the theory that matter does not exist does not logically require the existence of God as a premise, even though Berkeley argues for both these theses.[2]

Idealism is the opposite of materialism. Materialism is the theory that if something exists then it is physical. Idealism is the theory that if something exists then it is mental. According to the tenets of materialism, what we pre-philosophically take to be mental is in fact physical. According to the tenets of idealism, what we pre-philosophically take to be physical is in fact mental. Thus materialism is essentially the view that the mental is physical and idealism is essentially the view that the physical is mental. (This raises the interesting question of whether materialism and idealism, far from being diametrically opposed, actually imply one another. If the physical is mental then the mental must be physical, and if the mental is physical then the physical must be mental.)

Hobbes, Locke and Berkeley exemplify the three main ontological options in the philosophy of mind.[3] Hobbes was a materialist, Locke a dualist and Berkeley an idealist. Hobbes thought that only physical objects exist; Locke thought that both minds and physical objects exist; and Berkeley thought that only minds exist. Notice, then, that empiricism does not force one to subscribe to one of these three ontologies rather than either of the others. It is possible to be an empiricist and a materialist, or an empiricist and a dualist, or an empiricist and an idealist. *Prima facie* at least, empiricism is logically consistent with any of these three ontologies.

George Berkeley was born on 12 March 1685 in the farm adjoining Dysert Castle in Kilkenny, Ireland. Little is known of his mother, but his father was an English immigrant who had arrived in Ireland some time during the preceding fifteen years. We do not know whether Berkeley's family was half-Irish, half-English, or wholly English. What is clear, however, is that he always regarded himself as Irish and not English. He was brought up a Protestant during the years of the Irish campaigns of the War of the League of Augsburg (1689–99) and was five at the time of the victory of the Protestant king of England, William of Orange, over the Catholic ex-king of England, James II, at the Battle of the Boyne (1690).

Berkeley started school in Kilkenny in 1696 and must have been considered an able pupil because in 1700 he obtained a place to study philosophy, science and theology at the prestigious Trinity

College, Dublin. He very quickly developed his idealist world-picture and by his mid-twenties had written three of his most influential books: *An Essay Towards a New Theory of Vision* (1709), *A Treatise Concerning the Principles of Human Knowledge* (1710) and *Three Dialogues Between Hylas and Philonous* (1713). In composing his idealism Berkeley had been well acquainted with the prevailing philosophical and scientific ideas of his time through the open-minded and up-to-date syllabus at Trinity. The young Berkeley avidly read and discussed Hobbes, Locke, Descartes, Malebranche, Gassendi and Leibniz. He also immersed himself in the new science not only of Descartes but of Bacon, Boyle and Newton. Indeed, it would be a serious mistake to assume that Berkeley was anti-scientific in his thinking. He admired the new science. His quarrel was with its prominent ontological assumption which horrified him for the threat it seemed to pose to Christianity: the assumption that the universe is ultimately material, composed of a substance called 'matter'. Berkeley thought the new science should jettison this assumption and could proceed quite consistently without it. Accordingly he made his life's work the refutation of materialism.

Berkeley obtained his B.A. degree in 1704 and his M.A. in 1707, and immediately became a Fellow and tutor of Trinity College. He remained in this post until 1720, teaching and writing. In 1709 he was ordained.

In 1713 Berkeley began to travel. He visited England for the first time in that year to promote the *Dialogues* in London, and make the acquaintance of intellectuals there. He met Swift and Pope and was received at the court of Queen Anne. From 1710 to 1714 he was in France and Italy, part of that time in the service of the Earl of Peterborough as his chaplain and part in the service of the Bishop of Clogher as tutor to his son. He returned to London in 1714, only to go back to Paris the following year. It has been said that there he met Malebranche and even that the heated dispute between the dualist and the idealist contributed to Malebranche's death in that year. Certainly Malebranche's Cartesian view that both minds and physical objects exist is logically inconsistent with Berkeley's thesis that only minds exist. The story of the meeting is perhaps apocryphal, because other sources suggest that Berkeley did not in fact visit Paris in 1715. However, we know that Berkeley was in Italy from 1717 to 1720, travelling and writing, that he was in London in 1720, and that he returned to Dublin that year. During his seven years' absence Trinity College seems to have awarded him multiple sabbaticals.

In 1721 Berkeley published a short but philosophically significant work called *De Motu* ('Concerning Motion'). In it he tried to reconcile some of the new science with his own idealism by demonstrating that there is motion but not matter. Motion was one of the central concepts of the seventeenth- and early eighteenth-century scientific world-picture and Berkeley tried in that book to separate 'motion' from its seeming conceptual dependence upon 'matter'. Motion is the result of the operations of conscious minds, in Berkeley's view, and matter does not exist. That he wrote this book, and that he took such care over notions of vision, space and distance in his works on vision, in my opinion shows beyond doubt that Berkeley had a profound respect for the natural sciences of his time and that his only fundamental quarrel was with the assumption that scientific method implied materialism.

Berkeley was not only concerned that false metaphysical doctrines were finding widespread acceptance; he was appalled by the practical living conditions of much of the British and Irish populations of that time. The tendencies which dismayed him were linked: materialism caused the spread of atheism, which caused in turn moral, social and economic decay. By 1721 he had formulated a utopian politics which, retrospectively, may be characterized as a kind of Christian socialism. His travels had made him familiar with a variety of social conditions and his interests turned from the problems of metaphysics to politics and applied philosophy. By his mid-thirties Berkeley had not given up trying to understand the world but he had definitely decided to change it.

He seems to have thought the moral, social and economic reform of European societies too large a task for him to undertake, so he turned his eyes to the New World where, it seemed to him, societies existed which were almost pre-political. He resolved to go to Bermuda and set up Christian educative institutions which would promote his utopian ideas in a real society. During the 1720s he had meetings with Newton's disciple Clarke, and it is more than likely that they discussed the nature of space and time. However, suddenly, in September 1728, Berkeley sailed for America.

In January 1729 the ship arrived at Rhode Island. Berkeley quickly became disillusioned by the practical difficulties of establishing a college in the West Indies, and realized he had been grossly optimistic in his project of transforming the societies of the Americas. His interests returned to metaphysical and scientific matters and in 1731 he sailed back to England. There he published his *Alciphron* (1732) and *A Theory of Vision, or Visual Language, Vindicated and Explained* (1733).

By 1734 Berkeley was in Ireland once more and in that year he became Bishop of Cloyne, a post he held until his death in Oxford in 1753.

2 MATTER

Berkeley is an idealist philosopher. Idealism is the doctrine that what exists is fundamentally mental or spiritual in character and idealism is logically incompatible with materialism, the theory that what exists is fundamentally material or physical in character. Berkeley's major works therefore not only contain a defence of idealism but also a systematic attempt to refute materialism – an attempt, in fact, to show that matter does not exist. Locke and Newton are frequently the implicit targets of Berkeley's arguments, even though he sometimes ascribes to them views rather different from the ones they actually held. However, his philosophy may be read with profit by anyone who believes in the existence of a mind-independent self-subsistent spatio-temporal material constituting the universe. Berkeley deploys several arguments against the existence of matter. I shall examine the main ones in this section.

The Arguments from Qualities

Berkeley argues that secondary qualities are relative, so they must be subjective. By 'relative' I mean: *A* exists relative to *B* if, and only if, the existence or nature of *A* is at least partially determined by the existence or nature of *B*. By 'subjective' I mean: *A* is subjective if, and only if, the existence or nature of *A* is determined only by the existence or nature of a mind. Berkeley argues that because secondary qualities exist relative to minds they are subjective. For example, from the fact that an object feels cold to one hand but hot to another it follows that temperature is not an objective, subject-independent, property of the object but a subjective, mind-dependent, property of the perceiver. Further, primary qualities are just as relative as secondary qualities: for example, objects look large or small, in motion or at rest, depending on the state of the perceiver. If it is rational to deduce the subjectivity of secondary qualities from their relative nature, then it must be rational to deduce the subjectivity of primary qualities from their relative nature. It follows that the primary qualities of an object do not exist independently of the perception of them. But the primary qualities of a physical object are its essential properties, so it follows that physical objects essentially only exist perceived:

... in short, let anyone consider those arguments which are thought manifestly to prove that colours and tastes exist only in the mind, and he shall find they may with equal force be brought to prove the same thing of extension, figure, and motion. (P 15)

Notice that the primary/secondary quality distinction Berkeley considers is not exactly Locke's, even if it is intended as such. For example, Berkeley accepts that 'heat and cold are only affections of the mind' (P 14), but there is an important sense in which Locke does not accept this. Locke says our ideas, or experiences, of secondary qualities are wholly mental, but as dispositions of the object to produce those ideas, secondary qualities are properties the object intrinsically possesses in virtue of its primary qualities (see pp. 76–8 above). The broad difference between Berkeley and Locke may be put this way: for Locke, ideas are in the mind but qualities are in the object, but for Berkeley all qualities of physical objects are nothing over and above ideas (in the sense of 'ideas' that include 'experiences'). There is a way of reading Berkeley which does not make him misrepresent Locke. On this reading, by 'secondary qualities' Berkeley does not mean what Locke means: he means colours, sounds, tastes, and so on, as we pre-philosophically or commonsensically think of them – that is, not as dispositions of objects but as contents of experience. Berkeley would then be perfectly correct in the exegetical sense in maintaining that Locke thought that secondary qualities construed in that way are completely mind-dependent. Clearly, however, the interesting philosophical question of the subjectivity or objectivity of the properties of physical objects remains, whether Berkeley misconstrued the historical Locke's position or not.

Berkeley also argues that primary qualities logically depend upon secondary qualities, secondary qualities depend upon minds, so primary qualities depend on minds. This argument seems to me valid but not sound. It is valid because of the transitivity of 'depends upon' – if A depends upon B and B depends upon C, then A depends upon C. The problem is that the first premise is false. Berkeley says he cannot *imagine* the existence of a primary quality without a secondary. He says: 'It is not in my power to frame an idea of a body extended and moving, but I must withal give it some colour or other sensible quality which is acknowledged to exist only in the mind' (P 69).

I can imagine this. Think of invisible physical objects. More significantly, from the fact that P cannot be imagined it does not follow that 'necessarily not-P'.[4]

The Argument from Meaning

Locke, it will be recalled, uncomfortably postulated a material substance to answer the question of what the properties of a physical object are properties of (see pp. 78–80 above). Berkeley finds 'material substance' a meaningless expression. It divides into two putative semantic components, the concept of bearing or supporting properties and the concept of being. It bears properties and it exists: these are the only two claims that may be extracted from the concept by way of verbal definition. Berkeley points out that to say substance 'bears' or 'supports' properties is to speak metaphorically.

It is reasonably clear what these terms mean literally when used to describe, for example, the pillars supporting part of a building. That is to use the terms empirically. However, we could not possibly be acquainted with the relation between a putative substance and its primary qualities in the same way, and once the notion is shorn of its metaphorical content it becomes utterly vacuous.[5] Berkeley's empiricism about meanings is here directed against Locke's metaphysical concept of matter.

If we ask what other meaning 'material substance' has, this can only be 'being in general' and Berkeley says about this: 'The general idea of Being appeareth to me the most abstract and incomprehensible of all other' (P 17). Berkeley is right in thinking the concept of 'being' unclear. It is tremendously difficult to say what you have said about something when you have simply said that it exists, and the concepts of 'being' and 'existence' have repeatedly resisted any more primitive analysis in philosophy.[6]

Berkeley argues that because the concept of material substance is meaningless, material substance cannot exist. He is correct in the belief that putative entities which have only meaningless descriptions cannot exist, but it is less clear that he has shown that 'material substance' is wholly meaningless. Because we are unable to define a concept verbally it does not logically follow that that concept cannot denote. 'Red', for example, construed phenomenologically rather than in terms of physics, resists verbal definition but we are not thereby entitled to claim that nothing is red; similarly with 'exists'. Clearly, however, from the fact – if it is a fact – that 'being' or 'exists' is meaningful it does not follow that 'material substance' is wholly meaningful, and from the fact that something exists it does not logically follow that it is material. It is not open to the defender of material substance against Berkeley's argument to mention primary qualities in the definition of 'substance' (save as what substance supports) because substance is what has or bears those properties. It is not logically constituted by them. In any case, Berkeley argues that primary qualities are mind-dependent.

The Epistemological Argument

Suppose, however, the notion of material substance is meaningful so that it is logically possible that there should exist mind-independent physical particulars. Berkeley thinks this assumption false, but even if we accept its possibility, according to Berkeley we can never know it to be true. There are two, and only two, putative routes by which we could know that there are mind-independent physical objects: 'Either we must know it by sense or by reason' (P 18).

The senses cannot inform us that physical objects exist unperceived because through them we are directly acquainted only with 'our sensations, ideas' (P 18), and it does not logically follow from the having such experiences that they are experiences of mind-independent physical objects. Also, from the fact that physical objects exist perceived it does not necessarily follow that they could exist unperceived. Indeed, if Locke is right that only ideas are perceived, then no one has ever perceived a physical object and it is logically possible that there are no physical objects. It follows from that that the senses cannot inform us that physical objects exist. If we hold, conversely, that physical objects are perceived, that cannot prove that they exist unperceived because from the fact that an object exists perceived it does not logically follow that it exists unperceived. For sense experience to establish that conclusion it would have to be possible to perceive an unperceived object, but that idea is self-contradictory so it is logically impossible that sense experience should prove physical objects exist unperceived.

Reason is powerless to inform us of the existence of physical objects precisely because there is no sound inference from the existence of experiences to the existence of physical objects. If reason and experience are the only putative means of knowing that physical objects exist independently of minds, and if reason and experience cannot provide this knowledge, then it is impossible to know that mind-independent physical objects exist. So Berkeley concludes: 'if there were external bodies, it is impossible that we should ever come to know it' (P 20).

Berkeley's epistemological argument does not prove that mind-independent physical objects do not exist. It proves at most that we cannot know that they exist (or perhaps only that we do not know that they exist). It does not prove that they do not exist, because from the fact that we do not or cannot know that something exists it does not logically follow that it does not exist; the concept of epistemologically inaccessible existants is not self-contradictory. If the reason why some putative entity is epistemologically inaccessible is that its concept is contradictory, then it does logically follow from that that that object does not exist. The incoherence of 'material substance' does not feature in any premise of this particular argument of Berkeley's, however.

Berkeley's argument that we cannot know that physical objects exist independently of our thoughts and perceptions seems to me sound. Even if we discard the Lockean representational theory of perception and hold that physical objects are perceived directly, it does not logically follow from the truth of that new view that they could exist unperceived and that they do not depend on our perceptions of them. No one has refuted Berkeley, even though most people insist that his view is false.

The Argument from Causation

Reason is powerless to establish the existence of mind-independent physical objects because there is no sound inference from the existence of experiences to the existence of physical objects. Nevertheless, Berkeley considers the possibility that mind-independent physical objects probably exist as the causes of our ideas. Even if it does not logically follow from the fact we have experiences that physical objects exist, 'it might be at least probable there are such things as bodies that excite [our] ideas' (P 19). On this view, even if it is not deductively certain that physical objects exist, it is inductively probable. We postulate physical objects as the overwhelmingly likely cause of our experiences, and we are most likely correct in this postulation.

Berkeley rejects this argument because it leaves wholly mysterious the nature of the causal relation between physical objects and ideas – the problem that dogged traditional Cartesian dualism. Berkeley maintains that causal relations may only obtain between minds and each other, or minds and the contents of minds. Nothing as senseless and inert as the purported 'material substance' could have causal efficacy. Berkeley's idealism is a monism as materialism is a monism, and Berkeley, like the materialist monists, rejects mind–body dualism partly because the alleged psycho-physical causal relation is a confused idea. Idealists and materialists often hold it in common that causal relations may only obtain between ontologically homogeneous kinds of entity, and it is impossible to conceive of a psycho-physical causal relation.

If it is true that there are no psycho-physical causal relations, and ideas are mental and material substances material, then it logically follows that material substance cannot be correctly postulated as the cause of our ideas – it cannot exist under that description.

This argument does not prove that material substance does not exist: it proves at most that material substance does not exist as the cause of our ideas. It is logically consistent with material substance not having that causal role that it should exist because the notion of a physical existant that does not have a particular causal role is not contradictory. It is, perhaps, part of the concept of a physical object that physical objects have *some* causal efficacy, but not the specific efficacy of causing mental states.

The Argument from Imagination

Berkeley argues that not only is it impossible to know that physical objects exist independently of minds, but also that it is impossible to imagine that physical objects exist independently of minds. Any such putative imagining of mind-independent physical objects is 'framing in your mind certain ideas', and this is necessarily only a mental occurrence. To imagine something unimagined, as to perceive something unperceived, is contradictory, or, as Berkeley puts it, 'a manifest repugnancy' (P 23). However psychologically compelling it may be to believe that we do imagine mind-independent objects, this belief is illusory because its content is self-contradictory.

It does not follow from someone's, or indeed everyone's, inability to imagine that something is the case that it is not the case. What is the case and what is not the case is logically independent of the psychology of our imaginative powers. However, if what is putatively the case is self-contradictory to describe, it is logically impossible that that should be the case. It is impossible to imagine logically impossible states of affairs; therefore in those cases where the reason why we are unable to imagine what is the case is that what we are trying to imagine is self-contradictory in its description, it will logically follow that what is putatively the case is not. If Berkeley has shown that the notion of an object existing unimagined is contradictory, he has succeeded in demonstrating that there are no imagination-independent physical objects even when there seem to be.

Notice that in an important sense Berkeley's idealism is consistent with the world appearing just as it does commonsensically or pre-philosophically. If Berkeley were with you now he would agree that you are reading this book and that this book exists. He would, however, deny two claims about the book. He would deny that it exists over and above some perception or idea of it, and he would deny that it is made of a material substance called 'matter'. He is manifestly not asserting that there are voids or gaps in our experience where commonsensically we take there to be books, tables, etc. All those objects exist, but certain fundamental beliefs about them – that they have a mind-independent and material character – are false. Berkeley's idealism is consistent with everything in the course of our experience. Nothing empirical refutes it. In that sense, Berkeley's idealism leaves the world intact.

Having said that, it may be that our beliefs in the mind-independent and material nature of the objects we perceive cannot be so readily divorced from the content of experience. Those beliefs may, so to speak, be 'read into' experience so that the world about us looks and feels mind-independent and physical. If that is right, then giving up those two beliefs does imply qualitatively altering our experience, not leaving it intact and just relinquishing beliefs about it. In that case, Berkeley's idealism is less consistent with the world as it appears commonsensically.

Whether or not Berkeley's 'immaterialism' is consistent with commonsense, it is not to be dismissed lightly. In my opinion there is no historically perennial commonsense, or at least, any would-be historically perennial commonsense has a metaphysical content sufficiently vague as to be consistent with competing ontologies in the philosophy of mind. Commonsense is historically constituted and historically changing. We late twentieth-century Westerners have a commonsense which is largely Newtonian and Cartesian, and central to it is the belief in mind-independent matter. It may well be that this view is false. If it is objected to this that the reality of matter is not only commonsensical but scientific, I think that view is certainly false. Science has not proved the existence of matter and Berkeley may well be right when he denies that there is any material substance of which the universe is made. It may well be that the science of the twenty-first century is logically incompatible with materialism. If so, Berkeley's idealism will be taken much more seriously than it is now.[7]

3 ABSTRACT IDEAS

In a strikingly modern turn of phrase, Berkeley diagnoses philosophical problems as results of 'Abuse of Language' (P 6). This abuse essentially consists in thinking that the meanings of words can be abstract ideas, and that abstract ideas can denote. This twin doctrine is false, so Berkeley argues, because it is logically impossible that there should be any abstract ideas. Clearly, if Berkeley is able to prove that, then he has proved there are no abstract ideas, and if there are no abstract ideas it both follows that the meanings of words are not abstract ideas and that there are no abstract ideas which denote. Logic and metaphysics deal in abstract ideas, so to that extent those two putative intellectual disciplines are bogus.

Berkeley begins by attacking abstraction, the alleged process by which abstract ideas are acquired. As in the case of secondary qualities and substance, there is a debate between historians of philosophy about whether Berkeley is attacking a position which the historical Locke held. Locke is certainly Berkeley's target in the attack on abstract ideas and is mentioned by him as such, and in at least one passage in the *Essay* Locke does advocate the view Berkeley attacks.[8] However, as philosophers, we must not read Berkeley simply as a critic of Locke. We want to know whether his arguments are sound.

Berkeley attacks several kinds of abstraction and one of them is the thesis that it is possible to think of the properties of objects as independent of one another, even if they cannot exist independently of one another. Berkeley accepts that the properties of objects do not exist independently of one another. Colour, for example, does not really exist without size, or movement without shape. However, the mind is alleged to have the power to think of one property in abstraction from the others upon which it depends. Hence we have the putative power to think of size, colour and motion independently of one another.

Not that it is possible for colour or motion to exist without extension; but only that the mind can frame to itself by abstraction the idea of colour exclusive of extension, and of motion exclusive of both colour and extension. (P 7)

To say that an idea is abstract is to say that it is acquired by a process of abstraction: by the psychological process of ignoring the properties upon which it depends. Abstract ideas are also allegedly general, so that our abstract idea of colour is the idea of colour in general and not of one particular colour, and our abstract idea of extension is an idea of extension in general and not of some particular extension. The process by which it is alleged that abstract ideas become general is this: the mind perceives what is common to all and only, say, the extensions it has perceived or the colours it has perceived, and 'it considers apart or singles out by itself that which is common, thereby making a most abstract idea of extension' (P 48) or colour. The abstract idea of extension is not that of any particular size, nor is the abstract idea of colour the idea of a particular colour such as red or blue or white. The abstract idea of motion is not the idea of any particular velocity or direction, and the abstract idea of 'man' or 'humanity' is not the idea of any particular person. Even though 'man' includes the ideas of colour and size, because any person is of some colour and size, those too are abstract ideas because there is no single colour and no single size common to all people.

Berkeley's first attack on abstract ideas is an appeal to introspection. He maintains he has the capacity to imagine particular people and objects, but says: 'I cannot by any effort of thought conceive the abstract idea above described' (P 10). He cannot conceive of motion without thereby conceiving of some particular object moving, or frame any idea of colour without size, or any idea of size without shape.

Berkeley maintains that in these cases the constraints on what can be imagined are governed by the constraints on what can exist independently: 'I deny that I can abstract from one another, or conceive separately, those qualities which it is impossible should exist so separated' (P 10). Clearly, from the fact that Berkeley cannot frame abstract ideas it does not logically follow that no one has this power, or that abstract ideas are logical impossibilities. However, Berkeley has an inductive argument which he hopes will convince us that others too lack this power of conceiving abstract ideas. He notes that most people – people in non-philosophical contexts – do not use abstract notions, and this is good evidence that they do not have them. Berkeley says, with more than a touch of irony, 'they are confined only to the learned' (P 10).

In general, from the fact that it is impossible to imagine something, we cannot logically conclude that it does not exist. For example, it may be that we are unable to imagine colours we have not experienced but it does not follow from that that they do not exist. However, abstract ideas are putatively necessarily conceivable, and putatively necessarily conceivable by us, so if it is true that abstract ideas cannot be conceived, or cannot be conceived by us, it logically follows that abstract ideas do not exist. If Berkeley's premise is true, it follows it is true that there are no abstract ideas.

Berkeley accepts that there are general terms in language, words which may be used to refer to more than one thing, but denies that the meanings of general terms are or depend upon abstract ideas. Words, for Berkeley, as we shall see in section 8, become general not by standing for general ideas but by standing for several particular ideas.

We come now to Berkeley's central and most devastating objection to the concept of an abstract idea: that it is inconsistent – self-contradictory. The abstract idea of *x* must be the idea of all the properties common to all and only *x*s. The decisive objection is that such a putative idea must both possess and lack some of the same properties. For example, the abstract general idea of a triangle 'is neither oblique nor rectangular, equilateral nor scalenon, but all and none of these at once' (P 13). The composite idea of *x* in general is impossible because the properties of *x*s which the putative idea would have to include are so qualitatively diverse that it is logically impossible that they should be subsumed under the same idea. They exclude one another. For example, any triangle is either equilateral or non-equilateral, but the putative abstract idea of a triangle must be both equilateral and non-equilateral and that is contradictory. That the description of some putative idea or entity is contradictory is a sufficient condition of the logical impossibility of that putative idea or entity, and what is logically impossible cannot exist. It follows that there are no abstract ideas.

Not only does Berkeley argue that the properties of xs subsumed under the putative idea of x are so diverse as to be mutually exclusive, but he also holds that it is logically impossible that there should be an idea of x possessing characteristics unique to xs sufficient to distinguish any x from any non-x and yet subsuming every x. Berkeley denies that there are any properties common to all and only xs.

If Berkeley's arguments are sound, there are no abstract ideas. In his repudiation of abstract ideas Berkeley is a more thoroughgoing empiricist than Locke.[9]

4 THE SELF

In the case of physical objects, to be is to be perceived, but in the case of spirits, to be is to perceive. Berkeley makes a fundamental distinction between the ideas or objects of perception and the perceiver of them. Indeed, he thinks it impossible that there should be ideas without someone or something to have those ideas. It does not make sense to talk about perceiving unless it makes sense to talk about a perceiver:

> This perceiving, active being is what I call MIND, SPIRIT, SOUL, or MYSELF, by which I do not denote any one of my ideas but a thing entirely distinct from them, wherein they exist. (P 2)

I am not one of my ideas. I am not even all of my ideas, I am that which has my ideas. Locke and Berkeley have in common the belief that the mind is an immaterial substance or soul, and in this they differ sharply from their predecessor Hobbes for whom the mind is a set of physical processes, and from Hume and the later empiricists for whom the self is nothing over and above a set of experiences, impressions or sense data. Berkeley departs abruptly from Locke, however, in being an idealist and so a monist, while Locke is a mind–body dualist. Locke holds that both mental and physical substances exist but Berkeley holds that only mental substance exists. Both differ utterly from Hobbes for whom only physical substance exists.

Berkeley realizes that there is *prima facie* a problem about being an empiricist and holding that the self is a soul. Empiricism implies that all knowledge is acquired through experience, but there is no experience of the soul, so the soul cannot be known to exist. Worse than this, every meaningful word corresponds to some idea, but we have no idea of the soul and that would seem to make 'soul' meaningless. As Berkeley puts it:

> It will be objected that, if there is no idea signified by the terms 'soul',
> 'spirit', and 'substance' they are wholly insignificant, and have no meaning
> in them. (P 139)

Berkeley's solution is as follows. It is certain that I exist – no one can deny their own existence without manifest absurdity. However, I am not identical with any of my ideas. It is not as though I am one of those ideas to be met with during the course of my experiences; on the contrary, I am that which has my experiences and ideas. What is meant by 'soul' or 'spirit' is that which perceives or that which experiences. Here is Berkeley's rather Cartesian claim about his own existence:

> If I should say that I was nothing, or that I was an idea, nothing could
> be more evidently absurd than either of these propositions. (P 139)

So the first premise of the argument is: 'I exist.' The second premise is that the existence of my ideas consists in their being perceived. Berkeley has maintained this all along. However, it makes no sense to claim perception without a perceiver, or to claim that the perceiver could be all or one of his ideas, so the 'terms "soul", "spirit", and "substance" . . . these words do mean or signify a real thing – which is neither an idea nor like an idea, but that which perceives ideas, and wills, and reasons about them' (P 139).

Thus I am what perceives my ideas and that which perceives ideas is a soul or spirit. It logically follows that 'What I am myself – that which I denote by the term "I" – is the same with what is meant by soul or spiritual substance' (P 139).

The soul and its ideas have, in a sense, opposite properties. The soul is a substance which actively perceives ideas, whereas an idea is something inert or passive the existence of which consists only in being perceived by a spirit. Souls are substances because they do not logically depend upon the existence of anything else for their own existence (although God created all souls and could in principle annihilate them). Ideas, in contrast, depend logically upon being perceived, but only spirits perceive, so ideas depend logically on spirits. Berkeley draws the distinction in this way:

> All the unthinking objects of the mind agree in that they are entirely passive, and their existence consists only in being perceived; whereas a soul or spirit is an active being, whose existence consists not in being perceived, but in perceiving ideas and thinking. (P 139)

It follows that for Berkeley 'spirit' and 'soul' are not meaningless. He accepts that strictly speaking we have no idea of the soul; however, we have a 'notion' of the soul.[10] This means that we can use the word meaningfully. We can on his view define it – even though it corresponds to no idea (in the way that 'blue' does, for example). 'Soul' denotes something that exists – a spiritual substance – even though no one is directly acquainted with a soul, even the one that they are.[11]

Berkeley maintains that as souls we are immortal. Indeed, he thinks this logically follows from his account so far: 'The Natural Immortality of the Soul is a necessary consequence of the foregoing doctrine' (P 141). What Berkeley means by 'Natural Immortality' here is that no natural event – no empirical event in accordance with natural law – could possibly destroy the soul. Nevertheless, as noted above, souls may be destroyed by their creator, God.

Berkeley derives the immortality of the soul from the definition of 'soul'. The soul is 'indivisible, incorporeal, and unextended' (P 141). It is simple in the sense that it has no parts. It is non-physical and it has no size. The natural destruction of something consists in its decomposition into separate parts. But the soul has no parts. It follows that the soul cannot be destroyed by any natural event because only complex things may be destroyed by such events. The soul is therefore 'naturally immortal' (P 141).

Whether or not we accept Berkeley's arguments that we are immortal spiritual substances, he has addressed an important issue: What is the self? It is precisely one's own individual, subjective, conscious existence with its point of view on the external world that has not been accommodated within the late twentieth-century scientific materialist world-picture. Explaining the subjective self usually takes the form of explaining it away. The major philosophical task of the twenty-first century is the reconciliation of the natural sciences with the subjectivity of human existence; the integration of the perceiving subject into our picture of the universe. The subject of science must become the subject of science.

5   GOD AND OTHER MINDS

There are two fundamental philosophical questions about God: What is God? and Does God exist? Berkeley attempts answers to both of them.[12]

Berkeley's argument for the existence of God is a version of the causal argument which contains a description of the essential properties of God in its conclusion. The first premise of the argument is that we persons have or perceive ideas. But we are not the cause of our own ideas. Berkeley means that the content of our experience – what we experience – is not the result of the exercise of our will. On the contrary, when we experience we have no control over what we experience. However, everything that happens has a cause, and the cause of ideas must be spiritual. Berkeley has ruled out all physical causes because he has ruled out the existence of matter and because psycho-physical causal interaction is incoherent: 'there is therefore some other Spirit that causes them; since it is repugnant that they should subsist by themselves' (P 146).

This yields the conclusion that everything we experience has a spiritual cause. But any cause of the whole of our experience must have certain attributes. The regularity and order of our experience implies that the cause of it is infinitely intelligent, the scale of experience is such that the cause of it must be omnipotent, and the beauty and perfection of the objects of nature found in experience are such that the cause of them must itself be perfect:

I say if we consider all these things, and at the same time attend to the meaning and import of the attributes One, Eternal, Infinitely Wise, Good, and Perfect, we shall clearly perceive that they belong to the aforesaid spirit. (P 146)

At work in Berkeley's argument is a suppressed Cartesian, indeed, Scholastic, premise. This is that there must be at least as much reality in the cause as the effect. (Hobbes remarked about this principle that it does not make much sense to talk about degrees of reality: either something is or it is not.) We may read the principle as the claim that if an effect has a certain property, then the cause of that effect must have that property in at least the degree that the effect has that property.

Although Berkeley's argument is valid as he interprets the premises it is less clear that it is sound, because each of its premises might be challenged. Philosophical arguments could be deployed against the theses that we are not the cause of our own ideas, that everything has a cause, that causes of ideas must be mental causes, and that experience exhibits sufficient regularity to imply the existence of an intelligent and perfect cause of it.

Nevertheless, Berkeley insists that 'the existence of God is far more evidently perceived than the existence of men' (P 147). The belief that other persons exist is an inference I make from the fact that I have certain ideas; some of them are such as to appear to be ideas of other people's bodies. The existence of other persons as conscious minds can only ever be an inference from *some* of my own ideas, but the belief that God exists is an inference from *all* my ideas, so the evidence for the existence of God is greater than the evidence for other minds. If we believe in other minds, the rational thing for us to do is to believe in the existence of God.

Berkeley realizes that, as in the case of the soul, there is a *prima facie* difficulty in being both an empiricist and a theist. God is not, after all, an empirical object and 'it seems to be a general pretence of the unthinking that they cannot see God' (P 148). However, all anyone is ever directly acquainted with is their own ideas, so it makes as much sense to say that we see God as it does to say that we see other people. The existence of other people and of God are both inferences from facts about experience, and 'We need only open our eyes to see the Sovereign Lord of all things, with a more full and clear view than we do any one of our fellow creatures' (P 148).

Thus there is a strong analogy for Berkeley between the two philosophical questions of the existence of God and the problem of other minds.[13] Indeed, they could be presented as one and the same question. The problem of other minds is: How can we know that other people have minds – have psychological interiors broadly like our own – given that we only perceive their bodies? The problem of the existence of God is: How can we know that there exists a spiritual cause or sustainer of the physical universe when all we perceive is the universe? God is a mind, an infinite, wise, benevolent, omnipotent and omnipresent one, but a mind none the less. So the problem of God's existence is part of the problem of other minds. Berkeley's position is that if we are confident that other human minds exist we should be still more confident that God exists.

Berkeley says that we perceive or 'see' God to a greater extent than we 'see' other people, if we are sufficiently attuned. What does this mean? Persons are essentially spirits, but we do not literally or directly see spirits because we only perceive ideas. Spirits perceive but are not perceived, so we never directly perceive persons as persons:

A human spirit or person is not perceived by sense, as not being an idea; when therefore we see the colour, size, figure, and motions of a man, we perceive only certain sensations or ideas excited in our own minds. (P 148)

It logically follows that 'we do not see a man' (P 148) if we mean by 'man' an active spirit like oneself. Our ideas are marks or signs which lead us to suppose that other persons exist. It is just in this way, too, that it makes sense to say we perceive or see God, the one difference being that only a sub-set of our experiences, at certain times, shows the existence of other minds, but the whole course of our experience at every time demonstrates the existence of God. The evidence for God's existence is therefore overwhelming. Everything we are acquainted with confirms it at every moment and nothing refutes it, 'everything we see, hear, feel, or anywise perceive by Sense, being a sign or effect of the power of God' (P 141).

Berkeley's universe therefore contains only minds and their ideas. Minds are either finite or infinite; there is only one infinite mind, and that is God. Finite minds do not interact but God causes them to have ideas which makes it seem to them that they share a material universe. In that sense, and in that sense only, God created a material universe.

6 SPACE AND TIME

Berkeley's philosophy of space and time is best read as an attack on the absolute space and time of Newton. Indeed, many of Berkeley's remarks may be read as close anticipations of the theories of Mach and Einstein, as Popper has pointed out.[14] To understand Berkeley, then, we have to understand something of Newton.

When Newton said that space and time are absolute he meant that they do not logically depend upon the existence of physical objects. Physical objects are literally, not metaphorically, 'in' space: if there were to cease to be any physical objects – if all physical objects were to disappear – space and time would still remain. The space and time the objects used to occupy would be left over. To say that a physical object exists in a particular place or at a particular time is not to specify that object's spatial and temporal relations with other objects, but rather to specify its location in absolute space and absolute time.[15]

Berkeley rejects this whole picture. It is not simply wrong in its details for Berkeley but is one wholly erroneous metaphysic. I shall say something first about Berkeley on time and then turn to space.

Newton makes a double mistake about time, according to Berkeley. He thinks time exists over and above physical objects and physical objects exist over and above ideas. In fact, time is nothing over and above the physical objects and the relations between them and physical objects are nothing over and above ideas and the relations between those. Thus Newton is at two removes from the truth. As we have seen, objects are mind-dependent, and time 'is

nothing abstracted from the succession of ideas in our minds'
(P 98). It follows for Berkeley that time is logically dependent upon
minds. If time depends on physical objects and physical objects
depend on minds, then time depends on minds because of the
transitivity of 'depends on': if *A* depends on *B* and *B* depends on *C*,
then *A* depends on *C*.

Berkeley's theory of time is both idealist and relativist. It is
relativist because time does not exist over and above temporal
things and the temporal relations between them. In this view
Berkeley falls on the side of Leibniz in the Leibniz–Newton
disagreement.[16]

We are misled into thinking there is a philosophical problem
about time because we wrongly try to think of time in the abstract:
in abstraction from temporal things. This attempt merely generates
an incoherent abstract idea of time:

> For my own part, whenever I attempt to frame a simple idea of Time,
> abstracted from the succession of ideas in my mind, which flows uniformly
> and is participated in by all beings, I am lost and entangled in inextricable
> difficulties. I have no notion of it at all. (P 98)

It does not make sense within the Berkeleyan framework to speak
of time 'flowing uniformly' any more than being 'infinitely divisible'.
Notice he is not claiming that time is nothing over and above our
idea or concept of time. He is saying that time is nothing over and
above the temporal properties of our ideas. The temporal properties
of our ideas include the facts that some arise before others, some are
simultaneous, they all last, and so on. 'Ideas', it will be recalled, is
sufficiently broad in reference to denote what we call 'experiences'.
Berkeley's theory of time is thus thoroughly empiricist.

Berkeley represents Newton on space as follows: 'this celebrated
author holds there is an Absolute Space, which, being unperceivable
to sense, remains in itself similar and immovable' (P 111). Berkeley's criticism is that it makes no sense to speak of space in
abstraction from spatial things, and it makes no sense to speak of
spatial things as independent of minds. Space logically depends
upon minds because space logically depends upon spatial things
and spatial things logically depend upon minds. Thus we may talk
of this being to the left of that, this being such-and-such a distance

from that, and so on, but it makes no sense to talk of absolute space. To say that all physical objects are located in the whole of space means nothing unless it means there exists a set of spatial relations between all the physical objects there are. And, as we have seen now, to talk about physical objects at all is to talk about ideas or sensations, and not about mind-independent material substances. Space then, like time, is not absolute, but relative and subjective.[17]

The question of whether space and time are absolute or relative has re-emerged in a new form in modern philosophy and physics as the question of whether space-time is absolute or relative.[18] It remains to be seen whether a holistic unified science which locates the conscious subject in the universe will ascribe subjective properties to space-time.

7 NUMBERS

Berkeley's idealism includes the thesis that 'number is entirely the creature of the mind' (P 12). There are two reasons why he thinks this is so. Firstly, it makes no sense to speak of numbers of objects without reference to counting beings, and counting beings are minds. Secondly, objects counted are mind-dependent because objects are nothing over and above collections of ideas.

Berkeley maintains that how many there are of some kind of counted objects depends on the way the mind perceives those objects: 'the same thing bears a different denomination of number as the mind views it with different respects' (P 12). Therefore there being a certain number of things is not an objective property of those things but depends upon some mind picking out those things as those things. Things are not objectively ready-classified into sorts, it is the imposition of our own classificatory schemes which makes there be sorts of things, and specific numbers of them. Berkeley's example of this is, however, rather unfortunate: 'the same extension is one, or three, or thirty-six, according as the mind considers it with reference to a yard, a foot or an inch' (P 12). This point is terribly weak because in the case of three different units the length could be mind-independently one yard, three feet, and thirty-six inches. Berkeley needs an example where relativity to a subject proves the subjectivity of number through the mutual inconsistency of the lengths. In his example, being one of those lengths logically implies being the other two.

Berkeley may well be right to suggest that it is meaningless to talk about there being numbers or numbers of objects except within a system of counting and unless there are counting beings, and agreed criteria for discriminating sorts of objects to be counted. However, it would require more argument to show that

Number is so visibly relative, and dependent upon men's understanding, that it is strange to think how anyone should give it an absolute existence without the mind. (P 12)

The fact is we do not know whether numbers could exist without mathematical beings. This is part of a wider problem which is still unsolved. We do not know what numbers are.

8 LANGUAGE

Berkeley agrees with Locke that the meaning of a word is an idea, and that the meaning of a general word is a general idea, but differs from him on what a general idea is. As we have seen, Berkeley rejects the theory of abstract ideas so he denies that a general idea is an abstract idea.

Clearly, most words are general because a general word may be used to refer to more than one thing and most words may be used to refer to more than one thing. For Berkeley, 'a word becomes general by being made the sign, not of an abstract general idea, but of several particular ideas, any one of which it indifferently suggests to the mind' (P 11). In order to understand propositions containing general terms it is not necessary to have the thought of an abstract idea in the sense criticized above (p. 116–19). Rather, the proposition, if true, will hold true of any objects referred to by its general terms. Thus a claim about extension, if true, is true of all extensions. In understanding a proposition we know what it would be for that proposition to be true, and this does not logically or psychologically require us mentally to entertain abstract ideas. Berkeley says, 'I do not deny absolutely there are general ideas, but only that there are any abstract general ideas' (P 11).

It is Berkeley's theory that a particular idea becomes general by standing for a class of particular ideas. Thus the generality of one idea consists in a relationship between that and other ideas, and this relationship is 'standing for' or 'representing'. Unfortunately it is not clear what it consists in for something to 'stand for' or 'represent' something else, and Berkeley does not have an explanation of this relation. It is not as though any satisfactory theory of meaning may take these concepts as primitive. However, it is possible to make more sense of Berkeley's position through examples. The general idea of colour considered by itself is one particular idea, but in so far as it represents blue, red, and so on, it counts as a general idea. To use Berkeley's own example, a geometrician might use a particular line, say one inch in length, to stand for any line or all lines. Crucially, for that line to stand for or represent other lines, what the geometrician proves of that line must hold for those other lines (and this is perhaps intended by the geometrician). In close anticipation of a doctrine of Wittgenstein, Berkeley hints that in so far as the one-inch line has a use, it makes sense to talk of its standing for all lines.[19] He says:

This which in itself is a particular line, is nevertheless with regard to its signification general, since, as it is there used, it represents all particular lines whatsoever; so that what is demonstrated of it is demonstrated of all lines, or, in other words, of a line in general. (P 12)

It is clear from this passage what Berkeley thinks generality consists in. To speak of x in general is to speak of all instances of x, or the class of x. The line example is intended by Berkeley not only to demonstrate the relation between a general idea and the particular ideas it represents, but also as an analogy to show how particular words become general. Particular words stand for particular ideas, but a general word stands for a general idea. It is in fact a 'sign' of a general idea. It is not clear what relation obtains between A and B if A is a sign for B, but it could be that A is a sign for B if, and only if, A either represents or stands for B, and, as we have seen, representation is to be explained in terms of use. Here is the analogy: 'As that particular line becomes general by being made a sign, so the name "line", which taken absolutely is particular, by being a sign is made general' (P 12). Berkeley adds to his view that a general word stands for a general idea the claim that a general word denotes a class of ideas; for example, 'line' not only stands for a general idea but for the class of lines, which on Berkeley's idealist account is a class of ideas. Although this may not be quite incoherent, Berkeley should perhaps have added as a point of clarity that 'line' refers to the set of lines via its reference to the general idea of a line. A general word refers to a general idea and a general idea refers to a class of ideas, so a general word refers to a class of ideas. Berkeley maintains here that if A refers to B and B refers to C, then A refers to C, a principle which does not hold generally.

In another anticipation of Wittgenstein, Berkeley argues that the philosophical error of postulating abstract ideas is the result of being misled by language.[20] He claims that philosophers correctly note that language exhibits a certain generality – contains general terms – and they hold, also correctly, that the meaning of a word is an idea; but they then argue, unsoundly, that the idea must be an abstract general idea to account for the generality of language.

Part of the way in which 'words have contributed to the origin of that mistake' (P 18) is via the assumption that to each name there corresponds one, and only one, fixed and precise meaning. Abstract ideas are then postulated in a misguided attempt to say what constitutes such settled meanings. Berkeley, in contrast, substitutes a view close to the Wittgensteinian doctrine of the indeterminacy of sense: 'In truth there is no such thing as one precise and definite signification annexed to any general name' (P 18). Berkeley replaces the incoherent concept of an abstract idea by the view that general ideas signify particular ideas. The diversity of the particular ideas subsumed under one general idea accounts for the incoherence of abstract ideas, and in a quasi-Wittgensteinian way, for the indeterminacy of sense.

That each word may be given a single definition is no objection to the thesis that each word signifies a variety of particulars. Even if it were true that each word had one, and only one, definition, that is consistent with the word's denoting many qualitatively dissimilar particulars. Suppose, for example, the definition of 'triangle' is 'a plain surface comprehended by three right lines' (P 18), there would nevertheless exist a large variety of triangles with different lengths of sides and different-sized angles: 'Consequently, there is no one settled idea which limits the signification of the word triangle' (P 18). Although definitions are useful they are only guides to denotation, and it is useless to try to make general words stand for abstract ideas because that is impossible.

Berkeley accepts from Locke the two theses that 'language has no other end but the communicating our ideas' and 'every significant name stands for an idea' (P 19). Words are used meaninglessly by philosophers when they do not denote ideas.[21] For example, where a philosopher thinks a word denotes an abstract idea there exists no abstract idea, so that word is used meaninglessly. However, in using words we do not actually have to think the ideas they stand for in order to use the words meaningfully. Although every meaningful word stands for an idea, the idea itself does not have to be mentally entertained during the meaningful use of the word.[22]

There is a sense, then, in which Berkeley shares yet another doctrine about language with Wittgenstein. Wittgenstein denies that meaning is a mental process, and that implies what Berkeley also holds to be true: meaning is not necessarily an occurrent mental process. Of course Berkeley thinks the meaning of a word is an idea and Wittgenstein rejects this, but both have it in common that meaning is not the experience you have when you use a word, nor must mental imagery accompany the use of the word:

A little attention will discover that it is not necessary (even in the strictest reasonings) [that] significant names which stand for ideas should, every time they are used, excite, in the understanding the ideas they are made to stand for. (P 19)

Both Berkeley and Wittgenstein point to the variety of uses of language. For Berkeley the communication of ideas is just one use amongst others, and not even the chief one. Language excites the emotions, incites or prevents actions, causes mental dispositions. Indeed, many connative states are caused by hearing words without the intermediary of any ideas. Berkeley's advice, like Wittgenstein's, is not to theorize too much about language but rather to reflect upon our experience of it. Wittgenstein and Berkeley are both pragmatists about meaning.

HUME

1 HUME IN HISTORY

David Hume, Scot, empiricist and Tory, was born and died in
Edinburgh. Although his life, from 1711 to 1776, was outwardly
uneventful and his political outlook conservative, the implications
of his philosophy are revolutionary. His sceptical empiricism
unearths a set of philosophical problems subversive of both of the
massive and competing trends of Western thought since the late
Middle Ages: the Christian religion and the natural sciences. In his
ridiculing criticisms of the argument from design and the belief in
miracles he produces objections to religious faith which no theist
can afford to disregard. In his insistence on the contingency of
causal relations, his scepticism about induction, and his making our
belief in the mind-independence of matter depend upon the psychology of imagination he shows us that science rests on metaphysical assumptions. Neither theologian nor scientist may draw comfort
from Hume's philosophy. Nor does Hume give any hint that the
claims of science and religion may be reconciled. The greatest
synthesis of the two ever attempted – that of Descartes – is equally
the subject of his attack. Descartes's two-worlds ontology, his
division of what is into mental and physical substance, is exposed
to a radically empiricist critique in Hume's destruction of the
Cartesian idea of the self.[1]

Hume was born into an affluent and educated family of Scottish
lowland gentry. He never knew poverty and had the privilege of an
excellent classical education at the University of Edinburgh from
1723 to 1727. There it seems likely that he read and discussed
Locke's empiricism and the ideas of the leading exponents of the

new sciences, including Newton. There too he must have familiarized himself with the then prevailing proofs of the existence of God. It is hard to discern the historical cause of his lively scepticism. It is possible that his reading of Greek and Latin authors impressed him with the knowledge of alternative ways of thinking to the scientific and religious orthodoxies of his day. Perhaps it was the seeming incompatibility of the scientific and religious world-pictures that led him to discover shortcomings in both. In any case, it is clear that the young Hume had both time and money to pursue his philosophical interests. His parents made him an allowance which exempted him from the need to earn a living. He used his economic freedom to great profit in the disciplined business of writing books on philosophy, once he had received his M.A. from Edinburgh. He spent the years from 1734 to 1736 in France and there he wrote the massive and brilliant *Treatise of Human Nature*. This was published in three volumes during 1739–40, and hard on its heels in 1741–2 appeared the *Essays Moral and Political*. The first volume of the *Treatise* is called 'Of the Understanding' and it is there that Hume's empiricist epistemology is to be found. The second volume, 'Of the Passions', is Hume's examination of emotion as the title suggests, and the third volume, 'Of Morals', includes not only his ethics but the central tenets of his political theory. The third volume contains his attack on the whole principle of basing political theory on the idea of a social contract, and this attack is continued in 'Of the Original Contract' in *Essays Moral and Political*.

Despite the publication of his books, the early 1740s must have been a period of disappointment for Hume. In 1744 he was turned down for the post of Professor of Philosophy at Edinburgh and the *Treatise* had gone unnoticed in most philosophical circles and had been reviewed badly in others. However, Hume in his mid-thirties was not lacking in confidence, energy and determination and set about writing a fresh exposition of his philosophy which he hoped would reach a wider audience. The result was the *Enquiry Concerning Human Understanding* (1748) and the *Enquiry Concerning the Principles of Morals* (1751). These were much better received than the *Treatise*, and Hume's international reputation as a philosopher dates from the 1750s: a full ten years after the publication of the *Treatise*. One cannot help feeling that if Hume had not had the courage and persistence to rewrite his thoughts in a more palatable form he would, like Frege, have gone unrecognized in his own lifetime.

However, Hume's impact as a historian was greater in his lifetime than his impact as a philosopher. Feeling, perhaps, that he had said all he fundamentally could say about philosophical problems, he embarked on a six-volume history of England after he had finished the two *Enquiries*. The *History of England* was published between 1754 and 1762. During this concentrated period of writing Hume also spent some time as tutor to the Marquis of Annandale in 1745–6, and as private secretary to General St Clair in 1747. In 1752 he was turned down for another chair in philosophy, this time at Glasgow University; so in that year he became a librarian in Edinburgh, a post he held until 1757. In 1763 he accepted another position as private secretary, on this occasion with the English ambassador to France. Clearly this was an appointment of some importance and prestige, because Franco-British relations were highly sensitive in the immediate aftermath of the Seven Years War (1756–63). Until his retirement in 1769 he worked as a civil servant, becoming Under-Secretary of State in 1769. One cannot help feeling that Hume would have preferred an appointment as a university lecturer, and that by neglecting to offer him such a position Britain in general, and Scotland in particular, failed to recognize one of their greatest philosophers.[2]

2 IMPRESSIONS AND IDEAS

Hume's philosophy is motivated by a fundamental problem concerning empiricism. Empiricism is the thesis that all knowledge is acquired through experience, but some knowledge, or at least some concepts, do not seem straightforwardly derivable from experience. It is possible that there is no single experience which provides an empirical origin for our concepts of God, private property, morality, the self, causation and even physical objects. The problem is how to be an empiricist in the face of recalcitrant – seemingly non-empirical – concepts, and Hume's philosophical works are best approached as an extended attempt to solve this problem.

Hume's empiricism is often summed up by the slogan 'No ideas without impressions', but to appreciate this we have to make sense of 'idea' and 'impression'. For Hume, ideas are thoughts, or, more generally, mental contents. If someone is thinking, imagining, or remembering, the contents of those mental operations are ideas. Impressions are sense experiences, or perceptual contents, so if someone is seeing, hearing, touching, or otherwise sensing something, then the immediate objects of those perceptual operations are impressions.[3]

The distinction between ideas and impressions is one of degree. Ideas are, in fact, faded impressions. Impressions have a greater 'force and vivacity' than ideas, and unless a person is mentally deranged, it is impossible for someone to mistake the idea (thought) of, say, being in love, with the impression (experience) of being in love (E1 II.11). Hume says: 'By the term impression . . . I mean all our more lively perceptions, when we hear, or see, or feel, or love, or hate, or desire, or will', but 'impressions are distinguished from ideas, which are the less lively perceptions, of which we are conscious, when we reflect on any of those sensations or movements above mentioned' (E1 II.12). So, an idea of a sound is a faded impression of a sound, an idea of a colour is the faded impression of a colour, and so on.

Everything with which we are directly acquainted is either an idea or an impression, and impressions place a constraint on possible ideas because all imagination consists in the manipulation of ideas which are ultimately derived from impressions. It seems at first that our imagination is boundless. We can imagine anything that is not contradictory to describe – fictional monsters as readily as mundane objects. While we are physically limited to one planet our imagination may transport us to distant parts of the universe. However, this power of imagination really only exists 'within very narrow limits' (E1 II.13). If we imagine a gold mountain we combine two ideas, gold and mountain; if we imagine a centaur we combine the ideas of person and horse, so 'all this creative power of the mind amounts to no more than the faculty of compounding, transposing, augmenting, or diminishing the materials afforded us by the senses and experience' (E1 II.13).

We may imagine what we have not experienced only in the sense of imaginatively rearranging the ideas of what we have experienced. Each idea is closely dependent on some single impression. Ideas are representations of the impressions they resemble and from which they have faded. Not only is it the case that 'all the materials of thinking are derived either from the outward or inward sentiment', but also 'all our ideas, or more feeble perceptions are copies of our impressions of more lively ones' (E1 II.13). It follows that ideas depend upon impressions, in several ways. Ideas represent impressions. Ideas are copies of impressions. Ideas are faded impressions. Ideas are caused by impressions, although, as we shall see, Hume has a special account of causation so that particular concept needs to be treated with caution.

Hume maintains that if we reflect on our mental contents we will notice that they may be analysed into simple ideas which depend upon impressions. Even a seemingly wholly non-empirical concept like 'God' is acquired by exaggerating empirical ideas of the human powers of wisdom and intelligence. All our imagining, and even our most abstract thinking, has an empirical origin: 'every idea which we imagine is copied from a similar impression' (E1 II.14).

Apart from this appeal to introspection, Hume has an argument to show that ideas depend upon impressions. If a person has a defective sense organ which prevents him from receiving certain impressions, he is thereby prevented from acquiring certain ideas: 'A blind man can form no notion of colours: a deaf man of sounds' (E1 II.15), but if the physiological defect is remedied and the requisite impressions acquired, then the ideas too are acquired. Similarly, persons from different cultures are unacquainted with some of the impressions, and so of the ideas, of other cultures. Hence Laplanders have no impression, and so no idea, of the taste of wine (E1 II.15). According to Hume, it is possible that there should be beings with different sense organs from our own, and hence with different impressions and ideas, but we would not be able to understand the nature of their mental lives because our ideas are constrained by our impressions. Clearly, we may make the supposition that there could be such creatures without knowing what it would be like to be one.[4]

Hume does allow one exception to his thesis that there are no ideas without corresponding impressions. If a person has had the impressions of a series of shades of blue, from dark to light, but the impression of one member of the series is missing, then Hume thinks that person could imaginatively reconstruct – entertain the idea – of the missing shade of blue, even though he never had the impression corresponding to exactly that shade.

Hume, in common with the other British empiricists, has an aversion to 'all that jargon, which has so long taken possession of metaphysical reasonings' (E1 II.17). He thinks of his empiricism as introducing greater clarity and exposing nonsense in philosophy. The test of whether an idea is genuine or spurious is to ask of it: 'From what impression is that supposed idea derived?' (E1 II.17). If there is no impression, the idea is bogus. Nevertheless, Hume wishes to preserve as genuine several seemingly non-empirical ideas. Now we shall turn to the first of these.

3 PHYSICAL OBJECTS

Hume thinks there is a genuine and a spurious question concerning physical objects. The spurious question is whether matter exists, the genuine one is what is the cause of our belief in matter: 'We may well ask, What causes induce us to believe in the existence of body? but 'tis vain to ask, Whether there be body or not?' (T 1.4.2). Berkeleyan scepticism about the existence of the physical world is vacuous because it is psychologically impossible to doubt the existence of matter, and that there are physical objects 'is a point we must take for granted in all our reasonings' (T 1.4.2). There are some assumptions so fundamental it does not make sense to doubt them, and that physical objects exist is just such an assumption. There remains, then, the useful question of how we come by our belief in physical objects and, more specifically, whether a wholly empirical account may be given of the concept of a physical object.

Hume divides the question of the causes of our belief in the existence of physical objects into two sub-questions. It is reasonably clear that in answering each of these he is not only showing what causes our belief in physical objects, but also justifying that belief – despite his avowal that doubting that belief is spurious. The two sub-questions are: What is the cause of our belief in the continued existence of physical objects? and, What is the cause of our belief in the distinct existence of physical objects? If an object has a continued existence, then it exists before, during and after the perception of it. If an object has a distinct existence it exists independently of the perception of it. It exists whether or not it is being perceived. These questions are not the same, even though they are mutually dependent: the resolution of the one question resolves the other (T 1.4.2). If an object has a distinct existence, then it has a continued existence, and if it has a continued existence it has a distinct existence. Nevertheless its continued existence is not its distinct existence.[5]

Hume thinks there are three putative means by which physical objects may be known to exist, continued and distinct from our perceptions: the senses, reason, and the imagination. He examines each of these in turn.

The senses cannot establish the continued existence of physical objects because that would require the logically impossible state of perceiving an unperceived object. Nor can the senses prove the distinct existence of objects because 'they convey to us nothing but a single perception, and never give us the least intimation of anything beyond' (T 1.4.2). We are presented with impressions only, not both the impression and the independently existing physical object of which it is an impression. That would require us to be presented with a 'double existence' (T 1.4.2), and according to Hume, our sense experience simply is not of that kind. It is true that illusions are possible, and they do require us to make a distinction between an object and our impression of it. However, a correct understanding of illusions does not imply that we are acquainted with two sorts of entity in sense-perception: objects and the impressions of them. Illusions are both generated and corrected by the 'relations and situation' of impressions. Knowledge of impressions *qua* impressions is incorrigible because 'all sensations are felt by the mind, such as they really are' (T 1.4.2). Perceptual mistakes are false beliefs derived from relations between impressions.

We are never in a position to compare a physical object with our impression of it, nor can the senses provide us with a clear distinction between what pertains to ourselves and what pertains to the external world: "tis absurd . . . to imagine the senses can ever distinguish betwixt ourselves and external objects' (T 1.4.2). For all these reasons, our sense experiences do not cause us to believe in the continued and distinct existence of physical objects.

Reason is as powerless as sense experience to justify our belief in physical objects, because even if a clear distinction could be drawn between a physical object and our perception of it, nothing would logically follow about the former from facts about the latter: 'Even after we distinguish our perceptions from our objects . . . we are still incapable of reasoning from the existence of one to that of the other' (T 1.4.2). The only remaining plausible justification for our belief in physical objects would seem to be the imagination.

The force and vivacity of our impressions is not sufficient to make them impressions of mind-independent physical objects because our pains are sometimes most forceful and vivid, yet they do not exist over and above the impression of them. According to Hume, two features distinguish physical objects from the impressions of them. These two features are 'constancy' and 'coherence'. Unfortunately, Hume sometimes ascribes the properties to impressions, sometimes to physical objects themselves. By the constancy of physical objects Hume means that they 'present themselves in the same uniform manner, and change not on account of any interruption in my seeing or perceiving them' (T 1.4.2). As a point about physical objects this claim is clearly question-begging. Hume is trying to explain what causes our belief in the continued and distinct existence of physical objects, and this is only a partial explication of what that belief consists in, not a justification or explanation of that belief. As a point about impressions the claim is less question-begging. In the case of impressions putatively of physical objects, qualitatively similar impressions are often to be had when the same physical object is putatively perceived. The degree of constancy of our impressions is one of the causes of our belief in the mind-independence of physical objects.

As in the case of 'constancy', in describing 'coherence' Hume assimilates discussion of impressions and of physical objects. The argument works better if being coherent is a relation between impressions. By the coherence of physical objects Hume means their 'regular dependence on each other' (T 1.4.2). He says that even if physical objects change, and so their constancy is not absolute, they still exhibit the feature of coherence and this too causes us to believe they exist over and above our perception of them. Although physical objects change over time, their changes display a regularity which enables us to think of them as interacting causally, to predict their future states, and to infer their previous ones. Maybe; but it is not clear what entitles Hume to invoke this as a premise about physical objects. He says something more useful about the coherence of impressions: 'The opinion of the continued existence of body depends on the coherence and constancy of certain impressions' (T 1.4.2). Coherence could feature in a premise in this way: although numerically distinct impressions gained at different times differ qualitatively, this qualitative difference is not so great as to preclude those impressions being of one and the same physical object. Indeed, numerically distinct but qualitatively similar impressions exhibit repetitious patterns within experience. The mind-independence of physical objects does not logically follow from the coherence of impressions, but we need to bear in mind that Hume is only trying to show what causes us to believe in objective physical objects, not to prove that there are such things. That our perceptual experience is logically consistent with the existence of objective physical objects is plausibly one such cause.

According to Hume, it is a fact about us that we take a coherent series of impressions for impressions of one and the same physical object. We assume the physical object exists continuously, not only during but also between intermittent perceptions of it. This assumption is provided by the imagination. The imagination continues, so to speak, where the perception leaves off; the perceptual assumption continues even when the perception ceases. The imagination thus fills the perceptual gaps between our perceptions by 'feigning a continued being'. As he puts it, 'We have a propensity to feign the continued existence of all sensible objects' and this 'makes us believe in the continued existence of body' (T 1.4.2). If the belief in the continued existence of body is true, then it logically follows that the belief in the distinct existence of body is true. It must be emphasized, however, that Hume does not claim to have proved either of those propositions. Indeed, although he thinks it psychologically impossible to doubt that physical objects exist, the whole of his account is logically consistent with the supposition that there are none. From the fact that it is impossible to doubt that something is true it does not necessarily follow that it is true. So, despite what Hume says, there might not be any physical objects.

4 SPACE AND TIME

Space and time are clear ideas when taken for granted commonsensically, but become contradictory when made the objects of philosophical reflection. Hume is concerned to refute those doctrines which he thinks lead to the contradictions: 'the infinite divisibility of extension' and 'an infinite number of . . . parts of time, passing in succession, and exhausted one after another' (T 1.2.2).

Hume deploys a single kind of argument against the infinite divisibility of both space and time. If something is infinitely divisible it must contain an infinite number of parts, so if a finite object is infinitely divisible it must contain an infinite number of parts; but it is contradictory to suppose that a finite object could contain an infinite number of parts, thus no finite object is infinitely divisible. Hume assumes that if no finite portion of either space or time is infinitely divisible, space and time as wholes are not infinitely divisible.

Hume has an extra argument for the impossibility of the infinite divisibility of time. The parts of time are successive, not simultaneous, so that 'each of its parts succeeds another, and . . . none of them, however contiguous, can ever be co-existent' (T 1.2.2). It follows from this that not only is time divided into moments (discrete durations) but also that it is composed of indivisible moments, because one moment could not be divided from another without its being co-existent with that other. That supposition is contradictory because each moment of time is posterior or anterior to every other (T 1.2.2).

Hume also claims that 'the infinite divisibility of space implies that of time' (T 1.2.2) and concludes from this that if time is not infinitely divisible then nor is space.

In these passages Hume makes the correct assumption that something is impossible, logically impossible, if the thought of it is contradictory, and possible, logically possible, if the thought of it is not contradictory. If his argument that the thesis of the infinite divisibility of time and space is contradictory is sound, he has shown that it is impossible that space and time should be infinitely divisible, not just that they are not.

Are the concepts of space and time empirical? Hume argues that they are. His empiricism includes the doctrine that 'every idea, with which the imagination is furnished, first makes its appearance in a correspondent impression' (T 1.2.3), and therefore the ideas of space and time cannot be exceptions. The idea of spatial size is thoroughly empirical because it is acquired only through the senses of sight and touch. We receive visual or tactile impressions of physical objects, imagine the distances between the objects when they are not being perceived, and thus acquire the idea of extension; 'the idea of space or extension is nothing but the idea of visible or tangible points abstracted in a certain order' (T 1.2.4). Hume tends to assimilate the ideas of space and extension because he believes there is no empty space. The idea of a vacuum where in principle there is nothing visible or tangible is not a coherent one for us to formulate. Space does not exist over and above the spatial relations between physical objects, and what we know of those we know through our impressions.

Time does not exist in abstraction from our ideas and impressions:

As 'tis from the disposition of visible and tangible objects we form the idea of space, so from the succession of ideas and impressions we form the idea of time, nor is it possible for time alone ever to make its appearance, or be taken notice of by the mind. (T 1.2.3)

Time is nothing over and above ideas and impressions replacing one another in a before-and-after relation. The more rapid the train of ideas or impressions the shorter seems the period of time in which they occur. If there were only one changeless object there would be no time, because 'time . . . is always discovered by some perceivable succession of changeable objects' (T 1.2.3).[6]

5 KNOWLEDGE

Hume maintains a fundamental distinction between two kinds of knowledge. There exists knowledge of relations of ideas and knowledge of matters of fact. Relations of ideas are propositions which may be decided wholly intellectually, without any empirical observation. That is, they are *a priori*. In contrast, matters of fact may only be decided empirically, so they are *a posteriori*. Hume gives as examples of relations of ideas the sentences of geometry, algebra and arithmetic, and includes all definitions and tautologies under this heading. Relations of ideas 'are discoverable by the mere operation of thought, without dependence on what is anywhere existent in the universe' (E 1.4.20). The claim that the sun will rise tomorrow morning is a matter of fact, as equally is the proposition that the sun will not rise. No purely intellectual procedure could determine with certainty the truth or falsity of these propositions. They are made true or false by the state of the universe and their truth or falsity may therefore only be decided by observation – that is, empirically.[7]

The negation or denial of a proposition which is a relation of ideas is or implies a contradiction. For example, 'a triangle has three sides' is a relation of ideas, so the claim that something is a triangle but does not have three sides is contradictory. However, 'the contrary of every matter of fact is still possible; because it can never imply a contradiction' (E 1.4.21). The putative states of affairs denoted by the negations of relations of ideas are logically impossible, because those negations are contradictions, but the negations of matters of fact denote logically possible states of affairs, even if those states of affairs do not actually obtain. The distinction between relations of ideas and matters of fact is intended by Hume to be mutually exclusive and collectively exhaustive. Thus every meaningful proposition is either a relation of ideas or a matter of fact. If a proposition is not a relation of ideas it is a matter of fact and if a proposition is not a matter of fact it is a relation of ideas, and if a proposition is a matter of fact it is not a relation of ideas and if a proposition is a relation of ideas it is not a matter of fact. So, 'the operations of human understanding divide themselves into two kinds, the comparing of ideas and the inferring of matters of fact' (T 1.3.1).

Relations of ideas and matters of fact are the content of knowledge. They are what is known. So if someone knows something then what they know is either a relation of ideas or a matter of fact, but not both. This raises the central question of epistemology: What is it to know? What exactly have we said about someone when we have said that he 'knows' such-and-such? For that matter, what does it mean to say someone 'believes' such-and-such? Are beliefs mental, physical, or neither? Where, if anywhere, are all the beliefs? What are they?

Hume maintains that ideas are components of beliefs: 'the idea of an object is an essential part of the belief of it, but not the whole' (T 1.2.7). It follows that having an idea of an object is a necessary condition for having a belief about that object, but it is not logically sufficient. Hume's ground for this is that 'we conceive many things, which we do not believe' (T 1.3.7). Hume is sensitive to the philosophical problem of stating the difference between believing something to be the case, and simply entertaining the thought that something is the case. Clearly there is a distinction between my merely entertaining the thought that a bomb is about to fall on the place where I am standing and my actually believing that a bomb is about to fall on that place. If my thought is idle imagination I remain where I am, in idle imagination. If my thought is a belief I race off in sheer terror for the nearest shelter. But, clearly, I must be able to distinguish in advance my beliefs in particular from my thoughts in general if I can act accordingly. How is that done?[28]

Hume distinguishes beliefs in particular from thoughts in general by claiming that beliefs, although ideas, are more lively ideas than those which are not beliefs. They are ideas which have the vividness of impressions, to which they are specially related: 'An opinion, therefore, or belief may be most accurately defined, a lively idea related to or associated with a present impression' (T 1.3.7).

This account of belief is rather weak. From the fact that you or I have a vivid idea we cannot conclude that that is a belief. After all, we may experience many intense psychological states sharing Hume's 'vivacity' which we should not call beliefs, and we may have beliefs which lack that intensity and seem to fall into Hume's 'faded' category. Also, Hume says beliefs are related to impressions, but he does not say how in particular. It cannot follow from the bare fact that an idea is related to an impression that that idea is a belief, because all ideas are related to impressions: 'all our ideas are copy'd from our impressions' (T 1.3.1), but not all ideas are beliefs. That cannot distinguish beliefs in particular from ideas in general. Furthermore, the claim that beliefs are necessarily related to present impressions leads Hume dangerously close to the view that all beliefs are about present sense-contents. The passage at T 1.3.7 suggests that. However, there is another passage in which Hume allows beliefs about the past and present, even if it is unclear whether he leaves room for beliefs about the future: 'belief or assent, which always attends the memory and senses, is nothing but the vivacity of those perceptions they present, and . . . this alone distinguishes them from imagination'. Again, the problem is that our imaginings may be vivid but our beliefs faint. Nor is it clear that the central questions about belief have been answered. What is the relation between believer and what is believed? Suppose a person, A, believes some proposition, p. What thereby minimally has to be true of A and p? Hume neglects all but the psychological properties of belief. We do believe waveringly, emphatically, and so on. But beliefs have semantic, and logical, as well as psychological, properties. For example, beliefs are truth-valued and truth is a semantic concept. If you believe that p then you believe p is true, but p may be true or false, so your believing that p is true is consistent with the truth or the falsity of p. Also, logical relations obtain between beliefs. One belief may logically imply another, people may be consistent or inconsistent in the beliefs they hold. Furthermore, beliefs are about some subject-matter, so they exhibit the psychological property of 'aboutness' or intentionality. Belief states are intentional states. Any satisfactory account of belief has to address these issues.

Within Hume's epistemology no clear distinction is drawn between belief and knowledge. He does not point out, for example, that if it is true that A believes p, then that is logically consistent with either the truth or the falsity of p, but that if it is true that A knows that p, then it logically follows that p is true. There is a reason, I think, why he does not adopt this distinction. He lays great stress on the fallibility of our senses and our intellectual faculties, and the resultant provisional nature of what we call 'knowledge'. He says that 'our reason must be considered as a kind of cause, of which truth is the natural effect' (T 1.4.1). The trouble is that we are not utterly reliable truth-generators.[9] Although the rules and proofs of logic are infallible our powers of reasoning are not, so we have only a certain probability of generating true beliefs. Indeed, on Hume's view, if someone knows something, they know it only with a certain probability: 'by this means all knowledge degenerates into probability' (T 1.4.1). Hume does not make this point but it is logically consistent with his view that that probability should be one, not between one and zero. To be realistic about knowledge, if A knows that p then it logically follows that p is true, whatever degree of probability the knower may allocate to that knowledge.

6 CAUSATION

Hume's problem of causation is how an empirical account can be given of the origin of the idea of causation when that idea does not seem to be straightforwardly empirical. To see this, contrast the concept of causation with the concept of red. The concept of red is straightforwardly empirical. An impression of red causes an idea of red, and our idea of red is a faded copy of the impression that caused it. The idea of red represents the impression of red. In the case of causation, however, this genetic account is less feasible:

When we look about us towards external objects, and consider the operation of causes, we are never able in a single instance, to discover any power or necessary connection, any quality, which binds the effect to the causes, and renders the one an infallible consequence of the other. (E1 VII.50)

Our idea of A causing B is that A necessitates B, that A is related to B such that if A happens, B cannot fail to happen. Hume points out that the idea of this putative relation is not empirical. If A causes B, and if A and B are both perceived, then there is no additional perception to be had of the causal relation which obtains between *A* and *B*. No such relation is observed over and above the occurrence of *A* and the occurrence of *B*. It follows that there exists no impression of the causal relation. Causal relations are not perceived, so they are not empirical. Crucially, this is a putative case of an idea without an impression. There is only an impression of the string of events which we hold to be causally related, not of the causal relation itself. Still less is there any impression of a connection between cause and effect which would make the second the inevitable and infallible consequence of the first: 'We only find, that the one does, in fact, follow the other' (E1 vii.50).

Therefore the idea of causation seems, *prima facie*, to violate the central principle of Hume's empiricism; there are no ideas without impressions. We certainly have an idea of causation, but if Hume is right we have no impression of causation, only of constantly conjoined events. We observe that events of one sort are regularly followed by events of another sort. But that is all. We do not perceive causal relations between them. Hume's task is to show that, nevertheless, the idea of causation has an empirical origin.

That there is no single impression of causation has several important consequences: 'From the first appearance of an object, we never can conjecture what effect will result from it' (E1 vii.50). Hume means that no empirical scrutiny of an object will reveal to us what sorts of effects it will have, indeed we may not know what these effects are until we have witnessed the events which follow it chronologically. Knowledge of which causes bring about which effects is completely *a posteriori* for Hume, and not *a priori*: 'Were the power or energy of any cause discoverable by the mind, we could foresee the effect, even without experience' (E1 vii.50). We need observation to discover causes and effects, so they are not knowable *a priori*.

Hume also thinks causal relations are contingent. Even if it is true that *A* causes *B*, it is logically possible that this should have been false. *A* could have had a different effect. *B* might have had a different cause, *B* might not have been an effect and *A* might not have been a cause. Contingent facts are facts that could have been otherwise. If *p* is contingently true, then *p* is true, but it is logically possible that *p* should have been false. 'Contingent' contrasts semantically with 'necessary'. If p is necessarily true, then p is true, but it is not logically possible that p should have been false. Hume is saying that where p reports some causal relation, p is contingent, not necessary. All causal relations might not have been, and given that they are, they might not have been as they are.

So, from the fact that A exists it does not logically follow that A is a cause of B, and if B exists it does not necessarily follow that B is an effect of A. There is nothing intrinsic to an event or an object which could make it either an effect or a cause. The qualities of a physical object such as 'solidity, extension, motion . . . are all complete in themselves, and never point out any other event which may result from them' (EI VII.50).

All that is directly given through impressions of the outward senses is one event following another in time; 'we only learn by experience the frequent conjunction of objects, without being ever able to comprehend anything like a connection between them' (EI VII.54). It would seem to follow, if the meaning of a word is always derived from some impression, that the expression 'necessary connection' is meaningless (EI VII.58).

Hume provides a psychological account of our idea of causation, to explain its empirical origin. We perceive that many events of type A are regularly followed in time by many events of type B, and the repetitive nature of this process leads us to suppose that a type A event will be followed by a type B. This happens so often that it is psychologically almost impossible for us not to expect a B after an A. This expectation is conditioned into us by our experience of regularities: 'After a repetition of similar instances the mind is carried by habit, upon the appearance of one event, to expect its usual attendant, and to believe that it will exist' (EI VII.59). The idea of necessary connection, or causal efficacy, or causal inevitability, is only the impression of expectation that the second event will follow the first. We mistake the subjective expectation for an objective necessity, but really there is no impression of necessary connection, only of our own expectation. For Hume, the universe is thoroughly contingent, not necessary. That there is a universe at all is a contingent fact, and it is a contingent fact about it that what happens in it does. Although it is ingrained in our psychological habits to foist necessities, forces and inevitabilities on the universe, in empirical reality

the scenes of the universe are continually shifting, and one object follows another in an uninterrupted succession; but the power or force, which actuates the whole universe, is entirely concealed from us, and never discovers itself in any of the sensible qualities of body. (E1 VII.50)

It is possible to analyse the concept of causation more thoroughly than Hume has done. For example, suppose A is the cause of B, then this could mean that A is a necessary condition for B ('that without which not'), so that unless A happens, B does not happen. Or, again, suppose A is the cause of B, then this could mean that if A happens then B happens, perhaps not with logical necessity but, nevertheless, always and everywhere. Perhaps the set of necessary conditions for B, which will be very large, are jointly sufficient for B. It is possible to develop sophisticated accounts of causation on these lines, and, further, to ascribe real causal powers to mind-independent physical objects. It could be, conversely, that Hume's scepticism about the causal relation is an important first step to the abolition of that concept. Hume does not say this, but perhaps there is no causation.[10]

7   PERSONAL IDENTITY

One putative solution to the problem of what it is for a person at a later time to be numerically identical with a person at an earlier time is that they are one and the same person if, and only if, they are numerically the same self. It is not clear what a self is, and it is not clear whether a self exists, and consequently it is not clear whether continuation of the self is necessary and sufficient for continuation of the person. Hume launches an attack on the idea of the self, because it is not an idea derived from any impression.

Hume points out that some philosophers suppose we are directly acquainted with the self as something that exists as self-identical and simple, in the sense of 'indivisible'. It is possible that Hume has in mind here certain of his rationalist predecessors.[11] His objection is that no introspective act seems to produce any such idea of the self. It discloses no impression from which such an idea could be copied: 'nor have we any idea of self, after the manner it is here explained. For from what impression could this idea be derived?' If there is a genuine idea of self, it must have been acquired from some impression because 'It must be some one impression, that gives rise to every real idea' (T 1.4.6). The problem is that the self is not derived from, and is not identical with, any impression. The self is putatively that which has impressions, and so is not to be found amongst them. The self is not one idea or impression amongst others, but the owner of them: 'that to which our several impressions and ideas are supposed to have a reference' (T 1.4.6).

If there were any single impression of self, then that impression would have to continue to exist during the whole time a person exists in order to be what the identity of that person consists in: 'But there is no impression constant and invariable' (T 1.4.6), according to Hume. As so often in Hume, his argument would be strengthened if he made a clear distinction between impressions themselves and what they are impressions of. It is the self, not the impression of self, which is putatively constitutive of the identity of the person. That there should be an impression of self is neither necessary nor sufficient for that identity. It is the self that would have to exist 'constant and invariable', not the impression of it. Hume confuses an impression of a 'constant and invariable' self with a 'constant and invariable' impression of a self.

On his own premises Hume is right to conclude that there is no genuine idea of self, because there is no single impression from which such an idea could be derived.

So far Hume's account of the self has appeared wholly negative and destructive and among its clear targets is the Cartesian substantial soul. He has, however, a positive account of the self. He thinks each of us is essentially the set of our mental states, or, as he puts it, a bundle of perceptions. I am, so to speak, the set of my thoughts, sensations and emotions, but there is no 'I' or 'me' over and above these. For Berkeley, it will be recalled (p. 119–22 above), it makes no sense to talk about a thought without a thinker, a perception without a perceiver, and so on. For him there is always some irreducibly subjective source of consciousness doing the thinking or the perceiving. Hume rejects this. In Hume's view, the thinker is nothing but the thoughts, the perceiver nothing but the perceptions. There is no subjective subject:

For my part, when I enter most intimately into what I call myself, I always stumble on some particular perception or other, of heat or cold, light or shade, love or hatred, pain or pleasure. I never catch myself at any time without a perception, and never can observe anything but the perception. (T 1.4.6)

So if my perceptions cease, I cease. Death is the cessation of my mental life. It follows that for Hume I am not a mental substance. There is no soul and *a fortiori* no immortal soul, 'and were all my perceptions remov'd by death . . . I should be entirely annihilated, nor do I conceive what is further requisite to make me a perfect non-entity' (T 1.4.6). I am co-extensive with my mental life. When that ceases I am nothing at all.

A person for Hume is best thought of as a process rather than an entity or object. A person is a set of perceptions and these perceptions replace one another with rapidity. They are, as he puts it, 'a perpetual flux and movement' (T 1.4.6). The problem of personal identity therefore becomes the problem of the identity of a process over time. The problem of what makes a later person numerically identical with an earlier person is what makes a later process part of the same process as an earlier process. The later person would have to be a person-process-slice and the earlier person would have to be a person-process-slice and each person-process-slice an episode in the history of one and the same person-process. Hume has no solution to the problem of personal identity, but his rewriting of the problem is perhaps a promising stage towards that solution.[12]

8 MIND AND BODY

Hume says of mankind: 'they are nothing but a bundle or collection of different perceptions' (T 1.4.6). As we have seen, Hume denies the existence of the Cartesian soul, and his concept of a physical object does not depend on the idea of material substance but on the coherence and constancy of certain impressions. Impressions them-selves are intrinsically neither mental nor physical. Hume therefore rejects each of the ontological options in the philosophy of mind which have been introduced so far in this book. He is not a materialist because he does not believe in material substance. He is not an idealist because he does not believe in mental substance. He is not a dualist because he believes in neither mental nor physical substance. Rather, Hume's philosophy of mind anticipates the 'neutral monism' of Bertrand Russell – the view that mind and matter only exist in relation to some more primitive, fundamental, 'neutral' entity or entities.[13] If neutral entities did not exist, mind and matter could not exist, or the distinction between them. In Hume's philosophy, the neutral entities are impressions. As we have seen, physical objects are only intelligible because impressions are intelligible, and if we ask: What is the mind? then Hume's reply is that the mind 'is nothing but a heap or collection of different perceptions united together by certain relations' (T, Appendix).

Hume famously compares the mind to a theatre, but says this analogy must not mislead us. A theatre is something over and above the various actors who pass through it, but a mind is nothing over and above the succession of its perceptions: 'The mind is a kind of theatre, where several perceptions successively make their appear-ance; pass, re-pass, glide away, and mingle in an infinite variety of postures and situations', but 'They are the successive perceptions only that constitute the mind' (T 1.4.6).

Clearly, in a sense, minds and physical objects are logical constructions out of ideas and impressions (see pp. 237–8 below). The existence of minds and physical objects depends logically on the existence of ideas and impressions. Although Hume does not state his philosophy of mind in this way, it is consistent with the claim that any sentence or set of sentences about either minds or physical objects may be translated without loss of meaning into a sentence or set of sentences about ideas and impressions. In other words, minds and physical objects are 'reducible' to ideas and impressions. If, as is plausible on Hume's epistemology, ideas may be reduced to impressions, then minds as well as physical objects may be ultimately reduced to just impressions.

One of the most valuable aspects of Hume's philosophical psychology is his sustained critique of the Cartesian doctrine that psycho-physical causal interaction is possible. In a pre-philosophical and commonsensical sense this is possible for Hume: 'The motion of our body follows upon the command of our will. Of this we are every moment conscious' (E1 VII.52), but this cannot be explained within a dualist framework. How a mental substance can interact causally with a physical substance is as obscure as telekinesis.

The problem of psycho-physical causal interaction is a special case of the general problem of causation (see section 6 above). There is no outer impression of the causal connection between natural events and there is no inner impression of the causal connection between an act of will and a bodily movement. It follows that 'we are totally ignorant of the power on which depends the mutual operations of bodies, we are no less ignorant of that power on which depends the operation of mind on body, or of body on mind' (E1 VII.55). We have no empirical grounds, and so no good grounds, for believing in such a power.

Hume's solution to the question of how psycho-physical causal interaction is possible is to give up the dualist assumption presupposed by the question. If it is not the case that there exist two kinds of substance, one mental and one physical, then the problem of causal interaction between them disappears. That there is causal interaction between *A* and *B* logically presupposes that *A* and *B* are numerically distinct: that *A* is not *B* and that *B* is not *A*. Hume unequivocally denies the assumption that 'soul' and 'body' denote discrete substances. He uses the terms 'soul' and 'substance' to denote sets of impressions and ideas, not any spiritual owner of them. 'Substance' in the Cartesian sense is incoherent, so 'the question concerning the substance of the soul is absolutely unintelligible' (T 1.4.5). Material substance is a 'fiction' (T 1.4.3).

In arguing that both mental and physical are logical constructions out of impressions, Hume offers us a philosophy of mind which avoids the difficulties of materialism, dualism and idealism. These competing ontologies are logically secondary to contents of experience which are inherently neither mental nor physical. Clearly, in a commonsensical sense Hume thinks we have bodies and minds. As human beings we may think and move our limbs, and his philosophy leaves our psychological and physical lives intact. However, his philosophy is radically anti-Cartesian. Only one of his two anti-Cartesian tendencies has been exploited so far in modern philosophy: there are no minds. The other is: there is no matter. Contemporary philosophy of mind is one half of Cartesianism trying to refute the other. Cartesianism is the view that both minds and physical objects exist, and in its revolt against Descartes modern philosophy denies only the first of these two claims. The necessary next step is to deny the second.[14]

9 FREEDOM

Do we have free will or not? The problem of freedom and determinism is whether our actions really result from our choices, or whether our choices are illusions and our actions are inevitable because they have other causes or because what we choose is inevitable. Determinism is the doctrine that every event has a cause, and in its strong version it includes the view that caused events are inevitable. Libertarianism is the doctrine that thought and action are produced by choices which are free. By an action's being 'free' is meant, that if I choose to perform some action and perform it, I could have nonetheless chosen otherwise and not performed that action, and if I choose not to perform some action and do not perform it, then I nonetheless could have chosen otherwise and actually carried out that action. It seems, then, if I am determined I am not free and if I am free I am not determined. Hume tries to reconcile freedom and determinism; to show they are not incompatible after all.[15]

Hume argues that the above issue is 'merely verbal' (E1 VIII.73), and in common with certain twentieth-century linguistic philosophers argues that the problem will disappear once we have clarified 'liberty' and 'necessity'.

Liberty, or freedom, has to be distinguished from chance, and from something happening without any cause whatsoever. Actions are caused. They are caused by the 'motives, inclinations, and circumstances' of the agent (E1 VIII.73). They do not occur by chance because they are performed deliberately and follow from their causes with a certain uniformity. Indeed, there is no chance in nature, according to Hume. If we say something happens by chance we are merely reporting our ignorance of some of its causes. So freedom is not chance for Hume, but is the ability to make choices and act upon them. One's freedom consists in being, or being amongst, the causes of one's own actions: 'By liberty, then, we can only mean a power of acting or not acting, according to the determinations of the will' (E1 VIII.73). It follows that a person acts freely if, and only if, their action is at least partly caused by their choice to act, and they could have chosen not to act and not acted. So, 'a person did something freely' means they chose to do what they did and did it, but they could have chosen not to do what they did, and then not done it. In Hume's example: 'If we choose to remain at rest, we may; if we choose to move we also may' (E1 VIII.73).

According to Hume, liberty is properly contrasted with constraint rather than with determinism. To say that someone acted freely is to say that person was not forced to act in that way and could have either refrained from acting, or acted otherwise. As Hume puts it, 'This hypothetical liberty is universally allowed to belong to everyone who is not a prisoner and in chains' (E1 VIII.73). He considers this account of freedom both internally consistent and consistent with our experience as agents.

Is it consistent with determinism? To decide this we must distinguish strong from weak determinism. Weak determinism is the theory that every event has a cause. Strong determinism includes that theory, but adds that causes necessitate their events such that every caused event (i.e. every effect) is inevitable. Hume's theory of action is compatible with weak determinism but incompatible with strong determinism. He accepts that human actions are caused, that they are caused by choices, so he does not thereby provide an exception to the thesis that every event has a cause. (Both kinds of determinist are going to want to know whether our choices have causes.) Hume must reject strong determinism, though, because, as we have seen (pp. 147–8 above), he rejects the theory that causes necessitate their effects. In strong determinism, if *A* is the cause of *B* and *A* happens, then *B* not only happens but happens by necessity. If something happens by necessity, it not only happens but could not fail to happen. Hume rejects this whole picture of causation because, for him, causal connections are contingent, not necessary. There is no contradiction involved in the notions that an event could have had a cause other than its actual cause, or that a cause should have an effect other than its actual effect, or that event should be neither a cause nor an effect. Putative causal necessities are psychological expectations derived from the observation of regularities: 'Had not objects a regular conjunction with each other, we should never have entertained any notion of cause and effect' (EI VIII.74). Objective, perceiver-independent causality is only constantly conjoined events.

If nothing happens by necessity then it logically follows that no human actions happen by necessity, and it follows from that that they are not strongly determined. Thus strong determinism is false. Not only does Hume's epistemology of causation imply the falsity of strong determinism, but his theory of freedom is inconsistent with that same doctrine. Hume thinks we may act freely. When we do, we could have done other than what we did. But this can make no sense within the framework of strong determinism. If *A* causes *B* then *A* necessitates *B*, so *B* could not not happen given *A*. It makes no sense for there to be a kind of freedom which allows someone to possibly not do that which they do, nor, for that matter, to possibly do that which they do not do.

Although we perform our actions freely when not constrained, that does not imply that human actions are unpredictable:

> A man who at noon leaves his purse full of gold on the pavement at Charing-Cross, may as well expect that it will fly away like a feather, as that he will find it untouched an hour after. (EI VIII.70)

We predict human actions, as we would predict any other kind of event, by observing regularities. We observe consistencies in the exercise of choices and the behaviour they cause. We are not acquainted with any causal conditions which necessitate human actions, so there is no basis for prediction there.

Hume fails to draw one important implication of his arguments. The fact that we are able to predict human actions does not show that we are not free. Causal connections are contingent, so a person may always have chosen and acted otherwise. Contrary to a widespread philosophical assumption, predictability does not imply determinism. We predict a person's behaviour by coming to know the ways in which he exercises his freedom.

10 INDUCTION

The problem of induction is best appreciated through drawing a contrast between two kinds of argument, deductive and inductive. In the case of a valid deductive argument the conclusion logically follows from the premises. For example, from the premises 'All *A*s are *B*s' and 'This is an *A*', the conclusion 'This is a *B*' follows logically. This means that if the premises are true, the conclusion must be true. It would be self-contradictory to assert the premises but deny the conclusion. In the case of an inductive argument, in contrast, the conclusion does not logically follow from the premises. For example, from the premises 'Some *A*s are *B*s' and 'This is an *A*', the conclusion 'This is a *B*' does not logically follow. Notice that even if the premises were 'Every *A* that has so far been experienced is a *B*' and 'This is an *A*', the conclusion 'This is a *B*' would not logically follow because it would not be self-contradictory to claim that every *A* experienced so far is a *B* but that the next *A*, or any future *A*, is not a *B*. However, although every inductive argument is invalid as a putative deductive argument, we feel that in the inductive case the premises in some sense make it rational to accept the conclusion. Defining this sense is the problem of induction. The problem is sometimes called the 'justification of induction' because it requires us to justify the inference that 'All *A*s are *B*s' or 'This *A* is a *B*' from 'Some *A*s are *B*s' where this does not follow logically.

Hume provides us with this example:

The bread which I formerly eat, nourished me; that is, a body of such sensible qualities was, at that time, endued with such secret powers: but does it follow, that other bread must also nourish me at another time, and that like sensible qualities must always be attended with like secret powers? The consequence seems nowise necessary. (E1 IV.29)

It does not necessarily follow from the fact that past bread was nutritious that present or future bread will be. The conjunction of the claims that past bread was nutritious and present or future bread is or will be nutritious is not a necessary truth. Nevertheless, as Hume emphasizes, we do habitually depend upon our past experience as a guide to information about the present and future. On the basis of this proposition:

I have found that such an object has always been attended with such an effect

we conclude,

I foresee, that other objects, which are, in appearance, similar, will be attended with similar effects. (E1 IV.29)

Premises of the form 'Some *A*s are *B*s' do not justify the conclusion that 'The next *A* is a *B*' any more than that 'All *A*s are *B*s'.

The problem of induction is crucial not only to scientific method but to commonsense. The natural laws of the sciences are universal inductive generalizations of the form 'All *A*s are *B*s'. They ascribe properties to objects over the whole of space and time, yet any scientist has only sampled some finite portion of the universe and therefore his or her investigations only warrant the claim that 'Some *A*s are *B*s' or 'All the *A*s observed so far are *B*s'. There is a logical gap between the conclusions justified by observation and the wide generalizations based on those conclusions.

Induction is essential to the intelligibility of the world of everyday life. We assume, as Hume says, that our food will nourish us and not poison us. We assume that when we open the door to leave the room we will step on to a floor and not into total emptiness, that when we stand up we will be able to walk, that we are not about to go blind or deaf, that when we talk to the cat it will not talk back, that the objects about us will stay on the earth and not fly into the air – and so on for thousands and thousands of other beliefs. If it were not for induction our knowledge would be confined to the bare solipsism of the present moment. But perhaps even that is not true.

We assume the objects about us can function as books and tables and lights, but we only believe that because it has proved so in our experience up to now. Even the intelligibility of the content of the present moment depends on induction.

Historians give us knowledge of the past based on present evidence, but it does not follow that 'Past *A*s were *B*s' from 'Present *A*s are *B*s' any more than it follows that 'Future *A*s are *B*s'. The problem of induction opens an irrational gulf in the midst of all our knowledge of the universe. If induction cannot be justified, then none of our knowledge can be justified. The problem of induction is epistemologically devastating and it has not been solved.[16]

11 MEMORY AND IMAGINATION

On Hume's empirical theory, what we may remember and what we may imagine are closely constrained by what we have experienced: 'All the materials of thinking are derived either from our outward or our inward sentiment: the mixture and composition of these belong alone to the mind and will' (E1 II.13). There are no ideas without corresponding impressions, so any idea of memory or imagination is derived from some impression. Hume argues, perhaps rather weakly, that one difference between memory and imagination is that ideas of memory are more vivid than those of imagination. Nevertheless

neither the ideas of memory nor imagination, neither the lively nor the faint ideas can make their appearance in the mind, unless their correspondent impressions have gone before to prepare the way for them. (T 1.1.3)

Hume presents us with a second and more satisfactory criterion for distinguishing remembering from imagining. Memory and imagination are the same faculty in two different employments. If someone remembers, the ideas in their memory appear in the same order as the impressions from which they are derived; but if an event is imagined, the ideas in the imagination appear in a different order from the impressions from which they are derived:

The imagination is not restrained to the same order and form with the original impressions; while the memory is in a manner ty'd down in that respect, without any power of variation. (T 1.1.3)

Clearly, both memory and imagination depend on past impressions, and remembering may be veridical or non-veridical. However, Hume needs to distinguish remembering from imagining the past accurately, because someone might imagine accurately what happened without thereby remembering it. You or I might, for example, imagine the Battle of Hastings accurately without remembering it. Hume requires a specific causal criterion to mark this distinction; for example, this one: a memory of an event is caused by impressions of that event, but the imagining of an event (that happened), although caused by impressions, is not caused by impressions of that event. He half offers such a criterion when he says that 'the memory preserves the original form, in which its objects were presented', but still fails to distinguish remembering from *accurate* imagining when he speaks of 'the liberty of the imagination to transpose and change its ideas' (T 1.1.3).

Although there is no faculty more free than the imagination, ideas are not there juxtaposed by chance. Although 'all simple ideas may be separated by the imagination, any may be united again in what form it pleases' (T 1.1.2). There exist three principles or criteria which the imagination uses to transpose ideas. These are resemblance, contiguity in time and place, and cause and effect. For any two ideas, A and B, if A resembles B, or if A and B are ideas of two contiguous objects, or if A and B are ideas of a cause and its effect, then the mind is more likely to imagine B if it imagines A or to imagine A if it imagines B than if none of these relations holds. Of the three, the causal relation is the most efficacious: 'There is no relation which produces a stronger connection in the fancy, and makes one idea more readily recall another, than the relation of cause and effect betwixt their objects' (T 1.1.4).

It is not necessary for any one of the three relations to hold between A and B for A and B to be juxtaposed in the imagination. For example, if some third idea, C, bears one of those three relations to both A and B, even if A and B do not bear any of those relations to each other, then the imagination is more likely to imagine A and

B if it imagines *C* than if *C* did not bear any of those relations to *A* and *B*.[17]

12 RELIGION

Hume was an atheist. He also thought there was no sound argument for the existence of God, and believed religion in general and Christianity in particular had proved harmful to human beings in the course of history. His attack on the idea of the existence of God is concentrated in two places in his works: section X of the first *Enquiry*, and in *Dialogues Concerning Natural Religion*. In the first *Enquiry* he tries to show that it is irrational to believe in miracles, and so attempts to discredit one reason for believing in God. In the *Dialogues* he offers a sustained criticism of the argument from design. I shall treat each in turn.

Miracles

It only logically follows that God exists from the existence of miracles if miracles are acts of God. However, even if 'act of God' is not included in the definition of 'miracle', miraculous events might be thought to provide good inductive evidence for the existence of God; that is, to make the existence of God more probable than it would be if no miracles occurred.[18]

Hume says that 'a miracle is a violation of the laws of nature' (E1 x.90), so it is built into the very concept of a miracle that miracles are highly unlikely events. We would not call an event 'a miracle' if it were likely to occur. Hume's position is that we should always believe what is more probably true and always disbelieve what is less probably true. It is rational to proportion one's belief to the evidence. If the evidence for an occurrence is very great, then one should believe in that occurrence with a high degree of certainty. If the evidence for an occurrence is very small, one should believe in that occurrence only to a very small degree.

Highly probable events are events which accord with the laws of

nature. Indeed, it is more than probable that each person will
sooner or later die, that lead will fall through the air if released, that
wood will be burned by fire. We say these events are certain, not
probable, because they are repeatedly confirmed and never refuted
by our experience.

Even many relatively unusual events do not count as miracles,
because they are still often observed to happen even if less often
than other events. For example, it would not be a miracle for a
seemingly healthy person to die, because that is sometimes observed
to happen, but it would be counted a miracle for a dead person to
be restored to life because that has nowhere and never been observed
to happen.

No event is less likely than a miracle because the evidence against
a miracle is overwhelmingly greater than the evidence for it.
Although the concept of miracle is not self-contradictory, it has
built into it the notion of the vast improbability of its occurring:
'There must . . . be a uniform experience against every miraculous
event, otherwise the event would not merit that appellation'
(E1 x.90).

That the whole, or nearly the whole, course of our experience
rules out a certain occurrence amounts to a proof for Hume that the
occurrence does not occur. Short of an *a priori* proof – the discovery
of a contradiction in the concept of a miracle, for example – it is
hard to envisage a more satisfactory refutation of the claim that the
event happened:

> As a uniform experience amounts to a proof, there is here a direct and
> full proof, from the nature of the fact, against the existence of any miracle;
> nor can such a proof be destroyed, or the miracle rendered credible, but by
> an opposite proof, which is superior. (E1 x.90)

However, nothing could outweigh such an overwhelming body of
evidence to the contrary. Crucially, it is far more probable that the
purported witnesses to the miracle are lying or mistaken than that
the miracle actually happened. It would only be rational to believe
in a miracle if it is more likely that such an event happened than
that the witnesses were either lying or mistaken. Hume thinks it is
always and everywhere more likely that some human putative
witness is lying or mistaken than that a law of nature has been

broken. We should believe what is probably true. That is the rational thing to do. It is therefore irrational to believe in miracles.

In reply to Hume, the following might be advanced. From the fact that a belief is very unlikely to be true it does not logically follow that it is false; so there might be miracles. If holding a belief which is very likely false is irrational, which in a sense it is, nevertheless it is logically possible that an irrational belief in that sense could be true. The obstinate minority could have it right – even a minority of one. One of the ways in which knowledge opens and grows is through a persistence with and toleration of the highly unusual.

The Argument from Design

The argument from design is the argument that the universe exhibits such order as to resemble an artifact, and the scale and complexity of the universe is so great as to make it rational to conclude that its designer is infinitely more intelligent and powerful than the designer of any man-made object. This designer could, then, only be God.

Hume criticizes this argument in his *Dialogues Concerning Natural Religion*. In the dialogues Cleanthes is the theist and Philo ('Wisdom') the sceptical atheist. Hume has Cleanthes formulate the argument in this way:

Look round the world, contemplate the whole and every part of it: you will find it to be nothing but one great machine, subdivided into an infinite number of lesser machines, which again admit of subdivisions to a degree beyond what the human senses and faculties can trace and explain. All these various machines, and even their most minute parts, are adjusted to each other with an accuracy which ravishes into admiration all men who have ever contemplated them. The curious adapting of means to ends, throughout all nature, resembles exactly, though it much exceeds, the productions of human contrivance – of human design, thought, wisdom, and intelligence. Since therefore the effects resemble each other, we are led to infer, by all the rules of analogy, that the causes also resemble, and that the Author of nature is somewhat similar to the mind of man, though possessed of much larger faculties, proportioned to the grandeur of the work which he has executed. By this argument *a posteriori*, and by this argument alone, do we prove at once the existence of a Deity and his similarity to human mind and intelligence. (D 17)

Hume's objections to the argument are voiced through Philo. Hume first doubts the premise that the universe is very much like an artifact. The differences between the whole universe and, say, a house are much more striking than the similarities, and in particular the similarities are not sufficiently great to allow us to infer that human artifacts and the whole universe have a similar sort of cause.

When Hume raises this objection it is hard to arbitrate between him and the theist. No doubt everything is in some measure similar to everything else, and we lack good criteria in the present case for 'similar to'. It rather depends upon the descriptions we use, or what properties we single out for attention, whether or not the universe is like a house, or a clock, or a water-mill (or, for that matter, like a computer).

Hume next objects that from the fact that the universe contains order it does not follow that it had a designer: 'Order, arrangement, or the adjustment of final causes is not of itself any proof of design' (D 20). Hume here presents a difficulty for any *a posteriori* argument for the existence of God. From no set of empirical premises – no matter how long and complex – does it logically follow that God exists. This means that nothing within our experience, and no fact about the world as we experience it, can conclusively prove that God exists. Further, the problem of induction (see p. 157–9 above) arises for postulating a designer of order. Even if it is true that much of the order within our experience is the result of design, and even if the universe is ordered, it does not logically follow from that that the universe was designed, because there is no contradiction involved in the assertion that some order is not the result of design.

To support this objection, Hume suggests an alternative account of order in the universe. He says: 'For aught we can know *a priori*, matter may contain the spring of order originally within itself (as well as mind does)' (D 20). Perhaps matter is the cause of its own ordering. Perhaps matter is self-ordering, as, in Hume's interesting if debatable analogy, minds are.

Hume's next objection is that it is in general fallacious to draw conclusions about a whole from facts about its parts. Hume asks sceptically, 'But can a conclusion, with any propriety, be transferred from parts to the whole?' (D 21). We do not draw conclusions about the whole person from one hair, nor about the whole tree from one leaf. Similarly, we are not entitled to draw conclusions about the order and cause of the universe from observing persons and artifacts. Hume is right on the point of logic that if *A* is a part of *B* and if there is some fact about *A*, it does not logically follow that what is thus true of *A* is thereby true of *B*. However, it needs to be noted that *B*'s being a part of *A* does not logically preclude some fact about *A* being also a fact about *B*. That *B* is a part of *A* does not of itself imply that *A* and *B* may have no common properties. Clearly, parts and wholes may share some properties but not others.

According to Hume, the theist in propounding the argument from design is guilty of anthropomorphism: the imaginative projection of human qualities on to the non-human. The fact that we are ourselves human leads us into a profound bias or partiality. We so grossly overestimate our significance in the universe as to think that it, or its causes, must be like ourselves and our products:

Yet why select so minute, so weak, so bounded a principle as the reason and design of animals [a]s found to be on this planet? What peculiar privilege has this little agitation of the brain we call 'thought', that we must thus make it the model of the whole universe. (D 21–2)

Again, we do not have ready and good criteria to decide upon the 'significance' of human existence. Perhaps human existence is a cosmic accident preceded, surrounded and succeeded by an infinity of silent matter in motion. Or perhaps we are the reason why the whole universe exists. It is difficult to arbitrate between Hume and the theist. Perhaps God created us. Perhaps we created God.

Hume accepts that 'from similar effects we infer similar causes' (D 20), even though there is no logical justification for this inductive practice. If it is true that similar effects have similar causes, then 'the liker the effects are which are seen and the liker the causes which are inferred, the stronger the argument' (D 37). Hume then proceeds to draw a much closer analogy between human design and the putative divine designer than the theist would wish. Human artifacts are produced by trial and error, so 'Many worlds might have been botched and bungled, throughout an eternity, ere this system was struck out' (D 39). In any case, human artifacts are often the products of several persons, and consequently the universe might have been produced by more than one god: 'Why may not several deities combine in contriving and framing a world?' The theist has not proved 'the unity of the deity' (D 39). Pleasant and unpleasant people produce artifacts, so demons as well as gods might have produced the universe. If it is true that like effects have like causes, it should be noted that the universe is physical, and rationally we should conclude that God is physical: 'And why not become a perfect anthropomorphite? Why not assert the deity or deities to be corporeal, and to have eyes, a nose, mouth, ears etc.?' (D 40). The universe is in many respects imperfect, and therefore we should conclude that its creator is imperfect also. Perhaps God is an incompetent. Perhaps it was 'the first rude essay of some infant deity', or 'the work only of some dependent, inferior deity', or 'the production of old age and dotage in some superannuated deity' (D 41).[19]

13 ETHICS

Hume maintains that reason and emotion each have a role in the resolution of moral disputes. It follows that he is not a pure emotivist. He does not think making value judgements the mere expression and excitation of feelings, because he believes ethical disputes may be conducted rationally. Nor is he a pure rationalist because he believes that any ethical standpoint has an emotive content; 'reason and sentiment concur in almost all moral determinations and conclusions' (E2 1.137). We may ask, then, what the roles of reason and emotion are in Hume's moral philosophy.

Hume notably rejects the view that it is possible logically to derive an ethical conclusion from premises which are purely factual. This rejection is often summed up in the slogan, 'It is not possible to derive an ought from an is' (although it should be remembered that the slogan is only a label, because relations like 'logically follows from' may only obtain between propositions, or whole sentences, not pairs of words (unless those two words are two sentences expressing propositions). It has sometimes been maintained that Hume was ironic in advocating the is/ought distinction. I think not. In any case, here is the relevant passage:

> In every system of morality, which I have hitherto met with, I have always remarked, that the author proceeds for some time in the ordinary way of reasoning, and establishes the being of a God, or makes observations concerning human affairs, when of a sudden I am surprised to find, that instead of the usual copulations of propositions, 'is', and 'is not', I meet with no proposition that is not connected with 'ought', or an 'ought not'. (T III.1.1)

For Hume, it is 'altogether inconceivable' how the 'ought' sentences may be deduced validly from the purely 'is' sentences. It is clear, then, that in a logical sense Hume maintains a strict fact-value distinction. Attempts have been made to bridge the is/ought gap, none of them ultimately successful.[20] Perhaps a more promising strategy would be to deny that there are any purely factual propositions – ones devoid of any evaluative content whatsoever, and deny that there are any purely evaluative propositions – ones devoid of any factual content whatsoever. This would make the distinction between facts and values one of degree, and the is/ought distinction could not be posed in such a stark form.

So for Hume the kind of reasoning appropriate to moral disputes is not from facts to values. Clearly, however, there may be valid logical inferences between value judgements, as Hume accepts.[21]

Hume is as empiricist about morality as about epistemology, so he does not wish to offer an explanation of the origin of moral concepts in any except empirical terms: 'since vice and virtue are not discoverable merely by reason, or the comparison of ideas, it must be by means of some impression that we are able to mark the difference between them'. For this reason, Hume holds that 'morality . . . is more properly felt than judged of' (T III.1.2).

What is the nature of the impressions which facilitate a distinction between right and wrong? Hume's answer is thoroughly utilitarian. Utilitarianism is the meta-ethical theory that 'good' means, in the last resort, 'conducive to happiness' or 'conducive to the diminution of pain', and 'wrong' means 'conducive to pain' or 'conducive to the diminution of happiness'. Utilitarianism usually also contains the theory that some experiences are intrinsically pleasurable and others intrinsically painful. Not everything can be only instrumentally good or bad. Utilitarianism, as we shall see in the chapter on Mill, was strongly developed by Jeremy Bentham and John Stuart Mill, but Hume anticipates their moral philosophy in its central theme when he says: 'we must pronounce the impression arising from virtue, to be agreeable, and that arising from vice to be uneasy' (T III.1.2).

Hume does not maintain that the dependencies of good on pleasure and of wrongness on pain are causal. They are constitutive. We may only make the conceptual distinction between right and wrong, and so have a moral vocabulary, if we are acquainted with impressions which are intrinsically pleasurable or painful: 'The distinguishing impressions, by which moral good or evil is known, are nothing but particular pains or pleasures' (T III.1.2). Hume, as a utilitarian, is a consequentialist about actions. It is because actions cause happy or unhappy consequences that we judge them to be right or wrong. It is simply in virtue of those causal roles that they are the sorts of item which it makes sense to evaluate ethically.

Further, to evaluate an action, or a person, or a state of a person, as moral is essentially to feel a certain pleasure towards it; and to evaluate an action, or a person, or a state of a person, as immoral is essentially to feel a certain displeasure towards it: 'An action, or sentiment, or character is virtuous or vicious: Why? because its view causes a pleasure or uneasiness of a certain kind' (T III.1.1). It is not just that the action excites these emotions in us, but that our having those emotional reactions constitutes our judging that action morally. To explain the emotion is to explain the value: 'In giving a reason, therefore, for the pleasure or uneasiness, we sufficiently explain the vice or virtue' (T III.1.2).

At this point of Hume's argument his utilitarianism has become too separated from the emotivist component of his ethics. It could be objected that even if undergoing a certain emotion is a necessary condition for adopting a certain moral stance, it is doubtful that this is sufficient. It is quite possible to feel pain or pleasure as the result of an action without thereby evaluating the action ethically. Hume is therefore over-reductivist when he asserts: 'To have the sense of virtue is nothing but to feel a certain satisfaction of a particular kind from the contemplation of a character' (T III.1.2). It might be more convincing to make the emotion partly rather than wholly constitutive of the value judgement. Rather than say, 'The very feeling constitutes our praise or admiration' (T III.1.1), he should say the feeling is a prerequisite for those evaluations. It might, after all, be a condition of finding something morally wrong that an emotional repugnance be felt against it. That can hardly be the whole of morality, however.[22]

14 POLITICS

Hume's most significant contributions to political thought are his theory of justice and his criticisms of the idea of a social contract.

Justice

Justice is not a natural relation between human beings, according to Hume, but a product of social convention. Nevertheless, justice and the convention it depends on are both prerequisites for there being such a thing as society at all. The convention is not to be understood on the model of a promise or contract. This is not just because there has been no historical agreement or contract in the establishing of any particular society, but also because the social contract is a bad heuristic device for understanding the relations that ought to obtain between state and citizen. Hume thus makes a clean break not only with his empiricist predecessors Hobbes and Locke, but also with his contractarian contemporary Rousseau, in not being a contract theorist.

We are to understand conventions as they already obtain when someone is born into society. It is not as though anyone is ever in a position to make a contractual agreement with other members of society about what political relations should obtain. The set of conventions in our society constitutes us as political beings.

Justice is essential to society because it provides its cohesion.

Private property is also necessary for society, and it is in the
reciprocal respect for their private property that justice between
individuals consists. Human beings may desire each other's property but it would be the disintegration of society if they acted
impulsively and without justice on this emotion. According to
Hume, the social convention which maintains justice nevertheless
cannot be incompatible with our desire for the goods of others
because otherwise it could not exist: the tendency towards seizure
of the property of others would override the tendency towards
mutual respect of property.

Human beings need to live in a society in order to fulfil their
needs. The individual human being's needs cannot be met by that
human being alone, only the collective power of groups of humans
is sufficient to meet the needs of each one. It is thus in the interests
of each that there should be society rather than anarchy. This also
explains why it is not sufficient for the satisfaction of an individual's
interests that that individual should refrain from taking the property
of others. It is in the interests of each positively to sustain society
and not merely to refrain from damaging it:

> Instead of departing from our own interest, or from that of our nearest
> friends, by abstaining from the possessions of others, we cannot better
> consult both these interests, than by . . . a convention; because it is by that
> means we maintain society; which is so necessary to their well-being and
> subsistence, as well as to our own. (T III.2.2)

By this convention each person respects the property of every other
person in that society. It is in the interests of each person to respect
the property of every other, and each person knows or perceives
that this is in his or her interests. Justice consists in the obtaining of
this convention, and, Hume insists, it is not to be understood as a
promise or contract:

> This convention is not of the nature of a promise: for even promises
> themselves, as we shall see afterwards, arise from human conventions. It is
> only a general sense of common interest; which sense all the members of
> the society express to one another, and which induces them to regulate
> their conduct by certain rules. I observe, that it will be for my interest to
> leave another in the possession of his goods, provided he will act in the
> same manner with regard to me. He is sensible of a like interest in the
> regulation of his conduct. (T III.2.2)

Justice for Hume is reciprocal respect for interests.

Hume regards interests as essentially the possession of property. This raises the question of the relation between property and justice. Sometimes Hume makes it sound as though property depends upon justice, yet at other times it sounds as though justice depends upon property. Admittedly, in the following passage Hume says the 'idea' of property, not property, depends upon convention, but it could be read as suggesting there is no property prior to that convention:

After this convention, concerning abstinence from the possessions of others is entered into, and everyone has acquired a stability in his possessions, there immediately arise the ideas of justice and injustice; as also those of property, right, and obligation. (T III.2.2)

The solution is that Hume makes a distinction between possession and property. Property is possession legitimized by reciprocal respect. I may, after all, possess what is not my property.[23]

The Social Contract

It might seem *prima facie* that Hume is a social contract theorist. After all, the convention which establishes justice is a kind of agreement, albeit a tacit one. Hume says that, if we wish, we may call the convention an 'agreement' so long as the concept of a promise is not intended as any part of 'agreement'. The convention between the members of a society to respect each other's property depends upon mutual recognition. There was never any promise made between the members to honour the convention. Also, the convention is essentially nothing over and above the mutual respect for property which actually obtains in society. It is not an agreement in the sense of a single historical episode. To help us understand the notion of an agreement or convention without a contract or promise, Hume gives us this example: 'Two men, who pull the oars of a boat, do it by an agreement or convention, tho' they have never given promises to each other' (T III.2.2).

Reciprocal respect for property grows as a society matures. Citizens learn not to transgress it as they are exposed to the painful consequences of doing so. Thus for Hume the convention which holds society together is much more like a language than a promise. There was not a historical moment when language was invented, and there was not a historical moment when society was invented. Persons are born into and brought up to observe the political conventions of society as they are brought up to observe the linguistic conventions of society. No real person in any real society has any alternative. All humans have lived in societies, so the idea of a pre-social contract cannot be of any real human situation:

> Philosophers may, if they please, extend their reasoning to the suppos'd 'state of nature'; provided they allow it to be a mere philosophical fiction, which never had, and never could have any reality. (T III.2.2)

It is clear, however, that for Hume not only was there never a historical state of nature, but that the whole notion explains nothing in political theory. The premises for any political theory must be about human societies because there have never been any humans without a society.

MILL

1 MILL IN HISTORY

John Stuart Mill, liberal, empiricist and political reformer, was born in London in 1806, the son of James and Harriet Mill. James was a historian, political theorist and economist, and his book *The Elements of Political Economy* was published in 1821. It is possible that John Stuart Mill was a child prodigy but what is certain is that his father forced on him the most extraordinarily thorough, if stressful, early education. Rather than sending him to school, James Mill saw that his son was steeped in the classics at home. The young Mill was learning Greek, mathematics and history at the age of three. Before he was eight he had read the whole of Herodotus' *Histories* and large quantities of Xenophon, and had been made to familiarize himself with such modern historians as Hume and Gibbon. When he was eight he began to learn Latin, still keeping up his other studies. By the time he was twelve he had read most of the works of Virgil, Horace, Livy, Sallust, Ovid, Lucretius and Cicero. It is clear that his Greek studies were by no means neglected during this Latin phase, because – before he was twelve – Mill had read Homer's *Iliad* and *Odyssey*, plays by Sophocles, Euripides and Aristophanes (though Mill tells us he did not profit much from those), all Thucydides, more Xenophon, and works by Demosthenes, Aeschines, Lysias, Theocritus, Anacreon, Dionysius, Plato, Aristotle, and Polybius's histories. Again before he was twelve, Mill learned geometry, algebra and arithmetic, although, he says, calculus not so thoroughly. James Mill was an impatient teacher. If the young John Stuart's understanding wavered, old Mill would fly into a temper. This would even happen when, for example, his son had not been taught an elementary piece of mathematics presupposed by a more advanced element he was struggling with. Harriet Mill, too, had to suffer James's sour moods and irritable manner.

It was an important part of this education that John Stuart should have no contact with the outside world. He could of course converse with the rest of the family. He and his sister, for instance, were allowed to study Latin together. There were to be no friends of his own age, however, and no straying from home. James Mill made only one exception to this rule. John Stuart was allowed to meet James's own friends because they were philosophers, political theorists and economists. Thus the fourteen-year-old Mill had had no boyhood, but had as friends Bentham, Ricardo and Place. It would hardly capture James Mill's attitude to his son's education to characterize it as obsessional, even if we recognize that education had an important place in James Mill's political theory. As a teenager Mill was made to study deeply the utilitarian philosophy of Jeremy Bentham. There is something eminently paradoxical about Mill's education; it was at once the most liberal and the least liberal education possible. The world's greatest liberal was indoctrinated with liberalism.

In 1820, at the age of fourteen, came escape. John Stuart was allowed to spend a year in France, mainly on the French–Spanish border. True, he passed most of his time there in the charge of Bentham's brother Samuel, but mercifully Samuel liked mountain walks. The clean immediacy of the Pyrenean environment made a lasting impression on Mill and later led to his love of the English Lake District and its poets. He also found that the people he met in France knew how to be open and uninhibited.

On his return to England Mill's education continued more by means of private study than under his father's close supervision. In 1822 James Mill considered sending his son to Trinity College, Cambridge, but finally decided against it and arranged for John Stuart to work for the East India Company instead. Thus James Mill ensured that John Stuart missed a Cambridge education, and Cambridge missed a great Cambridge philosopher. While John Stuart spent his days on clerical tasks of an intellectually undemanding nature, the evenings were devoted to discussions of philosophy and political theory in a number of informal groups. The most important of these was the Utilitarian Society, which met at Jeremy Bentham's house. James Mill had succeeded in making a liberal, an atheist, an empiricist and a utilitarian out of his son, even if this had nearly cost John Stuart a nervous breakdown by the time he was twenty-one.

Mill's most important works are *On Liberty* (1859), a stringent defence of the liberty of the individual; *A System of Logic* (2 vols., 1843), an empiricist approach to a whole set of philosophical problems, which is one of the founding texts of modern liberal social science; *Dissertations and Discussions* (1859–75); *Representative Government* (1861); and *Utilitarianism* (1863). My remarks on Mill's life are based on his *Autobiography* (1873).

Mill was not only a philosopher but also a political reformer. He was appalled by the living conditions of the dwellers in Victorian London. He was sentenced to fourteen days' imprisonment in London in 1824 for distributing leaflets advocating birth control. He was a passionate supporter of parliamentary reform and was active in the Reform Movement which led to the great Reform Act of 1832. Throughout his life he made speeches and wrote pamphlets advocating greater liberty for the individual in British society, and he was a passionate advocate of the rights of women. Mill died in 1873.

Mill is arguably the founder of liberalism. His political theory is concerned with striking a balance between the will of the majority and the voice and interests of the minority. His philosophy provides us with something of a conscience for twentieth-century politics.[1]

2 LANGUAGE

In the first volume of *A System of Logic*, Mill develops a detailed and sophisticated empiricist theory of meaning. Central to it is the concept of a name, so in what follows I shall concentrate on what Mill means by 'name'.

In Mill's opinion, the initiator of an adequate empiricist theory of meaning was Hobbes.[2] Hobbes's account of names is a contribution to a correct definition. Hobbes described the necessary, but not the sufficient, conditions for a particular word being a name when he claimed that a name is both a mark which causes us to recall some thought and a sign for communicating that thought to others. According to Mill, names have at least the two functions Hobbes ascribed to them.

Hobbes's account of names is psychologistic – it explains how words come to be meaningful in terms of our psychology. Mill raises a question about this: 'Are names more properly said to be the names of things or of our ideas of things?' (SL 1.23), and decides that although it is true that names cause ideas, they are not usually the names of ideas but rather the names of the things our ideas are about. The function of using names is to communicate our beliefs, not our imaginings, and our beliefs are generally about things, not thoughts. In any theory of names we should be guided by the ordinary uses of names, so we should conclude that names are 'names of things themselves, and not merely of our ideas of things' (SL 1.24).

Mill distinguishes between sorts of names and distinguishes names from particles and adjectives. Adjectives count as parts of names for Mill, so are not called 'names'. The fundamental distinction within names is between general names and individual, or singular, names. A general name may be used to refer to more than one thing in the same sense, but an individual name may refer only to one thing in one sense. Mill also distinguishes names which have sense from those which do not. 'Man' and the complex name 'The king who succeeded William the Conqueror' (SL 1.27–8) both have sense because their use implies the possession of certain properties by what is named, but 'John' does not pick out any properties (SL 1.22–8).

General names should not be confused with collective names. A general name may be used to predicate a property of each member of a class considered singularly, but a collective name is the name of all those things considered jointly as that class. For example, 'The 76th Regiment of Foot of the British army' is both an individual and a collective name, whereas 'a regiment' is both a collective and a general name (SL 1.28).

Mill distinguishes abstract from concrete names. A concrete name is the name of a thing, an abstract name the name of a property of a thing. Mill allows us to call adjectives abstract names even though they are strictly speaking not names, because they are used to denote properties. Abstract names are neither general nor individual.

A distinction Mill considers fundamental to the structure of language is that between connotative and non-connotative names: 'A non-connotative term is one which signifies a subject only, or an attribute only. A connotative term is one which denotes a subject, and implies an attribute' (SL 1.31). A subject is whatever may possess an attribute, so a term is non-connotative if, and only if, it denotes only a subject or only an attribute. If a term denotes a subject and implies the possession of an attribute by that subject, then it follows that that term is connotative. Mill thinks that when we use an abstract name or a connotative name we predicate an attribute to a subject, so to call something 'white', for example, is not so much to refer to the property of whiteness as to ascribe the property of being white to some subject. Notice that the word 'subject' is ambiguous between 'grammatical subject' – a word or set of words – and 'subject' in the sense of what a grammatical subject picks out, usually in non-linguistic reality.

Mill holds that 'all concrete general names are connotative' (SL 1.32). This means that all names which refer to more than one thing imply the possession of attributes by those things. He provides the example of 'man'. 'Man' applies to any man, and implies the attributes of being physical, being alive, being rational, and having a particular kind of shape. Possessing each of these attributes is singularly necessary and possession of all of them is jointly sufficient for being a man. Connotative names function in this way:

> The name, therefore, is said to signify the subjects directly, the attributes indirectly; it denotes the subjects, and implies, or involves, as we shall say henceforth connotes, the attributes. (SL 1.32)

It is part of Mill's account that 'proper names are not connotative' (SL 1.33). If we call someone 'Paul', this is not by virtue of any properties. Indeed, something close to Hobbes's psychologistic account of names is true just of proper names, on Mill's account. A proper name is in itself simply a mark. The thought of the name causes us to have the idea of what the name refers to.

Mill also distinguishes positive names, which are used to ascribe properties, from negative names, which connote the absence of properties. To every positive name there corresponds the negative equivalent formed with 'not'. Mill distinguishes relative from non-relative terms. Relative terms 'are always given in pairs' (SL 1.43), so that if someone is truly called someone's 'son' that implies the other is a 'father', if any distance is 'shorter' that implies some other distance is 'longer', and so on. A relative term depends on its opposite for its meaning.

Mill's philosophical motivation in distinguishing types of name is ontological. He assumes the linguistic taxonomy – if accurate – will yield an ontological taxonomy. After a short critique of Platonic, Aristotelian and Scholastic ontologies based on muddled lists of categories, Mill outlines his own linguistically determined ontology. This comprises states of consciousness, substances, attributes and relations. Meaningful pre-philosophical language is empirical, so an analysis of that language should yield an empirical ontology.

Mill's word for a state of consciousness is 'feeling', and therefore his use of that term is much broader than ours. Indeed 'everything is a feeling of which the mind is conscious' (SL 1.55), so emotions, sensations and thoughts all count as feelings. Nevertheless, emotions, sensations and thoughts are to be distinguished from their objects. A thought, for example, is not what a thought is of or about. Nor is a sensation, emotion or thought to be identified with the physiological cause of it. Mill adds volition to the category of states of consciousness and urges us to recognize that many names denote agents and actions, an action being an act of will with an effect, and an agent being the subject of an action. (Mill has here curiously omitted bodily movement as a component of action. His account is consistent with our moving objects only by acts of will.)

A substance is something 'self-existent' (SL 1.61). A substance, such as a stone or the moon, does not logically depend upon anything else for its own existence. This ontological fact is revealed because 'a stone' and 'the moon' feature in the subject or object place in sentences but never in the predicate place. Despite his attack on Aristotle and the Scholastics, Mill shares something of their commitment to an isomorphism between an object-property ontology and a subject-predicate grammar.

Mill notes that traditional dualist metaphysics distinguishes mental from physical substance. Physical substance is defined as 'the external cause to which we ascribe our sensations' (SL 1.62) in that metaphysics, yet Mill maintains that talk of physical objects is logically equivalent to talk about sets of actual and possible sensations. In other words, Mill is a phenomenalist (see pp. 237–8 below). He wishes to dispense with the dualism of physical and mental substances, and analyses minds as complexes of experiences. It is not the case, however, that this anti-dualist ontology could be logically derived from his theory of language. On the contrary, Mill's philosophy of language is logically consistent with the truth of the metaphysics he seeks to repudiate.

3 CAUSATION

Mill maintains that any two events are either simultaneous or successive, so that if events A and B occur, then either A happens at the same time as B, or A happens before B, or B happens before A. Numerical and spatial relations between events may be charted by arithmetic and geometry, but there exist in addition causal relations. Indeed there is a law which, so far as our experience permits us to discern, applies universally to all events and this is the law of causation. As far as we know, every event has a cause, or, as Mill puts it, 'The truth that every fact which has a beginning has a cause is coextensive with human experience' (SL 1.376).

Mill holds it in common with Hume that knowledge that causation exists, and knowledge of which causal relations obtain, is *a posteriori* not *a priori*; 'Invariability of succession is found by observation to obtain between every fact in nature and some other fact which preceded it' (SL 1.377). The invariability we perceive is not any kind of logical necessity, but the inductive fact that throughout our experience certain kinds of event have been succeeded in time by other kinds of event. The preceding event or events we call the 'cause' and the succeeding event or events we call the 'effect'. Clearly, however, the fact that two events, A and B, are temporally ordered in a before-and-after relation is not a sufficient condition of their being causally related. It does not logically follow from the fact that A and B are successive events that A is the cause of B and B the effect of A. Mill assumes that if A is the cause of B, then A precedes B in time, and so is neither simultaneous with B nor succeeds B, but for him this is only a necessary and not a sufficient condition of 'A causes B'. Mill therefore inquires into what it consists in for one event to cause another. What does 'A causes B' mean?

Mill's answer is that the real cause of an event is the entire set of conditions necessary for that event to occur. By 'necessary' conditions is meant conditions which have to obtain or else the event in question could not happen. They are prerequisites, in the sense that they are needed. The set of necessary conditions for the occurrence of any event will, as Mill recognizes, be extremely large. It would be a practical impossibility, for example, to itemize all the conditions necessary for a stone thrown into water to sink to the bottom. Not only are there the conditions which follow logically or tautologically from any true description of the event – that the stone was thrown, that it hit the water, and so on – but also there exist necessary conditions not derivable in that way: that the planet earth exists, that gravity exists, that motion exists. Mill does not extend the list this far, but it should include the conditions that there is a universe, that there are physical objects, that there is something rather than nothing at all . . . All these conditions are necessary for the stone thrown into the water to sink to the bottom.

Despite the practical difficulties of listing all conditions necessary for a particular event to occur, it remains true for Mill that 'The real cause, is the whole of these antecedents' (SL 1.378). The set of necessary conditions for an event is sufficient for that event to occur. This means that where all the conditions necessary for an event to occur are met, then that event will occur. Each condition is singularly necessary. All the necessary conditions together are jointly sufficient. 'Sufficient' means here 'all that is necessary'.

Mill is aware, however, that in scientific contexts, and in ordinary language contexts, we do not use the concept of causation in quite this way. If we ask what the cause of a certain event is, we are not asking for an enormous inventory of prerequisites. Mill's answer is that we make a selection from the necessary conditions for an event and call one or some of those 'the cause' of that event: 'It is very common to single out one only of the antecedents under the denomination of cause calling the others merely conditions' (SL 1.378). In fact, no one necessary condition has any more warrant to be called 'the cause' than any other. They are all equally necessary just because they are all necessary, in the sense that without any one of them the event in question could not happen. To be philosophically accurate, 'cause' applies to the whole set of conditions necessary for an event.

Why, then, do we select a condition, or sub-set of conditions, as the cause? Obviously, we cannot enumerate all the conditions for any event because the list would be unpractically large. Why do we select the conditions we do and not others we could? Mill maintains that we tend to count as the cause of an event the last condition to obtain in time before that event: 'the fact which was dignified with the name of cause, was the one condition which came last into existence' (SL 1.380). According to our interests in the situation we could select differently, so there is something capricious for Mill about the manner in which we decide causes. In some explanatory context we may call a condition 'the cause' if it is the one we have just discovered, rather than one of the obvious ones like 'the existence of the earth'. Sometimes we select a condition as 'the cause' if it is in some way conspicuous to us, and the criteria for being conspicuous are rather subjective. In this way, Mill treads a careful path between the objectivity of causation – the set of necessary conditions as jointly sufficient – and the subjectivity of causation. The selection of causes is guided by human interests, or perceived interests.[3]

4   INDUCTION

Induction is the kind of reasoning which putatively establishes conclusions of the form 'All As are F' from premises of the form 'Some As are F'. The problem of induction is that it does not logically – deductively – follow from 'Some As are F' that 'All As are F', so induction seems *prima facie* irrational. If it is not a type of argument where the conclusion follows from its putative premises, it is hard to see those premises as giving any reason for believing the conclusion. In the case of a deductive argument it would be self-contradictory to assert the premises but deny the conclusion, but this is clearly not the case with an inductive argument. Take the deductive case. 'Some As are F' logically follows from 'All As are F' because it would be contradictory to maintain that 'All As are F' but assert that 'Some As are not F'. However, in the inductive case there is no contradiction in maintaining that 'Some As are F' while denying that 'All As are F'.

Mill defines induction as follows:

> Induction . . . is that operation of the mind, by which we infer that what we know in a particular case or cases, will be true in all cases which resemble the former in certain assignable respects. (SL 1.333)

Mill therefore defines induction psychologically, as 'an operation of the mind', but since the work of Frege and Russell it is customary to separate logic from psychology. An important reason for this is that any argument is either valid or invalid irrespective of any states of mind, in particular any beliefs about that argument's validity or invalidity. Mill construes the problem of induction as epistemological rather than as a problem in the philosophy of logic. He thinks of it as the question of how we can know that what holds true in a restricted number of cases holds true in all cases. The problem might be better construed as whether the truth of the premises of an inductive argument in any sense make true, or make probably true, the conclusion. Hence, although Mill says induction is 'a process of inference', he also says 'it proceeds from the known to the unknown' (SL 1.333).

Mill maintains that an appeal to the uniformity of nature is powerless to solve the problem of induction because it is itself an inductive principle. Although 'that the course of nature is uniform, is the fundamental principle, or general axiom of induction' (SL 1.355), such a law could only be established by induction, and so produces a circularity in any putative justification of induction employing it as a premise. The principle that nature contains uniformities is equivalent to the truth of a set of sentences of the form 'All As are F' and the establishing of just such sentences rests on inductive premises, if not an observation of each *A*. Mill therefore asks rhetorically: 'In what sense, then, can a principle, which is so far from being our earliest induction, be regarded as the warrant for all others?' (SL 1.356).

Indeed, it is not the case that nature is wholly uniform, and it is not the case that inductive generalizations hold true always and everywhere. The unknown does not always resemble the known and the future does not always resemble the past. However, even this distinction between where regularities obtain and where they break down rests on induction: it again being impossible to observe all possible cases of which a generalization is putatively true.

Induction is presupposed by our science and our commonsense. It is also essential to empiricist philosophy, but, it seems, cannot be established empirically. Mill does not solve the problem of induction; his conclusion would seem to be that induction is indispensable but unjustifiable.

5 DEDUCTION

In the case of a deductive argument, if that argument is valid then it is logically impossible for the conclusion to be false if the premises are true. The truth of the premises guarantees the truth of the conclusion because the conjunction of the premises with the negation of the conclusion is contradictory. Notice that the premises of a deductive argument do not in fact have to be true in order for that argument to be valid. To decide the validity of an argument we make only the supposition that the premises are true. Nor do we have to believe them. We say if the premises are true then the conclusion is true – a hypothetical statement.

If the premises of a valid deductive argument are true, are in fact true, then we say that argument is 'sound'. So an argument is sound if, and only if, it is valid and all its premises are true. Clearly, the conclusion of a sound argument is true, so soundness is a very valuable property of argument.

There is nothing novel about this broad characterization of the elements of deduction. Mill did not invent it, and it is prominent in

Plato and Aristotle. The interest of Mill's account of deduction is the extent to which he makes deduction rely on induction. That is unusual.[4]

To appreciate the dependence of deduction on induction according to Mill, consider one of his examples. The following is a valid deductive argument:

Major premise: All cows ruminate.
Minor premise: The animal which is before me is a cow.
Conclusion: The animal which is before me ruminates. (SL 1.240)

The argument is valid because if the premises are true then the conclusion must be true. However, the soundness of the argument depends on the actual truth of the premises, and this is where Mill maintains inductive principles are at work. The major premise is an inductive generalization based on observation of a finite number of cows, and the minor premise is confirmed or refuted by direct observation. In a sound argument, the truth of the conclusion is only guaranteed by the truth of the premises. It may be that in this argument there is no (practical) room for doubt about the truth of the minor premise, but both premises are in principle open to empirical falsification. There is no contradiction involved in the supposition that there are cows that do not ruminate, or in the supposition that the object before one is not a cow, even if it appears to be one.

The soundness of deductive arguments which include empirical premises therefore rests on inductive assumptions; that what is true of a sub-set of a set applies to a whole set, and that certain observations are veridical. This is no objection to the validity of deductive arguments, and no practical objection to the use of deduction and induction in science and commonsense. However, Mill would have us recognize that the soundness of our arguments is only as good as our inductive assumptions. In this he is right.

6 KNOWLEDGE

Two kinds of knowledge traditionally pose a problem for empiricism: *a priori* knowledge and knowledge of necessary truths. A proposition, *p*, is *a priori* if, and only if, *p*'s truth or falsity may be decided independently of observation. A proposition *p* is necessarily true if, and only if, *p* is not only true but could not (logically) be false. Notice that '*a priori*' and 'necessary' do not have the same meaning, even if (as some philosophers maintain) all and only *a priori* truths are necessary. *A priori* knowledge is a problem for empiricism because empiricism is the thesis that all knowledge is acquired by experience, but *a priori* knowledge may be established independently of experience; so *prima facie* to be an empiricist yet maintain there is some *a priori* knowledge is to subscribe to a contradiction. Necessary truth is a *prima facie* problem for empiricism because, arguably, experience only demonstrates that certain propositions are true, not that they are not only true but could not fail to be true. Possibly, empiricism allows knowledge of contingencies but not necessities. There seems, then, to be incoherence in holding to the position that all known truths are or could be established by experience, yet also maintaining that some truths are knowable independently of our experience, and some truths hold whatever our experience.

Mill's solution to these problems is to argue that putatively *a priori* knowledge is, when thoroughly understood, really *a posteriori* and inductive, and to argue that putatively necessary truths are, when thoroughly understood, really contingent. In this way he hopes to accommodate, when redescribed, both *a priori* and necessary truths within the empiricist framework.

He has already argued that 'Deductive or Demonstrative Sciences are all, without exception, Inductive sciences', because 'their conclusions are only true on certain assumptions' (SL 1.291), and, as we have seen, these assumptions are inductive, not necessary (see p. 184 above). Mill now asserts that any putative *a priori* or necessary truth is really inductive.

The sentences of arithmetic and algebra are perhaps paradigms of *a priori* necessities. Mill considers but rejects one prevalent attempt to explain their logical status. This is the claim that necessary and *a priori* truths are really verbal: true by definition only. If *p* is true, and true by definition, then *p*'s necessary and *a priori* status seems to be explained at a stroke. *p* is *a priori* because *p*'s truth may be decided by intellectual contemplation of the meanings of *p*'s constituent terms. There is no need to observe any extra-linguistic conditions for *p*'s truth because *p*'s truth is integral to *p*. *p* is necessary because *p* is true by definition. This means that *p* could not be false, given the way we use the words to express *p*. *p* is self-verifying and, so to speak, illustrates the use of words. So if *p* is a verbal truth, *p*'s truth is a condition of *p*'s meaning and, because meaningful, *p* is necessarily true. That *p* is known to be true is a condition of *p*'s being understood, so *p* is decidable without observation and therefore *a priori*.

Mill, although tempted, rejects this solution. He thinks we are misled by the generality of language into thinking *a priori* and necessary truths are only verbal. The generality of language masks 'a real induction, a real inference from facts to facts' in mathematical calculation, and the *a priori* and necessary propositions generally (SL 1.293). Mill accepts that the propositions of arithmetic are general, indeed 'they are propositions concerning all things whatever; all objects, all existences of every kind, known to our experience' (SL 1.293). However, the generality of language is a clue to the inductive nature of *a priori* and necessary truths, not to their verbal nature. Necessities are not verbal because no matter how we changed our linguistic conventions the facts expressed by necessary sentences would still remain facts.

The fact that two plus one is three 'is a truth known to us by early and constant experience; and inductive truth; and such truths are the foundation of the science of Number' (SL 1.295). For Mill, arithmetic ultimately depends on sense-perception, not just genetically but epistemologically. If only two pebbles are placed on the ground, and then only one pebble is placed next to them, and there were no pebbles there beforehand, then there are three pebbles there. This according to Mill is an inductive fact, not a necessary truth.[5] Mill accepts that 'three is two and one' is a definition of 'three' (SL 1.296), but that definition depends genetically and epistemologically upon experience. From the fact that hitherto if only one object is added to only two objects only three objects result, it does not logically follow that this process will hold good for the future:

> The Science of Numbers is thus no exception to the conclusion we previously arrived at, that the processes even of deductive sciences are altogether inductive, and that their first principles are generalizations from experience. (SL 1.296)[6]

From the fact that it is inconceivable by us, as human beings, that some proposition should be false, it does not follow that that proposition is true. Even if the whole of our experience seems to confirm *p* and none to refute *p*, it is still possible that not-*p*. Also, some future experience might demonstrate that not-*p*. For Mill, any proposition whatsoever is in principle open to empirical verification or falsification. If he is right, then this raises an interesting question: Can we ever know anything for certain?

7 FREEDOM

Mill distinguishes libertarianism from determinism as follows: 'Liberty is the thesis that the will is not determined like other phenomena, by antecedents, but determines itself' and determinism is 'necessity, as asserting human volitions and actions to be necessary and inevitable'. Libertarianism includes the doctrine that 'our volitions are not, properly speaking, the effects of causes, or at least have no causes which they uniformly and implicitly obey'. Determinism includes the doctrine that 'the law of causality applies in the strict sense to human actions as to other phenomena' (SL 1.413).

Determinism, here, is therefore the twin theses that every event has a cause and causes necessitate their effects, including human actions. If a cause necessitates its effect, then if the cause happens the effect could not fail to happen. Libertarianism is, here, the view that the will is the cause of its own actions, and what is willed could have been otherwise. The will has no cause other than itself.

Clearly, as defined, libertarianism and determinism are radically incompatible. Determinism is the view that every event has a cause, but if this means 'cause other than itself' and if the operations of the will are un-caused (save by itself), both theories cannot be true. Similarly, if causes necessitate their effects, those effects could not fail to happen, given their causes. But the actions of the will must be able not to have happened even if they do happen, otherwise the will is not free. Part of freedom consists in the ability to do otherwise, and this implies the contingency denied in determinism.

Mill is a determinist. However, what he means by 'determinism' turns out to be something rather different from the definition of 'necessity' given above. His determinism consists in the claim that if we knew enough about a person we could predict their actions with as much certainty as we could predict natural events:

> The doctrine called Philosophical Necessity is simply this: that given the motives which are present to an individual mind, and given likewise the character and disposition of the individual, the manner in which he will act may be unerringly inferred; that if we knew the person thoroughly, and knew all the inducements which are acting upon him, we could foretell his conduct with as much certainty as we can predict any physical event. (SL 1.414)

The problem with this as a kind of determinism is that from the fact that we are able to predict a person's behaviour it does not logically follow that that person is not free. From a very great knowledge of a person's motives and character we may predict their actions accurately, but this may only show that we are intimately acquainted with the ways in which they exercise their freedom. Notice that the claims of the above passage are logically independent of Mill's twofold definition of 'necessity'. The fact that we are able to predict human actions does not entail, and is not entailed by, either or both the theses that every event has a cause, and causes necessitate their effects.

Mill thinks his determinism is consistent with the experience but not the reality of freedom. I think Mill's predictivism is consistent with the experience and the reality of freedom.

8 MIND

It is characteristic of Mill's empiricism, and his hostility to speculative metaphysics, that he refuses to address the questions of what mind and matter are, independently of their putative appearance in experience. Mill accepts a commonsensical distinction between what pertains to the psychology of the person and what pertains to a person's body and its environment. He uses the term 'feeling' to denote both thoughts and sensations. Both of these are mental because even though they have physical causes they are 'internal' rather than 'external', and Mill maintains that 'If the word mind means anything, it means that which feels' (SL 1.428) – that is, that which has mental states.

Mill thus uses an internal–external distinction to mark the mental–physical distinction. However, it is not entirely clear what Mill means by 'internal' and 'external'. It is plausible to suggest that if x is internal then x is privately undergone in some way, but x is not observable, but if x is external then x is, at least in principle, observable, but x may not be privately undergone. He prefers this to any causal criterion, so the fact that x has physical causes, for example, is not a sufficient condition for x being physical. For example: 'The immediate antecedent of a sensation is a state of body, but the sensation itself is a state of mind' (SL II.428).[7]

For Mill, minds and physical objects are not Cartesian substances but logical constructions out of experiential contents. If minds and physical objects are not substances the metaphysical mind–body problem does not arise.

9 ETHICS

Mill's theory of ethics is utilitarianism. Mill did not invent this theory: it is to be found in the works of his father James Mill, and his friend Jeremy Bentham.[8] As Mill himself remarks, there are utilitarian strains in the thought of Plato, and the doctrine is partly anticipated by Epicurus.

What is utilitarianism? It is a meta-ethical theory designed to

distinguish between right and wrong. It offers us a criterion by
which to distinguish the good or moral from the bad or immoral.
The suggestion is that some action, person, character or other
phenomenon is morally good if, and only if, it is conducive to
happiness, and morally wrong if, and only if, it is conducive to
unhappiness or pain. 'Utility' is Mill's word for pleasure or happiness. Here is his definition of 'utilitarianism':

> The creed which accepts as the foundation of morals, Utility, or the
> Greatest Happiness Principle, holds that actions are right in proportion as
> they tend to promote happiness, wrong as they tend to promote the reverse
> of happiness. By happiness is intended pleasure, and the absence of pain;
> by unhappiness pain, and the privation of pleasure. (U 257)

Clearly, in order to appraise this definition of 'right' and 'wrong'
it is necessary to know what Mill has in mind when he talks of
happiness and unhappiness, pleasure and pain.

Mill distinguishes between 'higher' and 'lower' pleasures, and
long- and short-term pleasures. Lower pleasures are 'sensual indulgences' (U 261) and higher pleasures engage our intellectual and
artistic faculties. Mill's justification for making the distinction in
this way is as follows. If any of us, hypothetically, had the option of
becoming one of the non-human animals and so sacrificing our
intellectual and artistic faculties yet were told that our amount of
sensual pleasure would be greatly increased, Mill thinks that no one
would adopt this course. As Mill puts it: 'It is better to be a human
being dissatisfied than a pig satisfied; better to be Socrates dissatisfied than a fool satisfied' (U 260). Notice that Mill uses a hypothetical test to mark the distinction, but one which contains an empirical
component. This component is what our real preferences would be
in the hypothetical situation. I think an objection could be raised to
Mill's procedure here. If it makes even hypothetical sense to talk of
people becoming animals, the reason why most of us would opt for
what Mill calls the higher pleasures is not that we prefer them to
lower pleasures but because we would not wish to be turned into
animals. If we performed a more empirical test, some kind of
sociological survey, it is far from clear that people would be found
to prefer higher to lower pleasures.

Health is a higher pleasure than sensual indulgence, according to

Mill. However, we frequently pursue sensual pleasures at the expense of our health because this is the easier course to follow: 'men, from infirmity of character, make their election for the nearer good' (U 260–61). Human beings follow the line of least resistance, so to speak, in securing pleasure and avoiding pain. Even in such cases, however, Mill asserts that we are fully aware of the distinction between higher and lower pleasures. Through weakness of will we pursue immediate gratification rather than perform actions which will maximize pleasure in the long term. Again, in his example, 'They pursue sensual indulgences to the injury of health, though perfectly aware that health is the greater good' (U 261).

It is not straightforward or clear what happiness is and what pain is, and Mill recognizes this. However, Mill thinks the distinction is an empirical one. Human beings have a pre-philosophical, common-sensical distinction between pleasure and pain, and this should be the foundation of ethics. Moral philosophy takes its content from people's preferences for pleasure rather than pain: 'pleasure, and freedom from pain, are the only things desirable as ends' (U 257). In Mill's view, if something is desirable that is because it is pleasurable, or, if it is not pleasurable, then it is the means to something which is pleasurable.

It is an empirical fact that human beings seek their own pleasure at the expense of others, but Mill's utilitarianism is not to be confused with any kind of hedonism which might condone this fact. It is his opinion that what is good is conducive to the greatest happiness of the greatest number of people, and what is morally wrong is conducive to the maximization of pain. Thus, in acting, a person is not to evaluate the effects only on their own pleasure or pain but on the amount of pleasure and pain existing amongst all persons.

Utilitarianism is frequently subjected to severe criticism. What is pain? What is pleasure? How do we measure pleasure and pain? How do we predict the consequences of our actions? Who is to be included in the scope of persons whose pleasure is to be maximized – future generations? – non-human animals who feel pleasure and pain? Suppose we promote the happiness of the greatest number of people possible, this could be at the expense of some minority.

Suppose the happiness of the greatest number consists in persecuting some smaller number?

Two hypothetical situations may illustrate some of the objections. Suppose a hospital ward contains several patients each dying of a different complaint. One has something wrong with the heart, another the lungs, another the liver, and so on. Then a perfectly healthy person walks into the ward – perhaps a visitor with flowers and chocolates for the patients. It seems that the right thing to do within the utilitarian framework is to seize the visitor, dismember him and distribute the healthy parts amongst the several patients. In this way the pain of several persons is alleviated at the expense of only one.

It is just before D-Day, June 1944, and the Nazi forces have to be driven out of Western Europe by the forces of the Western democracies. However, the Germans have to be tricked into believing that the main attack will fall in the Pas de Calais, not in Normandy, or they will oppose the Allied landings with Panzer divisions and thousands of British, American and Canadian lives will be lost; Western Europe will remain under the heel of the dictator and Hitler may conquer the world. There is only one sure way to trick the German intelligence network. An Allied agent must be made to believe, falsely, that the landings will be in the Pas de Calais and he must be allowed to fall into the hands of the Gestapo, the German secret police. Then he will reveal under torture the false information and the Germans will deploy the Panzer divisions in the wrong place. If this is not too suspicious, the poison should be taken out of his suicide pill. In this way we save the free world and thousands of lives by sacrificing only one.

If we feel there is something immoral about dismembering the hospital visitor or deceiving the agent and sending him to certain death, we have to say exactly what is wrong with these actions. Perhaps they affront our sense of justice, or the liberty of the individual. After all, the visitor is an innocent and even altruistic character, and one feels the agent has as much right to life and liberty as the people for whom he is being sacrificed. Consider, however, the consequences of not killing them in those ways. The patients will die in the hospital and, in the other case, thousands of Allied soldiers will be killed and millions of civilians be enslaved and possibly exterminated. Indeed, both these horrendous consequences are avoidable by the sacrifice of just one person in each case.

Utilitarians sometimes make a distinction between 'act utilitarianism' and 'rule utilitarianism'. In act utilitarianism, the consequences of each act are to be considered on their own merits, in abstraction from any other even seemingly similar acts. In rule utilitarianism, one is to ask oneself what the consequences would be if a particular sort of action were adopted as a rule: if in similar situations that sort of action were to be performed. The difference between act and rule utilitarianism is roughly the difference between asking, What if this person does that? and, What if everybody (similarly placed) did that? It is possible that the act utilitarian is committed to killing the visitor and the agent, but the rule utilitarian is not.[9]

Utilitarianism is a consequentialist theory of ethics. This means that only the consequences of actions are to be taken into account in evaluating actions morally. The motives and intentions of the agent are irrelevant in themselves, so having good intentions is neither necessary nor sufficient for being moral. A person can have good intentions but be immoral through their actions, and a person can have bad intentions but be moral through their actions. Here, 'good intentions' are intentions to do good, and 'bad intentions' intentions to do wrong. Ted Honderich has pointed out, rightly I think, that if we had a choice between removing all evil intentions from the world or all evil consequences, we would choose the latter.

Despite the objections to utilitarianism I think there is much to be said in its favour. The utilitarians believe we should try to promote as much happiness as possible in the world and attempt to reduce suffering. It would be strange if they advocated the reverse. Also, we need to ask exactly what is the relation between pain and morality. Clearly, there is a great deal of pain in the world as well as pleasure – physical and mental. It is hard to imagine a world without pleasure and pain as they are so inextricably bound up with all our motives, thoughts and actions. Suppose, however, our world was without pleasure or pain. Could there be a distinction between right and wrong without the existence of pleasure and pain? Could morality and immorality exist in such a world? I think not.[10]

10 POLITICS

Mill's political theory is the classic statement of liberalism, the philosophy which advocates the maximum liberty of the individual and its protection against the power of the state and the liberty of other individuals. Mill's formulation of liberalism is to be found in his essay 'On Liberty'.

In 'On Liberty', Mill is not only concerned with the traditional problem of political theory in drawing a balance between the liberty of the individual and the authority of the state, although that is a problem that concerns him. He is worried by a more thoroughgoing and subtle erosion of liberty. This is the danger that the popularity of ingrained opinion within a society will stifle and repress the thoughts and opinions of minorities, including minorities of one. We could call this the repression of the individual by the social because it is a kind of enforced conformity, not only in action but also in thought and speech. Mill greatly prizes individuality – that each individual is qualitatively dissimilar from every other – but it is precisely individuality which is eroded by social pressures and made to conform to the values and perceptions of the majority. Even if the individual is protected against the tyranny of the institutions of state, he or she may still not be free.

> Protection, therefore, against the tyranny of the magistrate is not enough: there needs protection also against the tyranny of the prevailing opinion and feeling; against the tendency of society to impose, by other means than civil penalties, its own ideas and practices as rules of conduct on those who dissent from them; to fetter the development, and, if possible, prevent the formation, of any individuality not in harmony with its ways, and compels all characters to fashion themselves upon the model of its own. (OL 130)

This kind of tyranny, 'the tyranny of the majority' as Mill calls it (OL 129), is to be found in democracies as well as totalitarian dictatorships. Indeed, within democracies the opinions of the majority prevail at the possible expense of minorities, so the liberty of those minorities has to be safeguarded. Mill's liberalism is motivated by the need to draw a limit to social, collective, encroachments on the liberty of the individual: 'how to make the fitting adjustment between individual independence and social control' (OL 130).

A charge sometimes brought against liberalism is that it is unhistorical, or a-historical, in that it mistakenly assumes that political values do not change over time and space. This charge is, I think, unwarranted if brought against Mill, and in any case rests on a misunderstanding. Mill fully accepts the historical or sociological empirical fact that the line of demarcation between social pressures to conform and individual freedom vary culturally and historically. He says: 'No two ages, and scarcely any two countries, have decided it alike; and the decision of one age or country is a wonder to another' (OL 130). The misunderstanding is that Mill is not engaged in an empirical study, say political science, but in prescriptive political theory. He is stating what ought to be the case politically. In arguing this, he does adopt one fundamental premise: what matters to us is our individuality. What each of us values in ourselves is that which distinguishes each of us from every other; that which makes each of us just that individual which each of us is. The assumption is that if we were all qualitatively similar – submerged in a bland uniformity or obsequious conformity – then we would be interchangeable, and that which we each value in ourselves would be lost. It follows that the erosion of individuality is the erosion of what makes life valuable, meaningful, or worth living: 'All that makes existence valuable to any one, depends on the enforcement of restraints upon the actions of other people' (OL 130).

Two objections may be raised against Mill's individualist premise, one more plausible than the other. The first is that Mill neglects the fact that people are socially constituted, indeed constituted by their class location, so individuality is really a myth. The second is that it is false or one-sided to claim that individuality is what matters to people fundamentally. On the question of social class, Mill accepts there is a high degree of social determination and it is the point of his liberalism to place constraints on it. For Mill, as for Marxists, the ruling ideas are the ideas of the ruling class. Mill says explicitly:

Wherever there is an ascendant class, a large portion of the morality of the country emanates from its class interests, and its feelings of class superiority. (OL 132)

By 'morality' Mill means not only opinion but power relations of moral significance. In a striking list of masters and slaves Mill insists that power relations are determined by class interests:

The morality between Spartans and Helots, between planters and negroes, between princes and subjects, between nobles and roturiers, between men and women, has been for the most part the creation of these class interests and feelings. (OL 132)

It would thus be a severe misunderstanding of Mill to suggest that his social theory is utterly individualistic. Yet clearly, although our social locations determine the fact that persons share common properties, this determinism does not extend so far as to make us qualitatively identical.

On the point that our individuality is not what we value, I think two distinct but mutually consistent positions might be maintained. It could be argued, as by Mill, that we value that which differentiates each of us from every other, so that is what should be protected politically. Or it could be argued that we value that which each of us holds in common with others – shares with at least one other person. The second view makes people social in what they value. These views are only mutually inconsistent if it is urged that people must ultimately value what one of these views specifies rather than the other. I see no reason to urge this.

The criterion Mill advocates to demarcate the extent of legitimate social control over the individual rests on the premise that each individual has a right to do as they please with their own body and mind. This is not an empirical claim but the expression of a right: 'Over himself, over his own body and mind, the individual is sovereign' (OL 135). This premise is logically independent of Mill's claim that what matters most to each of us is our individuality. Clearly, it may or may not be true that there should be such a right irrespective of whether we value what is distinctive of ourselves as individuals. For Mill's argument, however, the connection between the two premises is crucially important. Because what each of us values should be protected, and because each of us values our individuality, we have a right to that individuality. It is exactly our individuality which is protected by the right each of us has to control our own body and mind. The central 'principle' of liberty which 'On Liberty' is written to formulate and defend is that the only limitation on the right to individual freedom is the right to self-defence, but self-defence is only the right to the protection of one person or several persons' individuality against another:

> The sole end for which mankind are warranted, individually or collectively, in interfering with the liberty of action of any of their number, is self-protection. (OL 135)

Each person may enjoy as much freedom as is consistent with the enjoyment of the same freedom by every other. Each person's freedom may be curtailed only in so far as it is incompatible with the enjoyment of that freedom by another. Mill is an egalitarian about freedom. Freedom must be distributed equally.

For Mill, liberty includes not only freedom of action but, importantly, freedom of thought and expression – both in speech and writing. 'Freedom of thought and discussion' is included in the egalitarianism regarding freedom which is the conclusion of the above argument. Mill has additional grounds, however, for defending the free expression of all opinions:

> . . . the peculiar evil of silencing the expression of an opinion is, that it is robbing the human race; posterity as well as the existing generation; those who dissent from the opinion, still more than those who hold it. If the opinion is right, they are deprived of the opportunity of exchanging error for truth: if wrong, they lose, what is almost as great a benefit, the clearer perception and livelier impression of truth, produced by its collision with error . . . we can never be sure that the opinion we are endeavouring to stifle is a false opinion; and if we were sure, stifling it would be an evil still. (OL 143)

Here Mill's liberalism rests on two epistemological premises: realism and falsificationism. Realism is the view that every belief is either true or false independently of its being believed or disbelieved. Falsificationism is the view that any of our beliefs could in principle turn out to be false. There is an anticipation here of the connection between liberalism and falsificationism in the philosophy of Karl Popper. Liberal societies are conducive to the growth of knowledge because they tolerate competing opinions, and it is through the test of being opposed that views are shown to be deficient and knowledge grows.

We should ask now whether Mill's liberal political theory is compatible with the rest of his philosophy. In particular, *prima facie* doubts arise about its consistency with his determinism and his utilitarianism.

Mill wishes to maximize the freedom of the individual in political society, and political freedom is to be distinguished from freedom of the will. The very first sentence of 'On Liberty' makes it clear that Mill's subject-matter is 'Civil, or Social Liberty', not 'Liberty of the Will' (OL 126). It is not clear, however, that the two are so easily separated. Suppose strong determinism is true, then every event has a cause, every caused event happens by necessity, and there is no human freedom. If there is no human freedom there is no human freedom *tout court*, and it is doubtful whether the individual can have a right over his own body and mind if he is not genuinely free in his thoughts and actions. Does political freedom presuppose freedom of the will?

Even if it does, this need not worry Mill too much. As we have seen (p. 188 above), Mill's determinism consists in the thesis that we could, given enough information, in principle predict any person's actions. I argued that that is consistent with that person possessing free will, so Mill is not committed to a determinism of sufficient strength to be incompatible with freedom: free will, or political freedom. Perhaps for this reason Mill also says in the first sentence of 'On Liberty' that 'Liberty of the Will' is 'unfortunately opposed to the misnamed doctrine of Philosophical Necessity' (OL 126).

Potentially more damaging is the *prima facie* mutual inconsistency between Mill's liberalism and his utilitarianism. It might be that the principle that the happiness of the greatest number is to be maximized is incompatible with the principle that each person should have as much freedom as is consistent with a similar freedom for every other. Whether the two principles conflict depends upon how individuals exercise their freedom. Suppose they exercise their freedom in such a way as to produce more pain and suffering than happiness. Should we then be liberals and say that this is their right? Or should we be utilitarians and say that this should be reversed because it is immoral? For example, suppose the individuals in liberal society decide to drink, smoke, gamble, and generally abuse themselves to the point that they maximize suffering over happiness in their society. It seems we have to choose between being utilitarians or liberals: we can give up liberalism and interfere with people's freedom to harm themselves, or we can give up utilitarianism and sacrifice the principle that we should maximize well-being.

Mill does not solve this problem. As long as people act in their own best interests it does not arise, but, of course, frequently they do not.[11]

RUSSELL

1 RUSSELL IN HISTORY

Had his philosophy not been eclipsed by that of his student, Ludwig Wittgenstein, it is possible that Russell would at this moment be regarded as the greatest philosopher of the twentieth century. Eclipses are temporary occurrences, however, and when philosophy again comes to recognize that its problems are genuine, Russell's solutions may come to be regarded as more than plausible.

Russell's philosophical career may be usefully divided into three phases. The earliest phase was a Cambridge education dominated by German idealism. The young Russell subscribed in one form or another to the world system of Hegel and was profoundly influenced by Kant. This phase I judge to have lasted from 1890 to about 1896. During that time he attended the lectures of John McTaggart Ellis McTaggart, one of the most rigorous Hegel scholars the English-speaking world has ever produced.

The second phase, which lasted from about 1897 to the First World War, was dominated by the philosophy of mathematics but included a concern with a wide range of metaphysical problems. His friend G. E. Moore, also at Cambridge, persuaded him that the systems of Hegel and the neo-Hegelians were philosophically vacuous, and from that time on Russell became one of the most virulent opponents of that tradition. He was always left, however, with a deep sense of the plausibility of idealism which perhaps only someone who has subscribed to the doctrine can share. It is this period leading to 1914 which was the most fertile in Russell's philosophical development. In 1897 he published *An Essay on the*

Foundations of Geometry which inaugurates his fascination with mathematics but still bears a heavy Kantian stamp. In 1900 he published in book form the lectures he had given in place of McTaggart: *The Philosophy of Leibniz*, a brilliant analysis which is often maligned but rarely read. The intense work on the foundations of mathematics continued with the publication in 1903 of *The Principles of Mathematics*, and culminated in the masterly and epoch-making *Principia Mathematica* (1910–13). Russell and his co-author A. N. Whitehead, who was also at Cambridge, argue that the whole of mathematics may be derived from certain logical axioms. This project had been partially anticipated by Frege, and it was shown later by Gödel that no consistent mathematical system has the resources within it to prove its own completeness. Nevertheless, Russell mathematized logic and logicized mathematics in a historical transformation of both subjects. Russell in fact made them into two aspects of one subject that superseded the archaic Aristotelian logic which had constrained philosophy for two and a half millennia.

In 1910 Russell published two works which remind the reader, if this is necessary, that philosophy is about trying to solve philosophical problems and nothing else: *Philosophical Essays*, and *The Problems of Philosophy*. *The Problems of Philosophy*, at once profound and readable by the non-philosopher, is an ideal introduction to our subject. Interestingly, it is a deeply Platonic work in its commitment to mind-independent entities. It is right to see in this, I think, a reaction against Russell's earlier espousal of German idealism. The relation between the mind and the external world is the topic of the work which ends this middle period: *Our Knowledge of the External World* (1914). The epistemological problem it addresses was to be central to the third phase: the relation between the world as described by science and the world of commonsense.

The third phase lasts from 1918 to around 1930. The *Introduction to Mathematical Philosophy* (1919) introduces Russell's pre-war work on the foundations of mathematics to the non-mathematical reader. The title of the 1918 collection of essays, *Mysticism and Logic*, reveals the range of Russell's philosophical mind. There are brilliant philosophers who are rigorous logical minds. There are brilliant philosophers who have a profound metaphysical imagination. I would place Frege in the first category, Hegel in the second. It is rare for both capacities to be combined in one individual but this was indeed the case with Russell. The synthesis is evident in *The Philosophy of Logical Atomism* (1918) and the paper 'Logical Atomism' (1924). The importance of science for the later Russell emerges clearly in *The Analysis of Mind* (1921) and *The Analysis of Matter* (1927). Russell knew too much about science to be a materialist in philosophy; in these two books he tried to do justice both to the reality of our psychological lives and the world of physics. He understood twentieth-century physics thoroughly and realized that its radical implications had not been absorbed – either by philosophers or by the non-philosophical public. He therefore wrote two popular introductory works: *The ABC of Atoms* (1923) and *The ABC of Relativity* (1925). Russell summarized his ideas in the later period in *An Outline of Philosophy* (1927).

It is well known that Russell was not only a philosopher but a political activist, a political theorist, a commentator on current affairs, a moralist and a historian of thought. Before the First World War he was an outspoken advocate of women's rights, and during it he was a pacifist. Despite the support of many colleagues this cost him his fellowship at Trinity College, Cambridge. In 1918 he spent a year in jail for speaking out against the war, and during his imprisonment wrote the *Introduction to Mathematical Philosophy*. His concern for the underprivileged and the downtrodden of the world made him an early enthusiast for the Bolshevik Revolution of 1917. The extermination of so many of those the Revolution was supposed to benefit, however, led Russell to break with Marxism by 1919.

Although Russell had been a pacifist, he supported the Second World War because he was an implacable enemy of Fascism and an eloquent defender of democracy. From 1945 the largest single problem facing the world, in Russell's view, was the possibility of nuclear war. He was often to be seen on the marches of the Campaign for Nuclear Disarmament, and once again he spent time in prison. He opposed the American war in Vietnam and in 1967 published *War Crimes in Vietnam*.

Russell is not easily located in any political taxonomy. Like his continental contemporary Jean-Paul Sartre, Russell promoted the causes of people subjected to deprivation and persecution whoever and wherever they were. His concern to alleviate abject poverty in the world is socialist, even if, after 1919, not Marxist. His vocal insistence on the liberty of the individual and his implacable opposition to all closed systems of thought is liberal.

Bertrand Russell was born in 1872 and died in 1970. He held numerous fellowships at Trinity College, Cambridge, the college where he was educated, and lectured widely throughout the world, especially in the United States. During the First World War, Harvard offered Russell a professorship, but to its discredit the British government would not allow him to leave the country. During the Second World War the roles were reversed, because a legal case was brought by the US government against Russell to prevent him taking up a post at New York University in 1940. He was thought to be an atheist who engaged in strange sexual activities. However, Trinity made him a temporary Fellow again in 1944 and this appointment was made permanent in 1949. He published his *History of Western Philosophy* in 1945 which, again, is more maligned than read. Russell is usually charged with doing scant justice to the positions of Kant, Hegel, Bergson, Heidegger and others removed from the British empiricist tradition. However, his metaphysical imagination was usually larger than that of his critics and there was a reason for his disparaging remarks. He believed there to be a connection between muddled metaphysical systems and totalitarian politics.

Russell never had any patience with the linguistic philosophy which came to dominate English-speaking philosophy from the 1940s. He and Wittgenstein fell out over this, Russell failing to find any philosophy in Wittgenstein's *Philosophical Investigations*. Nevertheless, Russell made important contributions to the philosophy of language, especially perhaps in *An Inquiry into Meaning and Truth* (1940) which was based on his William James Lectures at Harvard. In 1948 he returned to an old Russellian theme in *Human Knowledge: Its Scope and Limits*.

I said that Russell was a philosopher as well as a political activist. He clearly knew when his role was that of a professional philosopher and when it was not. Nevertheless, he believed it was the task of the philosopher to have a concern for the important political issues of his time. Like Sartre, Russell was a philosopher *engagé*. Perhaps we should add this as a third test of the truly great: logical rigour, metaphysical imagination and human commitment.[1]

2 PERCEPTION

In a sense, understanding an empiricist's thoughts on perception is a condition for understanding the remainder of his philosophy. If all knowledge is derived from experience, the nature of all knowledge arguably depends on the nature of experience and that derivation. Russell accepts this primacy by beginning *The Problems of Philosophy* with a discussion of appearance and reality.

Russell's opening question, and his prime epistemological motivation, is essentially Cartesian. He wants to know whether there is any knowledge which is so certain that it cannot rationally be doubted. Pre-philosophically, it seems to us unproblematical that we are surrounded by physical objects and other conscious beings, all in causal interaction in a spatio-temporal framework. However, when we try to specify more precisely what we know about ourselves and the world about us, our knowledge appears much less certain. A table appears to be a different colour in different lights, and to different people, and to the same person at different times, and from different points of view. It seems impossible therefore to speak properly of 'the' colour of the table. Rather the colour of the table is relative to the perceiver and the environment. Similarly, what texture the table has depends on whether it is perceived by the naked eye or under a microscope. What shape the table appears to have depends on your point of view, and how hard it seems to be depends on how hard you press it. Russell concludes from this rather Berkeleyan relativism about perception that 'the real table, if there is one, is not the same as what we immediately experience by sight or touch or hearing' (PP 11).

This gives rise to two questions: Does the real table exist? and, If so, what is it? To try to answer these, Russell makes a threefold distinction between what he calls sense data, our sensation, and the physical object. Sense data are the immediate objects of sensation, the colours, sounds, shapes, textures, and so on, exactly as they are

directly given in perception. The sensation of the sense data is not
the sense data but our experience of them. Thus if you visually
perceive a red patch, there are two discriminable components to
this occurrence: the red patch and your visual perception of it; that
is, the sense datum and the sensation of it. I think there are good
grounds for denying that sensations exist in addition to sense data,
but Russell, at least in *The Problems of Philosophy*, maintains this
distinction.[2]

Although it is possible, in principle, to doubt the existence of
physical objects, it is not possible to doubt the existence of sense
data. This claim is the foundation of Russell's empiricism.
Although, *pace* Descartes, it is possible to doubt the existence of an
enduring self as perceiver, and although it is possible to doubt the
existence of the physical objects we seem to perceive, it is not
possible to doubt the existence of the colours, sounds, shapes and
smells that appear in that perception. Russell calls this 'a solid basis
from which to begin our pursuit of knowledge' (PP 19). This is
clearly an empiricist foundation because it implies that unless we
have secure knowledge of the content of experience we cannot have
secure knowledge of anything else.

Russell rejects one argument that our perceptions are of public,
objective physical objects because it begs the question. This is the
argument that different people have similar sense data under similar
circumstances, and this would only be possible if they perceived the
same objects. The problem is not only that the argument assumes
people 'have' sense data, but I only know other people exist on the
basis of my sense data, and these are private to me. It is logically
possible that that solipsism is true: only I and my experience exist.

However, although there is no conclusive refutation of that
solipsism there is no proof of it either, and no reason to believe it.
Indeed, Russell argues that the simplest explanation of the regularities in our private sense data is the commonsensical one that
physical objects exist independently of our experience and its
contents; that is, physical objects exist before, during and after our
perceptions of them and would still exist if not perceived. Russell
maintains that simple explanations are to be preferred to complex
ones because, other things being equal, they are more likely to be
true.

So the sense data are sense data of physical objects, at least in

The Problems of Philosophy. Later Russell adopts the more sophisticated view that physical objects are logical constructions out of sense data (see p. 212 below). His answer to whether there is a real table is 'yes', although he accepts that it is logically possible his answer should be false.[3]

3 KNOWLEDGE

Russell distinguishes two sorts of knowledge, and the second sort in turn divides into two. There exists knowledge of truths and knowledge of things, and we may know things either by acquaintance or by description. Knowledge of truth is often called 'knowledge that' or 'propositional knowledge' because it is knowledge that such-and-such is the case, or knowledge that some proposition is true. For example, if I know I am in Edinburgh, then I know it is the case that I am in Edinburgh. If I know I am in Cambridge, then I know the proposition that I am in Cambridge is true. If I say, in contrast, that I know Edinburgh and I know Cambridge, this means that I have experienced those places in a way that makes me familiar with them. Russell says, usefully, that 'the distinction involved is roughly that between "savoir" and "connaître" in French, or between "wissen" and "kennen" in German' (PP 44).[4]

Acquaintance and Description

Chapter 5 of *The Problems of Philosophy* is devoted to the two kinds of knowledge of things: knowledge by acquaintance and knowledge by description. Acquaintance is direct awareness, unmediated by any reasoning or knowledge of truths. The objects of acquaintance are sense data, not physical objects, so strictly speaking it is correct to say that one is acquainted with the shapes, colours, sounds and so on which fall within one's immediate awareness, but only in a derivative sense may one speak of being acquainted with, say, cities. We are acquainted with appearances – sense data – through experience, and we are acquainted with sense data just as they are;

they do not admit of an appearance–reality distinction, so strict knowledge by acquaintance is incorrigible. Knowledge by acquaintance must not be confused with any knowledge of truths about sense data. Acquaintance with sense data is direct sensation of sense data, not knowledge of propositions which ultimately depends upon such sensation.

Although knowledge of physical objects depends upon acquaintance with sense data, it is not identical with it. It is not direct but indirect knowledge. As we have seen, by Russell's account we do not directly perceive physical objects, only sense data, and our knowledge of the existence and nature of physical objects is a set of inferences, a set of inferred truths. I sense sense data but I come to know the truth of some propositions of the form 'these sense data are caused by a physical object'. In other words, I come to know a description of a physical object even though I am only acquainted with sense data. For this reason, knowledge of physical objects falls into the category of knowledge by description.

Not all knowledge by acquaintance is knowledge of sense data, and not all knowledge by description is knowledge of physical objects, even though there is no knowledge by acquaintance of physical objects and there is knowledge of truths about sense data. We are directly acquainted with the contents of memory, according to Russell, even though knowledge of past events may be by description. In introspection we are directly aware of our own awareness, so we have knowledge of our own mental states by acquaintance. However, knowledge of the mental states of others is always by description. It is further possible, but by no means certain, that we are acquainted with ourselves in introspection. The reasons for Russell's scepticism on this point are Humean.[5] Russell also thinks we have knowledge by acquaintance of 'universals, that is to say, general ideas, such as whiteness, diversity, brotherhood, and so on' (PP 52). A universal is a concept for Russell, and he calls awareness of concepts 'conceiving' (see pp. 210–11 below).

Knowledge by description, by contrast, includes not only knowledge of physical objects, but of other minds and past events.

What is a description? A description is a phrase of the form 'the so-and-so' or 'a so-and-so', and we have knowledge by description if, and only if, we know the truth of a sentence in which at least one such phrase is embedded. Russell calls a phrase of the form 'the so-and-so' a 'definite description' because it picks out or denotes one definite, unique individual. He calls a phrase of the form 'a so-and-so' an 'ambiguous description' because one (but not one specific) individual is picked out by such a phrase.

Although knowledge of physical objects is never by acquaintance, knowledge of persons may be either by acquaintance or by description. Russell, for example, knew himself by acquaintance, but we – whether or not we ever met him – know him only by description.

Ultimately, all knowledge by description depends upon knowledge by acquaintance. Hence 'every proposition which we can understand must be composed wholly of constituents with which we are acquainted' (PP 58).

4 INDUCTION

Each of us is directly acquainted only with our sense data, universals, and perhaps ourselves. It follows that knowledge of anything else – the past, the future, other people, indeed anything outside our immediate private experience – must be by other means. Most of our knowledge depends upon induction, on inductive inference from facts about our immediate experience to other facts. It follows that the problem of the justification of induction is not only a problem in the philosophy of science; it is central to the possibility of nearly all our knowledge.

If we are asked why we believe the sun will rise tomorrow morning, we will reply, 'Because it always has risen.' If we are asked why we believe that, we reply, 'Because certain laws of motion hold.' If we are asked why we think those will continue to hold, we can only reply, 'Because they always have done.' In each case our reasoning is inductive. We argue that because something has happened, it will continue to happen. The problem is, as we saw above (pp. 157–9), that because x has happened n times it does not logically follow that x will happen again. Once this is realized it is hard to see how the occurrence of any finite set of events, no matter how large, is evidence that a further event of that sort will occur.

Russell carefully distinguishes the logical problem, the fact that there is no logical inference from 'Some *A*s are *F*' to 'All *A*s are *F*', or 'The next *A* is an *F*', from the psychological truth that the repetition of a type of event creates the expectation that an event of that kind will occur again. In Russell's example, 'the man who has fed the chicken every day throughout its life at last wrings its neck instead, showing that more refined views as to the uniformity of nature would have been useful to the chicken' (PP 63). Numerous qualitatively similar repetitions cause expectations of further such repetitions, but the problem of induction is whether such repetitions provide evidence for further repetitions.

Two proposed solutions to the problem of induction turn out to presuppose induction, and so beg the question. Any appeal to the uniformity of nature is circular, because the principle that nature is uniform is the thesis that nature operates in accordance with exceptionless natural laws. Those may only be established inductively, if at all. Any argument that we know the future will resemble the past because past futures have resembled the past is equally inductive, because only induction warrants the belief that future futures will resemble the past.

Russell's solution is to accept that we cannot logically, that is deductively, derive 'All *A*s are *F*' from 'Some *A*s are *F*', but we do not, in inductive contexts, wish to preclude the possibility of some *A*s not being *F*. The probability of all *A*s being *F*, or the next *A* being *F*, is all we should seek. Russell's principle of induction is therefore as follows: the greater the number of cases of *A* being *F*, the greater the probability of all *A*s being *F*, and the greater the number of cases of *A* being *F* the greater the probability of the next *A* being *F*. It is always more probable that the next *A* will be an *F* (other things being equal) than that all *A*s are *F*, because although 'All *A*s are *F*' makes 'The next *A* is *F*' true, 'The next *A* is *F*' does not make 'All *A*s are *F*' true.

Russell's probabilistic solution to the problem of induction is not refuted if, for a particular *A*, '*A* is not *F*' is true. Suppose we have seen only white swans, in a large and increasing population of swans. Suppose, however (as is the case), there is also a population of black swans. We were none the less rational in supposing all swans to be white even though that supposition was false. From the fact that an event is unlikely to occur it does not logically follow that it will not occur, and conversely if an event is likely to occur, it does not logically follow that it will occur.[6]

5 UNIVERSALS

Amongst the items that exist there are not only selves, sense data and physical objects but also universals, which exist in a radically different way from all these. I exist, this room exists, and I am in this room, but what is the ontological status of the relation 'in' here? Relations are in fact universals.

Universals are what examples exemplify, or what instances instance. Universals, whatever they are, are what generality consists in. All just actions are examples of the universal justice, all white things are examples of the universal whiteness, and so on. Russell's approach to the question of what universals are is part semantic and part Platonic.[7] 'Proper names stand for particulars' – the individual things that are instances of universals – 'but other substantives, adjectives, prepositions, and verbs, stand for universals' (PP 93). Universals are essential to language because every sentence necessarily contains at least one word that denotes a universal, that is, at least one general word. It follows that knowledge of truth depends upon acquaintance with universals, because such knowledge depends on knowledge of true sentences and all sentences denote universals. Russell assumes it is not possible to know the truth of a sentence without knowing what that sentence denotes.

Russell is a realist about universals. He believes universals exist independently of our thought and language. Thus 'things are white because they have the quality of whiteness' (PP 95). Universals are not words or sentences, nor are they our ideas, even though we do have general ideas and general words. Russell differs strongly from Locke on this. Locke, it will be recalled, thought there was no generality in mind-independent reality. Russell thinks there is. Indeed, the acquisition of abstract ideas according to Russell relies upon acquaintance with the mind-independent universal *resemblance*

(PP 96). Resemblance is a relation, and although philosophers have tended to reject the truth that relations as well as qualities are universals, Russell insists on this.

Russell's realism about universals is Platonic. If it is true that Edinburgh is north of London, 'we do not cause the truth of the proposition by coming to know it' (PP 97) and 'the part of the earth's surface where Edinburgh stands would be north of the part where London stands, even if there were no human beings to know about north and south, and even if there were no minds at all in the universe' (PP 98). Universals are mind-independent, knowledge-independent and language-independent.

Although universals exist, they are not spatio-temporal. There is no time or place in which we could come across 'north' or 'justice': 'It is neither in space nor in time, neither material nor mental; yet it is something' (PP 98). For this reason, Russell reserves the word 'exist' to refer to particulars. Minds, physical objects and sense data exist, but universals 'subsist' or 'have being'. If something subsists this means temporal predicates have no application to it: 'the world of universals, therefore, may also be described as the world of being' (PP 100).

Like Plato, Russell thinks of universals as perfect and timeless, and the proper objects of study for logic, mathematics and metaphysics. This 'world of being' contrasts with 'the world of existence' which consists in changing thoughts and physical objects. Russell differs from Plato, however, in insisting that neither of these worlds is more real than the other. Plato, of course, thought universals more real than particulars, but this, according to Russell, merely reveals a penchant for theory over practice.[8]

6 MIND AND MATTER

Russell rejects the three traditional principal options in the philosophy of mind: dualism, materialism and idealism. As we have seen, Hobbes is a materialist; he thinks everything that exists is ultimately physical. Locke is a dualist; he thinks there are ultimately two kinds of substance in the universe: mental and physical. And Berkeley is an idealist; he thinks everything that exists is ultimately mental. For Russell, 'mind' and 'matter' are naïve concepts, to be subjected to rigorous philosophical and scientific criticism. Indeed, Russell believes both idealism and materialism are inconsistent with the findings of modern science.

The universe is not fundamentally composed of minds or physical objects for Russell, but events. Events are intrinsically neither mental nor physical, and minds and physical objects are logical constructions out of those events called sense data. As are logical constructions out of Bs if, and only if, As are reducible to Bs – that is, if, and only if, any sentence or set of sentences about As may be translated without loss of meaning into a sentence or set of sentences about Bs, even if such sentences about Bs would have to be long and complicated.

Russell's attack on matter is a rejection of the claim that the universe is composed of a physical substance or material. On the contrary, 'a piece of matter, like a space–time point, is to be constructed out of events' (OP 289). On either of the two current theories of matter, matter is not a substance. On the Heisenberg theory, a piece of matter is a centre of radiation emissions but the centre itself is a 'mathematical fiction', and 'in the De Broglie–Schrödinger system matter consists of wave motions'. On either account the concept of an event logically precedes the concept of matter: 'we are led to construct matter out of systems of events, which just happen, and do not happen "to" matter or "to" anything else' (OP 289).

Similarly, the concept of mind is logically dependent upon the concept of a percept, and percepts are events. Indeed, a percept counts as mental only because a certain 'knowledge relation' (OP 289) called 'introspection' is possible in regard to it: 'Events to which a knowledge relation of this sort occurs are "mental"' (OP 291), and there can only be percepts if there are items perceived: sense data, which are in turn events.

Events are describable as physical or mental in so far as physics or psychology is the most appropriate science to explain them. Intrinsically, they are neither. In so far as an event is subsumed under the laws of physics it is physical. In so far as it is subsumed under the laws of psychology it is mental. As Russell puts it, 'In a completed science, the word "mind" and the word "matter" would both disappear and would be replaced by causal laws concerning events' (OP 292).[9]

7 LOGICAL ATOMISM

Logical atomism is a theory of meaning designed to solve philosophical problems. Russell's version of the theory is strongly influenced by that of his pupil and colleague, Wittgenstein, and is presented in the eight lectures *The Philosophy of Logical Atomism*, and the short essay entitled 'Logical Atomism'.

Russell tells us that his work in the philosophy of mathematics first suggested to him the correctness of logical atomism. It is not too misleading to say that in the philosophy of mathematics Russell attempts to reduce mathematics to logic, while in the philosophy of language he attempts to reduce language to logic: that is, to reduce ordinary language to a logical language. His ambition is to produce a logically perfect language which will not generate philosophical problems, the thought being that the imprecise and misleading nature of natural language leads us into those problems.

The title 'logical atomism' is intended to capture two aspects of the doctrine it names. Atomism is the thesis that the universe (and in logical atomism the language which names it) is intrinsically a plurality. There really are discrete elements constituting what exists, even if the set of such elements is infinite, and even if the elements are thoroughly interrelated. Atomism is thus opposed to the monism of, say, the neo-Hegelians, who think that the pluralistic nature of what exists is an illusion, or mere appearance.[10] Russell calls the theory 'logical atomism' because the atomic constituents of what exists are logical rather than physical, or, for that matter, mental. A physical atom could in principle be divided, but a logical atom could not even in principle be analysed into constituents.

According to Russell, 'the world contains facts, which are what they are whatever we may choose to think about them' (LA 35).

Logical atomism thus entails a kind of realism. Something either is or is not the case, regardless of whether we believe it to be the case. Propositions are either true or false, irrespective of whether they are believed to be true or false. A fact is whatever makes a proposition true or false, and a fact is a state of affairs that obtains quite independently of thought and language. No fact is any particular thing or person: 'a fact is the sort of thing that is expressed by a whole sentence, not by a single name like "Socrates"' (LA 36), so that A has property F, or that A bears relation R to B, are facts.

It does not make sense to speak of true or false facts: 'A fact cannot be either true or false' (LA 38). The bearers of truth values are propositions, and we may talk of beliefs, for example, as true or false because the propositions we believe are true or false. A proposition is treated by Russell as an indicative sentence – that is, a sentence used to assert what is or is not the case. Clearly, not all sentences are propositions because not all sentences are indicative. Some are imperative, interrogative, or exclamatory. Another way of explaining the concept of a proposition is to say that it is a sentence which is always capable of being prefaced by the propositional 'that', so '"that Socrates is alive" and "that two and two are four"' (LA 39) are propositions in Russell's terms.

It follows that no facts are propositions and every proposition is an indicative sentence. Every proposition is a complex symbol, a symbol that has symbols for its parts. For example, a sentence containing more than one word is a complex symbol and its constituent words are the simple symbols which are its parts. It is essential to clarity, and to the avoidance of error, not to mistake the properties of words and sentences for properties of objects and states of affairs. Meaning is a relationship between language and non-linguistic reality: nouns mean objects, adjectival expressions name qualities, and whole indicative sentences mean facts. Although names name objects, propositions assert or deny facts and do so truly or falsely, in virtue of those facts.

Facts are the objects of analysis in logical atomism. Complex facts are analysed into atomic facts, but the only way of doing this is via the analysis of propositions: the analysis of molecular (or complex) propositions into atomic (or simple) propositions, and the analysis of atomic propositions into simple symbols.

Simple symbols are the ultimate constituents of propositions, and they denote the simple components of the facts which make the propositions true or false. 'Red', for example, is a simple symbol because it cannot be analysed into constituent symbols, yet it may be a constituent of a symbol. Although 'red' can in one sense be defined (a description of what 'red' is can be given in terms of physics), it cannot be defined in the sense of 'analysed'. No verbal definition of 'red' could make a person unacquainted with the colour red know what red is. In this sense of 'red', ' "red" could not be understood except by seeing red things' (LA 49).

Atomic propositions are analysed into proper names and predicates. Proper names name particulars. A particular is a component of a fact which exists logically independent of other components and yet bears some relation to them. A predicate designates a quality, so 'red', for instance, is a predicate, but 'John' is a proper name. Russell says that 'to understand a name you must be acquainted with the particular of which it is the name' (LA 60).

Molecular propositions are truth functional. This means their truth or falsity depends upon the truth or falsity of their constituent propositions. Propositional functions are sentences with at least one uninterpreted constituent, and they are expressed in a symbolism. 'P', 'Q', 'R', etc. are propositional variables, and '$-$', '$.$', 'v', '$\rightarrow$', '$\equiv$' are logical constants. The logical constants may be defined by truth tables as follows:

$$
\begin{array}{c|c}
P & -P \\
\hline
T & F \\
F & T
\end{array}
$$

'$-P$' (read 'not P') is true if and only if P is false.

$$
\begin{array}{c|c}
P & Q \\
\hline
T & T \; T \\
T & F \; F \\
F & F \; T \\
F & F \; F
\end{array}
$$

'$P . Q$' (read 'P and Q') is true if and only if both P and Q are true.

$$\frac{P \lor Q}{\begin{array}{ccc} T & T & T \\ T & T & F \\ F & T & T \\ F & F & F \end{array}}$$

'$P \lor Q$' (read 'P or Q') is true if and only if either both P and Q are true or if only one of P and Q is true.

$$\frac{P \rightarrow Q}{\begin{array}{ccc} T & T & T \\ T & F & F \\ F & T & T \\ F & T & F \end{array}}$$

'$P \rightarrow Q$' (read 'if P then Q') is true if and only if either not P is true or Q is true or both.

$$\frac{P \equiv Q}{\begin{array}{ccc} T & T & T \\ T & F & F \\ F & F & T \\ F & T & F \end{array}}$$

'$P \equiv Q$' (read 'P if and only if Q') is true if and only if either both P and Q are true or both P and Q are false. The analysis of a propositional function may proceed in a purely logical, indeed algorithmic, manner. A complex propositional function is a tautology, a contradiction, or contingent, depending on the truth values of its constituent atomic propositional variables. A proposition is atomic if, and only if, it has no constituent propositions.

The truth-functional analysis of propositions leaves entirely on one side questions about the semantic constituents of propositions. Indeed, propositional functions are undetermined in the sense that P, Q, etc. may stand for any (mutually distinct) propositions whatsoever. Russell says that 'One may call a propositional function

> necessary, when it is always true
> possible, when it is sometimes true
> impossible, when it is never true' (LA 87)

but it does not make sense to ascribe these properties to propositions: 'Propositions are only true or false' (LA 88).

It is a source of philosophical error to confuse the properties of propositions with those of propositional functions, as it is to confuse properties of both of those with properties of facts. Being clear about grammar makes progress possible in philosophy. Indeed, 'practically all traditional metaphysics is filled with mistakes due to bad grammar' (LA 128–9).[11]

8   MEANING AND TRUTH

Meaning

Russell subscribes to a referential theory of meaning; that is, he thinks the meaning of a word is the thing the word refers to: 'Words all have meaning, in the simple sense that they are symbols that stand for something other than themselves' (PM 47). Russell's referential theory is, however, more sophisticated than most and contains attempts to forestall philosophical objections.[12]

If the meaning of a word is held to be the object the word refers to, then certain difficulties arise. An object may be referred to by a number of non-synonymous expressions: for example, 'the person with open eyes' and 'the person understanding this sentence' both refer to you but their meaning is not the same. Conversely, one description, say 'the head of department', may be used to refer to more than one person: a university professor at Cambridge and one at Edinburgh, for instance. If meaning were only reference, both these facts would be impossible. Again, if the meaning of 'The person writing this sentence is me' were me, then if I ceased to exist the meaning of that sentence would cease to exist. Clearly, however, the meaningfulness of that sentence does not depend so closely on my existence.

If you assert that 'Scott is the author of *Waverley*' (LA 105), what you assert is true but not tautologically true, as it would be if meaning were only reference. It is contingently true because a definite human being, Scott, wrote a specific book, *Waverley*. It is not true by definition but in virtue of a certain fact. 'Scott' is a name and 'the author of *Waverley*' is a definite description. The definite description is true of the person named by the proper name, and that is what makes the whole proposition true. If one were to substitute a proper name for the definite description in this example the result would be a different proposition, and if that proper name referred to Scott the new proposition would be a tautology.

The distinction between proper names and definite descriptions explains how identity statements may be informative. Although 'George IV wished to know if Scott was the author of *Waverley*', it is not true that George IV wished to know if Scott was Scott' (LA 105).

In *The Philosophy of Logical Atomism* Russell argues that 'the notion of meaning is always more or less psychological' (LA 40). Nevertheless, as we have seen, names name particulars, predicates denote qualities or relations, and indicative sentences express facts; thus there are three different kinds of meaning. Giving the meaning of an expression involves analysing that expression, and ideally the meanings of a logically perfect language would be clear. Ordinary language is riddled with ambiguities but this is not necessarily a disadvantage for non-philosophical work. Ambiguity gives ordinary language a certain richness and allows for originality in expression.

Russell's most influential contribution to the theory of meaning is his 'theory of descriptions'.[13] A singular definite description, a sentence of the form 'the so-and-so', may be true or false, but if it is false because what it putatively describes does not exist, then two philosophical problems arise. If we say, 'the present king of France is bald' is false, we seem to be covertly asserting the existence of what does not exist, and that is manifestly false. This is a problem concerning existence. If we claim that names name objects and propositions name facts, then objects and facts are the meanings of names and propositions. However, it then follows that if the king of France does not exist, the meaning of 'the present king of France' does not exist and the expression is meaningless. Similarly, if the king of France is not bald, then the fact that the king of France is not bald does not exist, so the meaning of 'the present king of France is bald' does not exist and that proposition is meaningless. This is a problem concerning meaning. The point of the theory of descriptions is to show in what way false existential claims are meaningful.

Russell's solution is to claim that 'a name has got to name something or it is not a name' (LA 100). If a putative name names nothing, it is a truncated description of the logical form '*x* has such and such properties' (LA 100). The proposition 'the present king of France is bald' is in fact two propositions:

(1) 'There is a *c* such that *c* is now king of France'
(2) '*c* is bald'.

Analysing the proposition this way avoids construing its denial, 'The present king of France is not bald', as entailing 'There is such a person as the king of France and that person is not bald' (LA 109), which is false. There are in fact two ways of denying the proposition: by denying the king of France exists and by denying the king of France is bald. So the denial of the proposition is not

(3) 'There is a *c* such that *c* is now king of France and *c* is not bald'

but

(4) 'Either there is not a *c* such that *c* is now king of France, or, if there is such a *c*, then *c* is not bald'. (LA 109)

If we wish to deny the proposition we have a choice of asserting either of the disjuncts of (4). In these ways we will not have said something meaningless and not have covertly asserted the existence of what does not exist.

Truth

Truth and falsity are properties of beliefs; but if I believe something, what I believe is a sentence; thus truth and falsity are derivatively properties of sentences. However, the truth or falsity of a sentence is logically independent of its being believed. Our beliefs may be true or false, and what is the case and what is not the case in no way depends on our beliefs.

A belief is true or false in virtue of the occurrence or non-occurrence of extra-linguistic states of affairs – 'facts' as Russell calls them in *The Philosophy of Logical Atomism*, or 'verifiers' as he calls them in *An Inquiry into Meaning and Truth*. For example, the truth of 'Caesar was assassinated' (IMT 215) consists in the occurrence of a particular event – the assassination of Caesar. This event is a fact which verifies the sentence.

Russell rejects the view that truth can be explained in terms of verifiability, perhaps for the very good reason that to 'verify' p means to demonstrate the truth of p, so any such explanation would be circular. Later, Russell subscribes to a correspondence theory of truth: p is true if, and only if, the fact expressed by p exists: 'The "verifier" is defined as that occurrence in virtue of which my assertion is true (or false)' (IMT 219).

A series of philosophical problems exists which concern what the truth of propositions about unobserved facts consists in: propositions about other minds, historical events, theoretical particles, for example. Russell, correctly I think, wishes to maintain that the truth of such propositions consists in the existence of these facts: 'on what may be called the realist view of truth, there are "facts", and there are sentences related to these facts in ways which make the sentences true or false, quite independently of deciding the alternative' (IMT 232), but 'the difficulty is to define the relation which constitutes truth if this view is adopted' (IMT 234). I should say the truth of the proposition lies simply in the existence of the fact and the proposition, and there is no residual relation and so no residual problem.[14]

9 MATHEMATICS

Russell argues in the massive and influential three-volume work *Principia Mathematica* that mathematics is reducible to logic. Indeed he maintains that essentially there is no difference between mathematics and mathematical logic because any putative distinction between the two is arbitrary. As he puts it in *The Principles of Mathematics*, 'All mathematics is symbolic logic . . . all mathematics is deduction by logical principles from mathematical principles' (PM 5), and in the *Introduction to Mathematical Philosophy*:

Logic has become more mathematical and mathematics has become more logical. The consequence is that it has now become wholly impossible to draw a line between the two; in fact the two are one. They differ as boy and man: logic is the youth of mathematics and mathematics is the manhood of logic. (IMP 194)

Russell wrote an enormous amount of outstanding quality on the philosophy of mathematics, but here I shall confine attention to one fundamental question: 'What is a number?' (IMP 11).

A number is not identical with the number of things there are that number of. For example, the number two is not identical with any two objects, the number three is not identical with any three objects, and so on. Rather, the number two is what is common to all pairs of objects, the number three is what is common to all trios, and so forth. All pairs of objects form a class of objects, the class of pairs; all trios form a class, the class of trios. Russell maintains that a number is a class of such classes. The number two, for example, is the class of pairs, the number three the class of trios, etc., but further argument is needed to reach this conclusion on pain of using 'number' in a question-begging way.

To analyse the concept of number Russell uses the notions 'class', 'member' and 'similar'.

Classes may be defined extensionally or intensionally. To define a class extensionally is to enumerate the members of that class (a, b, c, ... n). To define a class intensionally is to mention a defining property of the members of the class, a property such that if an individual possesses that property then it logically follows that it is a member of that class, and such that if it lacks that property it logically follows that it is not a member of that class. Intension is logically prior to extension for Russell because extension can always be reduced to intension but intension cannot always be reduced to extension. For example, we could not in principle enumerate all the members of an infinite set, but we could state the defining characteristic of all members. The series of natural numbers (0, 1, 2, 3 ... n) is infinite, so any definition of 'natural number' in terms of classes must be by intension and not by extension.

To define 'number' in terms of classes, it is necessary to know when two classes have the same number of members and so belong to the same class of classes. This is possible without knowing how many members those two classes contain. For example, if there were only monogamy the number of wives would be the number of husbands. Clearly, this is knowable *a priori* because the relation is 'one–one' (IMP 15). Russell distinguishes relations that are 'one–one', 'one–many', and 'many–one'. A relation is one–one if, and only if, 'if *x* has the relation in question to *y*, no other term *x'* has the same relation to *y*, and *x* does not have the same relation to any term *y'* other than *y*' (IMP 15). Clearly, a relation is one–many if, and only if, *x* has a relation to *y* and to *y'* but no term *x'* distinct from *x* has that relation to either *y* or *y'*; and a relation is many–one if, and only if, both *y* and some term distinct from *y*, *y'*, has a relation to *x* but does not have that relation to *x'*, some term distinct from *x*. Notice the concept of number is nowhere employed in these definitions.

Russell uses the idea of a one–one relation to provide a criterion for the similarity of classes: 'two classes are said to be "similar" when there is a one–one relation which correlates the terms of the one class each with one term of the other class' (IMP 15–16). If *a* is related to *b* by relation *R*, then *a* is the 'domain' of *R*, and *b* is the 'converse domain' of *R*. The relation 'similar' between classes has three logical properties:

(1) Reflexivity: 'Every class is similar to itself' (IMP 16).
(2) Symmetry: 'If a class *a* is similar to a class *b*, then *b* is similar to *a*' (IMP 16).
(3) Transitivity: 'If *a* is similar to *b*, and *b* to *c*, then *a* is similar to *c*' (IMP 16).

Russell defines 'number' in this way: 'A number is anything which is the number of a class' (IMP 19). There is no circularity here because he uses 'class' and 'similar' to define 'the number of a class' without using 'number': 'The number of a class is the class of all those classes that are similar to it' (IMP 18). Thus the number two comes out as the class of all couples, the number three is the class of all classes of three objects, and so on. Notice 'the class of all couples will be the number 2' (IMP 18). Numbers, then, are not Platonic, metaphysical or other-worldly, but classes of classes.[15]

Russell and Whitehead's attempt in *Principia Mathematica* to derive the order of mathematics from certain logical axioms was not entirely successful, as Gödel demonstrated.[16] However, it is in large part because of their efforts that mathematical logic is the thriving subject it is today.[17]

10 CAUSATION

There is a critical and a constructive side to Russell's theory of causation. He presents a neo-Humean set of criticisms of our commonsensical concept of 'cause', and then replaces this with an account he regards as scientific.

Our belief that causes necessitate their effects can be expressed as follows: If A causes B, then if A happens B cannot fail to happen. This belief is deeply embedded in commonsense. It is nevertheless an illusion because there is no compulsion or inevitability in nature. As Hume saw, the belief that A necessitates B is only a psychological product of our witnessing events of type A followed always by events of type B within our experience. We expect B to follow A and mistake our subjective expectation for an objective compulsion or necessity. Hence, Russell says, the ideas of 'compulsion' and 'necessity' are 'purely anthropomorphic' (OP 121).

Observing that Bs follow As, we feel justified in inferring that any A will be followed by a B. However, we are equally entitled to infer the reverse: that any B was caused by an A: 'When you get a letter you are justified in inferring that someone wrote it, but you do not feel that your receiving it compelled the sender to write it' (OP 121). Effects are no more necessitated by their causes than causes are necessitated by their effects. Our powers of prediction and retrodiction, and our expectations about past and future, are not to be taken for natural necessities. Thus 'science is concerned merely with what happens, not with what must happen' (OP 121). Russell's science generalizes probabilistically about Hume's constantly conjoined events. It dispenses with the idea of a force which, in Russell's view, 'is as mysterious as the influence of the stars in astrology' (OP 122).

Russell replaces the concept of causal necessity with the concept of a probabilistic law. If an event, A, occurs, then the probability of an event B occurring is greater or less depending on the number of previously conjoined events of sort A and sort B. Scientific generalizations are thus always probabilistic; the limiting deterministic case, where 'if A then B' has a probability of one, is rare and symptomatic of a young science: 'Genuine laws, in advanced sciences, are practically always quantitative laws of tendency' (OP 150).[18]

11 RELIGION

Russell is an atheist. He never maintained, as Ayer and the logical positivists were to do, that the claim that God exists is literally nonsensical.[19] Rather, Russell thinks there is no evidence whatsoever that God exists, and that every traditional argument for the existence of God is unsound. It might seem that this does not distinguish Russell's position from that of agnosticism, agnosticism being the view that it is possible that God exists and also possible that God does not exist; we do not know which is true. Philosophically Russell does subscribe to that agnosticism: he thinks God's existence cannot be proved or disproved. However, he thinks it foolish and damaging to believe something to be the case in the absence of any evidence for it, so he does not believe in God. This is as near as makes no difference to atheism, the belief that God does not exist.

Russell thinks all religions (with the possible exception of Buddhism) have been and continue to be extremely pernicious and damaging in their effects on human beings. The history of religion, and Christianity in particular, is a history of bloodshed, persecution and the enforcement of ignorance. For Russell, it is intellectual suicide to commit oneself wholesale to a world-picture, a kind of metaphysical map of the universe and our place in it. What one should try to do is accept or reject views according to the evidence for them and the arguments which may be brought against them. We should be prepared to give up any of our theories if the evidence counts against them, and listen with tolerance to the views of those who disagree with us. In that way we learn. Religion, almost by definition, requires the opposite of this. The claims of religion have to be believed whatever the evidence – or lack of it – for them, and they have to be held as true come what may. It follows that those who disagree with the doctrines of a religion are automatically counted as in error by the devotees of that religion. It is a short step from this to regarding one's opponents as either ignorant or wicked – to be converted or exterminated. Hence the history of religion is one of torture and murder of the proponents of one creed by those of another, and the export of intellectually closed world-pictures. Amongst the great world religions Russell counts not only Islam, Judaism, Christianity and Hinduism, but also Marxism. Marxism might have started with the pretension of being a science but has become a dictatorial religion like the others. Its central tenet, that 'as a result of social revolution, the division of classes is expected ultimately to disappear ... is a distant ideal, like the Second Coming; in the meantime, there is war and dictatorship, and insistence upon ideological orthodoxy' (HP 818). Marxism and Christianity alike are closed systems of thought which require the total commitment of the individual to the one fundamental 'truth', with the consequential repression, conversion, torture or elimination of opponents. In any of the world's trouble-spots religious intransigence, the view that the particular religion one is committed to is right, is conspicuous amongst the causes of bloodshed.

The effects of religious belief is partly an empirical and partly an ethical question, and is quite independent of whether the particular religious beliefs are true. Not all religions include the claim that God exists; Buddhism in its main variants does not, nor does Marxism. Central to most religions, however, is a belief in God or gods and it is the question of whether God exists in the Christian sense that Russell addresses in his essay, 'Why I am not a Christian'. Russell's approach is to seek to refute the most commonly used arguments for the existence of God.

The First Cause Argument

This is the argument that, as far as our experience shows, every event has a cause – that is, every event is an effect. However, an infinite regress of causes is impossible. Therefore there must be a first cause, the ultimate cause of all subsequent causes and effects. A first cause sufficiently powerful to initiate the entire subsequent causal chain could only be God.

Russell's objection to this argument is: 'If everything must have a cause, then God must have a cause. If there can be anything without a cause it may just as well be the world as God, so that there cannot be any validity in that argument' (NC 15).

Russell also remarks that the rather deterministic premise of the argument may be doubted, and the concept of causation as traditionally employed by philosophers and scientists may be on the verge of collapse. He clearly has not disproved the existence of God by criticizing this argument; his aim is to demonstrate that the conclusion does not follow from those premises. Russell offers us two alternative conjectures: 'There is no reason why the world could not have come into being without a cause; nor, on the other hand, is there any reason why it should not have always existed' (NC 15).

The Natural Law Argument

This is the argument that the universe operates according to natural laws: it exhibits the uniformities discovered by the sciences. There must be a reason why the laws are as they are and not otherwise; therefore they must be the result of a law-giver's design. This law-giver, as designer of the whole universe, can only be God.

Russell has three objections to this argument. Firstly, 'a great many things we thought were natural laws are really human conventions' (NC 16). Secondly, such laws as there are are statistical or probabilistic rather than deterministic. This makes it more likely that they are the outcome of chance rather than design. Thirdly, 'law' is perhaps being used in a misleadingly metaphorical way. Human laws in human societies are the result of legislation. However, natural laws are not 'laws' in a sense akin to that. They are simply regularities discovered by science, and, indeed, what counts as a natural law changes historically because science changes historically.

The Argument from Design

In the version Russell considers, this is the argument that everything in the world is exactly appropriate to the existence of life, including human life, and if it were just slightly different it could not sustain life. Therefore it was designed to be appropriate for life.

Russell replies that Darwin has shown that species adapt to their environments through evolution so it is life that adapts to conditions, not the conditions which were adapted to life. In any case, species die out and it is probable that the human species, and perhaps all life, will die out. This would seem a peculiar goal for God to give to the universe.

Moral Arguments

Russell's target here is the suggestion that 'there would be no right or wrong unless God existed' (NC 19), and Immanuel Kant's claim that we can make no sense of ourselves as moral beings without postulating the existence of God.

There are only two possibilities, if there is a distinction between right and wrong. Either the distinction depends on God having made it, or it does not: 'If it is due to God's fiat, then for God Himself there is no difference between right and wrong, and it is not a significant statement to say that God is good' (NC 19); but theologians wish to say that God is good and if that is right there is some independent criterion for the distinction. Russell suggests taking the other horn of the dilemma: what is right and what is wrong is logically independent of the existence of God. Thus Kant, for example, was quite wrong in making a moral life depend on belief in God.

The Argument from Remedying Injustice

On this argument there is great injustice in the world because frequently the good suffer and the evil prosper. If there is to be justice in the universe as a whole, God must exist to redress earthly injustices by consigning the good to heaven and the evil to hell.

Russell replies with an analogy: 'Supposing you got a crate of oranges that you opened, and you found all the top layer of oranges to be bad, you would not argue: "The underneath ones must be good to redress the balance"' (NC 20). So because there is injustice it does not follow that there is some unseen justice to come. In fact in Russell's view the world contains both justice and injustice and the existence of injustice is one good reason for not believing in a benevolent deity.

If there are no good reasons for believing in God, why do people persist in it? Russell's explanation is twofold. We are led to believe in God in infancy, and beliefs implanted in infancy are often extremely difficult to remove. If we are caused to believe something we cannot necessarily give reasons for believing it, and in Russell's view there are no such reasons. The other explanation of religious belief is fear:

> Religion is based, I think, primarily and mainly upon fear. It is partially the terror of the unknown, and partially . . . the wish to feel that you have a kind of elder brother who will stand by you in all your troubles and disputes. Fear is the basis of the whole thing – fear of the mysterious, fear of defeat, fear of death. Fear is the parent of cruelty, and therefore it is no wonder if cruelty and religion have gone hand-in-hand. (NC 25)[20]

AYER

1 AYER IN HISTORY

Ayer is the author of what may be regarded as the manifesto of logical positivism, perhaps the most radically anti-metaphysical movement Western philosophy has ever seen. For this reason, Ayer's place in the history of philosophy is assured. That manifesto is called *Language, Truth and Logic*, first published in 1936 but most effective in its impact in the immediate aftermath of the Second World War.[1]

What is logical positivism? The logical positivists were a group of philosophers and scientists who met in Vienna in the late 1920s and early 1930s to form what became known as the Vienna Circle. 'Positivism' is the name of the thesis that every problem may in principle be solved using the methods of the natural sciences. Logic is the exact study of inference. The logical positivists were impressed by the explanatory power of science and the rigour and precision of mathematics and logic. They hoped to make philosophy at least as rigorous as mathematics and put philosophy at the service of science. Their conception of philosophy was the Lockean one of clearing intellectual obstacles from the path of scientific progress.[2]

Traditionally, philosophy had been thought of as metaphysical, or at least as the study of metaphysical problems. By 'metaphysics' I mean 'the study of reality as a whole' – perhaps in its essential properties. Metaphysical philosophers often think it is the role of philosophy to tell us what the world is really like, with its intrinsic nature undistorted by the contingencies of our possible perceptions of it. Hence Plato's thesis that there exists a non-spatio-temporal, non-mental world of perfect universals called 'forms' is a metaphysical idea. So also is Hegel's claim that reality is ultimately spiritual and that the paradoxical nature of the world can be 'overcome' in Spirit's 'absolute knowing'. Similarly, the claims that what is is fundamentally material, mental, or both are metaphysical, as is Leibniz's postulation of non-spatio-temporal constituents of reality called 'monads'. Western philosophy contains innumerable metaphysical projects.[3]

The radical case advanced by the logical positivists was that the whole of metaphysics was meaningless: literally nonsensical. They did not think it false that forms exist, or that God exists, or that monads exist. Rather these putative claims were devoid of any literal meaning whatsoever. They did not even have the merit of being false. Metaphysics was nonsense.

In order to demonstrate the impossibility of metaphysics, the logical positivists advocated a criterion to distinguish meaningful from meaningless statements (or, to be accurate, putative statements which are in fact meaningless). This criterion became known as the 'verification principle'. It asserted that the meaning of a statement is the method of verifying it (or falsifying it) and there are two, and only two, methods of verification: empirical observation or logical analysis. By this criterion the logical positivists claimed that the various special sciences emerged as meaningful – genuinely capable of truth or falsity, but the whole of metaphysics and of theology were classified as nonsensical. For the logical positivists, many of the traditional questions of philosophy, such as: Does God exist? What are minds? What are numbers? Was there a first event? turned out to be meaningless questions to ask. At least, if there were meaningful questions thrown up by philosophy these were either in the last resort empirical, and so scientific, or else logical and so to be solved by producing definitions. Indeed, a major task of philosophy was to define the meanings of words precisely. 'What is x?' became 'What does x mean?' It is clear, then, that if logical positivism is a viable position the consequences for much else in philosophy are disastrous. The whole metaphysical tradition from Plato to Heidegger is called into question.[4] Admittedly, the logical positivists thought that many past philosophers were engaged in genuine logical analysis, but that many too were

engaged in meaningless metaphysics.[5] Logical positivism is a movement of potentially enormous eliminatory power, so I shall say a
little now about its most important exponent.

Alfred Jules Ayer was born in 1910. He was a King's scholar at
Eton, and a classical scholar at Christ Church, Oxford – Locke's
old college. At Oxford he studied under Gilbert Ryle, who was later
to publish the brilliant critique of Cartesian mind–body dualism,
The Concept of Mind (1949). After graduating, Ayer considered going
to Cambridge to study under the influential Austrian philosopher,
Ludwig Wittgenstein.[6] However, Ryle had recognized Ayer's ability
and suggested that instead he should go to Vienna to report back
on the activities of the Vienna Circle, whose anti-metaphysical
philosophy was then little known in England. This Ayer decided to
do.

Ayer arrived in Vienna in 1932, and quickly learnt enough
German to follow the debates of the Vienna Circle. The chairman
of the Vienna Circle was Moritz Schlick, then Professor of the
Philosophy of Science at the University of Vienna. Other prominent
members of the Vienna Circle included Rudolf Carnap (1891–1970),
whose work *Der Logische Aufbau der Welt* had been published in 1928;
the Marxist philosopher and sociologist Otto Neurath (1882–1945);
and Friedrich Waismann (1896–1959), whose specialities were the
philosophies of mathematics and of language. The circle was also
attended by Willard O. Van Quine, the American philosopher and
logician. Quine and Ayer were in Vienna at the same time.

It is sometimes maintained that logical positivism is a conservative movement politically and philosophically, in the history of
ideas. This view is wholly mistaken. In the 1940s and 1950s logical
positivism was a radical movement self-consciously iconoclastic in
its devastation of received philosophical orthodoxy. Central among
its targets were the concepts of God and the soul. Also, as noted,
Neurath was a socialist in his political views and Ayer himself
always remained a liberal humanist, implacably opposed, for
example, to any erosion of freedom of information by the British
state. Finally, the Nazis mercilessly hunted down the logical positivists, and the Vienna Circle had to be abandoned in 1938 in the face
of Hitler's *Anschluss*. It is to be noticed that the phenomenologist

and existentialist Martin Heidegger was happy to co-operate with the Nazis in their dark closure of the freedom of thought. When Schlick was shot to death by one of his students in 1936, the right-wing press in Austria thought this something of a joke – that it was, after all, what one might expect if one taught students logical positivism. The student may not have been a Fascist, but the apologists for totalitarian dictatorship fully appreciated that the logical positivists' claim that knowledge was tentative and provisional was incompatible with their own nationalistic Fascist mysticism.

Ayer took up a lecturing post at Christ Church in 1933, and became a research student in the same college in 1935. He served as an officer in the Welsh Guards at the beginning of the Second World War and was subsequently employed in military intelligence. In 1945 he became Fellow and Dean of Wadham College, Oxford. He was Grote Professor of the Philosophy of Mind and Logic in the University of London from 1946 to 1959, and Wykeham Professor of Logic in the University of Oxford from 1959 to 1978. He was knighted in 1970. Sir Alfred died in 1989, while this chapter was being written.[7]

2 MEANING AND METAPHYSICS

'Metaphysics' may be defined in two ways. It is sometimes thought of as the study of reality as a whole, where it usually means the study of what exists in its essential properties; and it is sometimes thought of as the study of what is as it really is in itself, independently of how it appears to us in experience. Ayer's logical positivism is a repudiation of metaphysics in both senses.

Ayer does not argue that metaphysical sentences are false; rather he seeks to establish that they do not even have the merit of being false. They are meaningless, or devoid of literal significance. Therefore, in Ayer's view, if someone claims that God exists; that there was a first event; that the empirical world is unreal; that what exists is ultimately mental; or if they make any similar metaphysical claim, then they do not make a false assertion. They produce sentences which are utterly nonsensical, notwithstanding their precise grammatical construction.

If Ayer's attack on metaphysics is sound, many of the celebrated philosophical systems of the past are discredited. Plato's theory of forms, Spinoza's view that there is only one substance, Leibniz's view that there are many substances, Hegel's concept of *Geist*, Heidegger's Question of Being and many others must turn out to be so much nonsense.[8] Logical positivism is thus a crucially important movement in modern philosophy, because its potential eliminatory power is so great. We should examine next Ayer's grounds for maintaining that metaphysics is meaningless.

Ayer argues that there are two, and only two, classes of meaningful statement. On the one hand there are sentences which may be confirmed or refuted by observation; on the other hand there are sentences whose truth or falsity may be decided by purely intellectual procedures. Into the first category fall the claims of science and the vast multiplicity of commonsensical claims we make in the course of our everyday lives. Into the second category fall the sentences of mathematics and logic, all definitions, and any sentence that is of a formal or self-proving nature. There are thus two, and only two, broad sorts of procedure for confirming and refuting statements: empirical observation and the inspection of meanings. If a sentence's truth or falsity is decidable in one of these two ways, then it is meaningful. If it is not decidable in one of these two ways it is not meaningful. Hence 'Water boils at 100°C' is the sort of claim that counts as meaningful on this criterion because it may be confirmed or refuted by observation. '2 + 2 = 4' and 'A square has four sides' also count as meaningful because they may be decided purely intellectually, by inspecting the meanings of their constituent terms. 'God exists' or 'The Absolute exists' do not count as meaningful because they are not decidable by observation, nor are they decidable by any formal system or analysis of terms.

Ayer expresses this position in a traditional philosophical terminology which I shall now explain. The indicative sentences of science and commonsense express propositions – that is, they are genuinely capable of truth or falsity. They are *a posteriori* or empirical sentences, meaning that the propositions they express may be confirmed or refuted by observation. They are also contingent, meaning that if they are true they could in principle have been false and if they are false they could in principle have been true. If something is contingently the case, then it is the case but it could possibly have not been the case. Finally, the sentences of science and commonsense are synthetic, because if true they are not true by definition but are empirically informative.

The sentences of logic and mathematics also express propositions, because they too are genuinely capable of truth or falsity. They are *a priori* sentences, meaning that the propositions they express may be confirmed or refuted independently of observation. They are necessary rather than contingent, meaning that if true they are not only true but could not have been false, and if false they are not only false but could not have been true. If something is necessarily the case, then it is not only the case but could not possibly have not been the case. Finally, the sentences of logic and mathematics are analytic or tautologous, because if true they are true by definition or in virtue of the meanings of their constituent terms and so are not empirically informative.

The two classes of meaningful statement are mutually exclusive and collectively exhaustive. Every meaningful statement is either *a posteriori*, contingent and synthetic, or *a priori*, necessary and analytic, but not both. Either some observation is relevant to deciding the statement's truth or falsity, or some inspection of meanings is relevant, but not both.

If a sentence falls into one of these two categories then it logically follows that that sentence is literally meaningful. If a sentence does not fall into one of those two categories, it logically follows that that sentence is literally meaningless. Thus verifiability by one or other of these two procedures is both logically necessary and sufficient for meaningfulness.

Devastatingly, metaphysical sentences fall into neither category. Claims about a putative reality transcending our experience, or reality as a whole, cannot be confirmed or refuted by observation. Nor, on the other hand, are they definitions or logical truths. It follows that they are literally nonsensical. As Ayer puts it, 'As tautologies and empirical hypotheses form the entire class of significant propositions, we are justified in concluding that all metaphysical assertions are nonsensical' (LTL 56). Notice that once again

Ayer is not claiming that they are false but that they are meaningless.[9]

Why does Ayer speak of empirical hypotheses? He thinks that no empirical claim may be absolutely certain because no sentence may be conclusively confirmed or refuted by observation. Although for practical purposes we count many empirical claims as certain, it is logically possible that any empirical claim we hold to be true may be false, and any we hold to be false may be true. Only analytic propositions, or tautologies, are conclusively verifiable because they are true by definition. An empirical claim has only a probability (less than one) of being true, even if this probability is very high. Ayer makes a distinction between strong and weak verifiability to accommodate this fact. If a proposition is weakly verifiable, observation makes its truth probable. If a proposition is strongly verifiable, analysis makes its truth certain. Either weak or strong verifiability is sufficient for meaningfulness.

Ayer also makes a distinction between verifiability in principle and in practice. Clearly, if someone says there are mountains on the far side of a distant planet, we may lack the practical means to verify or falsify that proposition. The proposition is still meaningful, however, because it is verifiable in principle. We may imagine without contradiction empirical procedures which would confirm or refute it. 'Verifiable' need not mean 'verifiable by us now', so propositions about remote regions of time and space are meaningful because some observer could in principle confirm or refute them. In this way Ayer protects the claims of historians about the past, or the wide empirical generalizations of the natural scientists, from the eliminatory power of his criterion.

Ayer calls his criterion for meaningfulness 'the verification principle' because it is the thesis that 'a sentence [has] literal meaning if and only if the proposition it expresses [is] either analytic or empirically verifiable' (LTL 7).[10]

Claims about God, about Being, about the Absolute and so on have no literal significance. They are at best of some emotional comfort to those who utter them, but they cannot be used to assert or deny anything of what is. Metaphysics is meaningless.[11]

3 PHILOSOPHICAL ANALYSIS

If philosophy is not metaphysics, what is it? Philosophy still has a critical role in demonstrating the meaninglessness of metaphysical sentences and in rewriting philosophical problems so that they may be solved scientifically. If a problem is not amenable to this treatment, and cannot be resolved by analysis either, it is not a genuine problem at all but a pseudo-problem; a piece of nonsense.

It is no part of philosophy's role to compete with the natural sciences. It is science's function to tell us what the world is like and philosophy's to clear conceptual obstacles from the path of science's progress. Ayer has enormous confidence in the explanatory power of the natural sciences:

> There is no field of experience which cannot, in principle, be brought under some form of scientific law, and no type of speculative knowledge about the world which it is, in principle, beyond the power of science to give. (LTL 64)

It is no part of philosophy's function to discover facts about the universe. Philosophy's function is critical for Ayer, and it is concerned not with the world but with the language we use to describe the world. Thus philosophy differs radically from any of the special sciences. It deals with the language we use to make the world intelligible, not with the world itself. This point is sometimes made by saying that philosophy is a second order subject, not a first order subject. For Ayer, philosophy is, in fact, a part of logic:

> The propositions of philosophy are not factual, but linguistic in character – that is, they do not describe the behaviour of physical, or even mental, objects; they express definitions, or the formal consequences of definitions. Accordingly we may say that philosophy is a department of logic. (LTL 76)

Thus the role of philosophy is not to generate empirical truths about, say, physical objects, but to define 'physical object'; or, to put it another way, to analyse the concept of a physical object. Similarly, philosophy does not discover causes and effects but states the logically necessary and sufficient conditions for the truth of sentences of the form '*A* causes *B*'. In other words, it analyses the concept of causation. Philosophy analyses the concepts of science and commonsense, so that our thinking about the world gains precision and is shorn of metaphysical illusions. Instead of asking 'What is *x*?' or 'What is the nature of *x*?', the philosopher should ask 'What is the definition of *x*?' or 'What is the analysis of *x*?' Instead of asking 'What are numbers?', the philosopher asks for an analysis of the concept of number, perhaps in terms of sets.

As Ayer says, it follows from this conception of philosophy that there can be no contradiction between the claims of philosophy and those of science, and 'It follows that philosophy does not in any way compete with science' (LTL 76).

Ayer maintains that many major figures in the history of philosophy anticipated the practice of conceptual analysis in their work. Even though Plato was guilty of generating much metaphysical nonsense he also produced valuable linguistic analyses. Aristotle and Kant were conceptual analysts, but Ayer reserves his greatest approbation for the British empiricists Locke, Berkeley and Hume. Indeed, he quotes with approval Locke's conception of philosophy as the under-labourer for science, clearing obstacles from the path of knowledge.[12]

4 PERCEPTION

A central example of linguistic analysis in action is provided by Ayer's solution to the problem of perception: the question of what the relation is between our sense experiences and the 'external world' of physical objects. Ayer's account also provides an analysis of the concept of a physical object.

Ayer's theory of perception is phenomenalism, the thesis that any sentence or set of sentences about physical objects may be translated without loss of meaning into a sentence or set of sentences about actual or hypothetical sense contents. As Ayer intends it, this is not an answer to the questions 'What is perception?' and 'What is a physical object?', but an analysis of the concepts 'perception' and 'physical object'.

To make sense of phenomenalism we have to understand the idea of a logical construction. *A* is a logical construction out of *B*s if, and only if, *A* is nothing over and above *B*s, or if all meaningful talk

about *A* may be expressed in meaningful talk about *B*s: 'The
English state, for example, is a logical construction out of individual
people' (LTL 85) in the sense that anything said about the English
state could in principle be expressed by a set of (long and complex)
sentences about a set of people. To say that the state is a logical
construction is not to say that it does not exist, or is a fiction, but to
say that 'state' is a shorthand term for a complex of individuals. In
a parallel way, 'physical object' is a shorthand term for a complex
of sense contents. This is not a factual, empirical, claim but 'a
linguistic assertion to the effect that the symbol "table" is definable
in terms of certain symbols which stand for sense contents'
(LTL 85). To say, for example, that a table exists is to say that
certain sense contents of hardness, brownness and squareness are
either actual or possible. Those two ways of speaking are logically
equivalent.

Another way of expressing the same claim is to say that physical
objects may be *reduced* to sense contents. If *A* is a logical construction
out of *B*s, then *A* may be reduced to *B*s. As Ayer puts it: ' "I am
now sitting in front of a table" can, in principle, be translated into
a sentence which does not mention tables, but only sense contents'
(LTL 86).

A physical object does not have sense contents as its parts. What
the parts of a physical object are is not a philosophical but an
empirical or scientific matter. Rather, the mentioning of sense
contents is necessarily required in saying what it is for something to
be a physical object. It is in this definitional sense that we must
understand Ayer's thesis that 'a material thing is constituted by
both actual and possible sense contents' (LTL 88).

The phenomenalist language has to contain both categorial and
hypothetical statements because it does not follow from any single
set of categorial statements about sense contents that a physical
object exists. However, to say that certain sense contents are
possible, even though not actual, allows translation into the sense
datum language of sentences about absent physical objects and the
unperceived properties of present physical objects. To say that a
physical object exists but is not present to perception, or to say that
a present perception is of a physical object, is to say that certain
sense contents are possible.[13]

5 CAUSATION

Typically, Ayer's approach to the problem of causation is not to ask 'What sorts of things are causes?' but 'What is it that we are asserting when we assert that one event is causally connected with another?' (LTL 73). His answer falls centrally within the empiricist tradition.

Ayer accepts much of Hume's account of causation.[14] For example, Ayer thinks Hume was correct to assert that no causal connections are necessary because the sentences reporting them are not necessary truths, and that in turn is because no negation of any causal statement is or entails a contradiction, even if it is false. He also agrees with Hume that knowledge of causal relations is *a posteriori*, not *a priori*, and that sentences expressing natural laws are not analytic but synthetic. It follows that Ayer's account of causation is essentially Humean, and we should think of Ayer as developing Hume's theory.

Ayer improves on Hume in two respects. Ayer's account of causation is less psychological than Hume's, so that causal relations may be safely asserted to hold between events which never have been, and may never be, observed. Though perhaps not impossible for Hume to maintain, this position would have been difficult because for him the idea of causal necessity is acquired from the impression of expectation habitually developed from the observation of constantly conjoined events. For Ayer, even though the observed constant conjunction of two events is excellent evidence for a causal relation between them, 'there is no self-contradiction involved in asserting the proposition "C is the cause of E" and at the same time denying that any events like C or E ever have been observed' (LTL 74).

The other improvement on Hume is the thesis that the making of a specific causal claim 'C causes E' is the invocation of a natural law that 'Cs cause Es', so that the sentences reporting particular causal connections are logically derivable from sentences expressing natural laws.

6 INDUCTION

The problem of induction is a pseudo-problem for Ayer because there is no possible method of solving it. No amount of empirical observation or inspection of meanings will resolve the putative sceptical issue, so 'it is a fictitious problem, since all genuine problems are at least theoretically capable of being solved' (LTL 67). It follows that the problem of induction is not a problem for the logic of the natural sciences because induction is not a problem at all.

Ayer describes the apparent problem of induction as that of proving that empirical generalizations about past experience will hold for the future. This is in fact a limited statement of the issue, because the problem of induction also includes the question of the rationality of non-deductive inferences from present to past and from some to many at least. If we assume the problem is genuine, according to Ayer, there are two, and only two, ways of trying to solve it. A claim about the future may putatively be derived from some formal, *a priori* claim or from some *a posteriori*, empirical claim, but neither of these is satisfactory. Ayer's view is that all true *a priori* propositions are tautologies, but no empirical claim may be derived from a tautology, therefore no claim about the future may be derived from a tautology, so no claim about the future may be derived from any *a priori* proposition. Nor, on the other hand, may a claim about the future be derived from empirical propositions about the past, on pain of circularity, because then 'one simply assumes what one is setting out to prove' (LTL 66). Ayer means that induction is at work in any such derivation but the justification of inductive inference is precisely what is at issue. If we assume, for example, the uniformity of nature, that begs the question because it is itself an inductive principle.

It follows from Ayer's premises that 'there is no possible way of solving the problem of induction' (LTL 67). Both the *a priori* and the *a posteriori* attempts at solution have failed, but as any meaningful statement is either *a priori* or *a posteriori* there remains no meaningful solution to the problem.

Ayer believes we should have confidence in induction as a practical principle and that this is all that is necessary for the conduct of science. It does not deductively follow from the past explanatory success of science that science will continue to be successful in the future, but it is wrong to hold this as an objection to scientific method because 'it is a mistake to demand a guarantee where it is logically impossible to obtain one' (LTL 67).

Nor does it follow from the fact that the problem of induction cannot be solved that it is irrational to suppose that the future will resemble the past. It follows, rather, that the problem of induction is a pseudo-problem. It is rational to believe scientific predictions because part of what it is to be rational is to be guided by the past: 'being rational entails being guided in a particular fashion by past experience' (LTL 67).

Scientific method is justified in practice and by experience, not by philosophy. Scientific prediction, for example, is justified in so far as scientific predictions turn out to be true, and no more than this. It is not the role of philosophy to construct *a priori* justifications of scientific method but to remove from its path pseudo-problems of which the problem of induction is one.[15]

7 MIND AND BODY

Ayer rejects the traditional positions in the philosophy of mind – dualism, idealism and materialism – as solutions to a pseudo-problem. His own thesis is that the distinction between mental and physical is a distinction between two kinds of logical construction out of sense contents; a view which approximates in its essentials to Russell's 'neutral monism' (see pp. 211–13 above).

As we have seen, for Ayer 'the existence of a material thing is defined in terms of the actual and possible occurrence of sense contents which constitute it as a logical construction' (LTL 162). The existence of mental items is equally to be analysed in terms of sense contents, such that something is mental if constructed out of introspective sense contents rather than out of sense contents which are parts of experience through the five senses. It follows that Ayer makes an epistemological distinction between mental and physical. We know about mental items through introspection, but we know about physical objects through sense perception. But these two modes of access are constitutive of the distinction, not just ways in which we become acquainted with items already distinguished. Ayer also says that mental items are constructed out of sense contents 'which are elements of one's own body' (LTL 163), but this cannot be criterial of 'mental' because one's body may have both mental and physical characteristics.

If we ask whether sense contents are mental or physical, this question makes no sense for Ayer: 'The answer to the question whether sense contents are mental or physical is that they are neither; or rather, that the distinction between what is mental and what is physical does not apply to sense contents' (LTL 162). This is because the mental–physical distinction only applies to logical constructions out of sense contents, not to the contents themselves, much as what is true of 'the British state' may not be true of each British citizen taken singly, or what is true of 'the average man' may not be true of each man considered individually.

Thus Ayer follows Russell in maintaining that sense contents are intrinsically neither mental nor physical. Depending on the epistemological relation a perceiver stands in with regard to them, and on the relation they have to one another, the constructions out of them are either mental or physical.

There is a complication in this account. A sense content is not an experience for Ayer, yet any sense content is part of some experience. It would seem to follow that sense contents are mental if experiences are mental, but that is not a conclusion Ayer wishes to draw. He does not in fact offer a solution to the problem, but one solution would seem to be that experiences are not intrinsically mental or physical but count as either mental or physical depending on whether their sense-content parts are accessible introspectively or through sense perception.

From Ayer's account it follows that the universe is intrinsically neither mental nor physical. Indeed, the putative claim that it is either is meaningless because it is neither analytic and *a priori* nor synthetic and *a posteriori*. Ayer's empiricism entails an explanation of 'mental' and 'physical' in terms of sense contents which fall under neither designation, so I should say that the most accurate characterization of Ayer's philosophy of mind is 'neutral monism'.

The so-called 'mind–body problem' is the problem of whether, and if so in what sense, mind and matter exist, and of the relation between them. This problem is clearly meaningless by Ayer's criteria. It may, however, be reformulated as a meaningful linguistic question which may be resolved through conceptual analysis: 'there is no philosophical problem concerning the relationship of mind and matter, other than the linguistic problems of defining certain symbols which denote logical constructions in terms of symbols which denote sense contents' (LTL 164).

It follows that there is no meaning in the claim that there are mental or physical substances. That claim is metaphysical and therefore a pseudo-claim, because it is not decidable *a priori* by analysis, nor *a posteriori*, empirically. Our commonsensical talk about mental and physical is empirical and depends upon our acquaintance with sense contents, so our ordinary language mental – physical distinction is meaningful.[16]

8 PERSONAL IDENTITY

If we ask the question 'What is the self?', Ayer's answer is that the self, like mental states and physical objects, is a logical construction out of sense contents. The claim that a self exists is logically equivalent to the claim that a set of relations obtains between certain sense contents. It follows that Ayer has a phenomenalist theory of the self which is, in its essentials, the same as Hume's. Like Hume, Ayer rejects the Cartesian notion of the self as a mental substance.[17] Self-consciousness reveals no such substantial self, but as self-consciousness is the only plausible experiential route to such a putative self the existence of the self cannot be known empirically. There is no empirical knowledge of the Cartesian self or soul, and it is not true by definition or true *a priori* that such a self exists. It follows that, if every meaningful claim is either *a priori* or empirical, the claim that Cartesian selves exist is devoid of literal significance. The claim is meaningless.

Any meaningful notion of the self must be grounded in experience and Ayer's phenomenalist account is designed to do just that.[18] The question 'What is the self?' is the same for Ayer as the question 'What are the conditions under which some experiences belong to one and the same self?' He says:

> To answer this question is that for any two sense-experiences to belong to the sense-history of the same self it is necessary and sufficient that they should contain organic sense contents which are elements of the same body. (LTL 165)

A body, like any physical object, is a logical construction out of sense contents and the criteria for the identity of a body are the same as the criteria for the identification of any physical object.[19]

9 RELIGION

The claim that God exists is not false but meaningless within the conceptual framework of Ayer's verificationism. Ayer's position therefore needs to be distinguished from traditional atheism. Atheism is the view that it is false that God exists; that, however, presupposes it is meaningful to claim that God exists and it is precisely this presupposition that Ayer denies.

The claim that God exists is not analytic and *a priori*, nor is it synthetic and *a posteriori*, but those two classes are mutually exclusive and collectively exhaustive of meaningful statements; thus the claim that God exists is meaningless: 'to say that "God exists" is to make a metaphysical utterance which cannot be either true or false' (LTL 152). It follows from this that there cannot possibly be any religious knowledge because knowledge is of what is the case – of truths – and religious claims are not truths because they are not true or false. They do not express propositions, so they cannot be known. Therefore there is no religious knowledge. It follows that religious talk is not meaningful talk, however emotionally significant it may be to the speaker. Atheism and agnosticism are as meaningless as theism because they depend upon religious language and that language is meaningless. If it is true that 'God exists' is meaningless, then it is true that 'God does not exist' and 'It is possible that God exists' are also meaningless.

If *per impossibile* the concept of God were significant then it would still be the case, according to Ayer, that no proof of God's existence is possible. This is because the claim that God exists would have to be derived either from *a priori* analytic premises or from *a posteriori* synthetic premises, these being the only two meaningful sorts of premise. However, the claim that God exists does not follow from any analytic truth, because only tautologies logically follow from tautologies and the claim that God exists is not a tautology. Nor does the claim that God exists follow from any empirical premise because no transcendent (and so non-empirical) claim follows from any empirical premises, and, in any case, all non-empirical claims that are not tautologies are nonsensical.

If someone were to claim that the truth of a particular set of empirical claims is both necessary and sufficient for the existence of God – for example, some set of claims about causal regularities in the universe – then it would follow that 'God' is being used in an unconventional sense. 'God' would then be a shorthand term for certain regularities in nature. This, Ayer maintains, would not prove God's existence as traditionally conceived: as the transcendent cause of the universe. The traditional concept of God is in any case incoherent: 'the notion of a person whose essential attributes are non-empirical is not an intelligible notion at all' (LTL 154).

It follows that all the claims of theology are senseless. Theology is either the study of God, or the study of human relations with God. On either account, the concept of God is incoherent and putative claims about God's existence or non-existence are literally nonsensical. So, as with the metaphysician, the theist 'says nothing at all about the world', so 'he cannot justly be accused of saying anything false or anything for which he has insufficient grounds' (LTL 153). Theology, like metaphysics, does not even have the merit of being false. It is meaningless.[20]

10 ETHICS

Value judgements may be neither true nor false for Ayer, so they, like metaphysical sentences, are literally senseless. To condemn someone or something morally is not to say anything informative but merely to express an emotion, and perhaps to cause another to have an emotion. For example, 'Stealing money is wrong' is 'a sentence which has no factual meaning – that is, [it] expresses no proposition which can be either true or false' (LTL 142). Ayer is not claiming that stealing is right or wrong – it is not the job of the philosopher to engage in value judgements; he is providing an analysis of what it is to judge something right or wrong. To say something is right is to express a feeling of approval, and to say something is wrong is to express a feeling of disapproval. It follows that if someone thinks something is wrong, say abortion or capital punishment, and someone else thinks that thing is right, then there is no contradiction between those two persons' ethical positions. Contradictions may only obtain between propositions – items capable of truth or falsity – but value judgements are not and do not express propositions. It follows that there can be no contradictions between value judgements. All that follows from moral disagreements between persons is that those persons have different emotional responses to some phenomenon:

> For in saying that a certain type of action is right or wrong, I am not making any factual statement, not even a statement about my own state of mind. I am merely expressing certain moral sentiments. (LTL 142)

Notice that ethical judgements are not to be construed as covertly autobiographical. It is not Ayer's position that in evaluating something ethically one is really making a report on one's emotions. Rather, one is expressing one's emotions, and causing emotions in others. Hence he claims that 'ethical terms do not serve only to express feeling. They are calculated also to arouse feeling, and so to stimulate action' (LTL 143).

Ayer's emotivist theory of ethics has two important consequences. Firstly, value judgements are in a sense relative; they are not truth-valued, so there is no rational way of arbitrating in ethical disputes. If two people disagree ethically there is no fact of the matter about who is right. Secondly, Ayer has the outline of a theory of how ethics function in social contexts that partially anticipates the theory of ethics called 'prescriptivism'. Prescriptivism is the view that value judgements have some of the logical features of commands and, indeed, that they logically entail imperatives. Ayer says that some value judgements have the effect of commands. This is clearly a claim about the causal efficacy of value judgements and not a claim about their logical status. Nevertheless, Ayer has it in common with prescriptivists like Richard Hare to maintain that value judgements are like imperatives. For example: 'The sentence "You ought to tell the truth" . . . involves the command "Tell the truth"' (LTL 143). Clearly, the imperative-like status of some value judgements is consistent with a theory of action which regards such value judgements as action-guiding and as action-causing.

It follows that Ayer's theory of ethics is emotivist but contains prescriptivist elements. Ayer makes a fourfold distinction between the kinds of claim to be found in philosophical writings about ethics. There are definitions of ethical words; descriptions and causal explanations of moral experience; prescriptions, and value judgements. Ayer says that only claims of the first sort count as genuinely philosophical. It is the business of the moral philosopher to analyse concepts like 'good', 'wrong', 'moral' and so on, and to justify these definitions.

It is also the role of the philosopher to separate value judgements from factual statements. It is no part of the philosopher's business to pronounce on ethical issues, to exhort people to virtue, or to produce causal explanations of moral experience. This latter task is an empirical one which belongs to the sciences, perhaps to psychology and sociology. Philosophy is a second-order inquiry into the logic of ethical concepts, not a first-order inquiry into what is right or wrong:

A strictly philosophical treatise on ethics should . . . make no ethical pronouncements. But it should, by giving an analysis of ethical terms, show what is the category to which all such pronouncements belong. (LTL 137)

NOTES

Hobbes

1. For an empirically detailed yet theoretically sophisticated survey of seventeenth-century England which gives due weight to political, socio-economic and intellectual developments, see Christopher Hill, *The Century of Revolution 1603–1714* (Edinburgh, 1961). For intellectual and radical political tendencies in England before and during the Civil War, see the same author's *Intellectual Origins of the English Revolution* (Oxford, 1980), and *The World Turned Upside Down* (London, 1972).

For an acute treatment of Hobbes's political philosophy in its historical context by an outstanding historian of ideas, see Quentin Skinner, 'The Ideological Context of Hobbes' Political Thought', *Historical Journal*, 9 (1966). Historical and intellectual connections between the thought of Hobbes and Locke are well exhibited in J. Bronowski and Bruce Mazlish, *The Western Intellectual Tradition* (Harmondsworth, 1963), Part II, Chapter 11, pp. 227–51. No one seriously concerned with the historical background to seventeenth-century political theory can afford to neglect Quentin Skinner's *The Foundations of Modern Political Thought* (2 vols., Cambridge, 1978), and on method in the history of ideas, see his 'Meaning and Understanding in the History of Ideas', *History and Theory*, 8 (1969).

2. The French mathematician and philosopher René Descartes (1596–1650) thought that there exist two, and only two, kinds of substance: mental substance, called 'mind' or 'spirit', and physical substance, called 'matter'. Hobbes is clearly opposed to this dualism because he thinks that only matter exists. The two best treatments of Descartes's philosophy are Anthony Kenny, *Descartes: A Study of His Philosophy* (New York, 1968) and Bernard Williams, *Descartes: The Project of Pure Inquiry* (Harmondsworth, 1978). By Descartes himself, see his 'Discourse on the Method' and 'Meditations on First Philosophy', in *Descartes: Philosophical Writings*, selected, translated and edited by Elizabeth Anscombe and Peter Geach with an introduction by Alexandre Koyré (London, 1970).

3. For the ideas of the English empirical scientist Francis Bacon (1561–1626), see Anthony Quinton, *Bacon* (Oxford, 1980).

4. For example, Kenneth Minogue in 'Thomas Hobbes and the Philosophy of Absolutism', in David Thomson (ed.), *Political Ideas* (Harmondsworth, 1966), maintains that 'There is no need to seek explanations of Hobbes' opinions in contemporary events' (p. 54) on just those grounds.

For a clear-minded introduction to Hobbes's political theory in its historical context, see Richard Tuck, 'Thomas Hobbes: The Sceptical State', in Brian Redhead (ed.), *Political Thought from Plato to Nato* (London, 1984); also Tuck's *Hobbes* (Oxford, 1989).

5. Here I endorse S. H. Steinberg's theory of seventeenth-century conflict in *The 'Thirty Years War' and the Conflict for European Hegemony, 1600–1660* (London, 1971) and reject that implicit in C. V. Wedgwood, *The Thirty Years War* (London, 1968).

6. See Immanuel Kant, *Critique of Pure Reason*, translated by Norman Kemp-Smith (London, 1978). For an introduction to Kant's philosophy, see Roger Scruton, *Kant* (Oxford, 1982). For philosophy's Kantian nature since Kant's death, see Stephen Priest, *The Critical Turn: Modern Philosophy's Kantian Assumptions* (forthcoming).

7. In the thesis that every problem may in principle be solved using the methods of the natural sciences, and in the logically related thesis of the unity of science, Hobbes shares the positivism of the twentieth-century logical positivists. The classic exposition of logical positivism is A. J. Ayer's *Language, Truth and Logic* (2nd ed., Harmondsworth, 1976). Hobbes and the logical positivists also chastise the metaphysical, and hence in their view, meaningless use of language in philosophy. Ayer recognizes the logical consistency of his own radical empiricism and linguistic analysis with these tendencies in Hobbes's thought. For Ayer on Hobbes, see *Language, Truth and Logic*, p. 74. For Ayer, see the chapter 'Ayer' in the present work.

8. I do not have conclusive empirical proof for my historical claim that it was the French experience which motivated Hobbes's political theory. However, early seventeenth-century France enjoyed only a precarious political and social stability, and it seems grossly improbable that such an acute political observer and sensitive personality as Hobbes should not be both apprised of and deeply worried by the possibility of imminent anarchic civil war. War, including civil war, was endemic in seventeenth-century Europe. Indeed, it seems to me that Steinberg's sophisticated analysis of war in that period is more than consistent with Hobbes's thesis that war is a disposition to battle. Hobbes's analysis of conflict is just what one would expect from an intelligent seventeenth-century theorist who feared anarchy

and war and wished to prevent it. See Steinberg, op. cit., especially Chapter 1, 'Background and Problems'. See also Hobbes, *Leviathan*, p. 185).

9. On the life and works of the Italian scientist and mathematician Galileo Galilei (1564–1642), see Stillman Drake, *Galileo* (Oxford, 1980) and Alexandre Koyré, *Galileo Studies* (Sussex, 1978). By the time of Hobbes's visit to Italy in 1610 Galileo had published *Dialogo della Stella Nuova* (Padua, 1605) and *Le Operazioni del Compasso* (Padua, 1606), and in that very year Galileo published his *Sidereus Nuncius* (Venice, 1610). All these have been translated by Stillman Drake; see, respectively, Drake's *Galileo Against the Philosophers* (Los Angeles, 1976), *Operations of the Geometric and Military Compass* (Washington, 1978) and *Discoveries and Opinions of Galileo* (New York, 1957). I cannot claim with certainty that Hobbes read these works, but it is certain that intellectual circles in the north-Italian states were alive to their contents, and these were the circles in which Hobbes moved.

10. See Johannes Kepler, *Gesammelte Werke* (Munich, 1938). The astronomy of the German mathematician-scientist was current in Italy during the time of Hobbes's visit, and was a source of much controversy. On Kepler's astronomy, see A. Koyré, '*L'Oeuvre astronomique de Kepler*', in *XVIIe Siècle* (Bulletin de la Société d'Étude du XVIIe Siècle, no. 30, Paris, 1956), pp. 69–109. 'Circles Vanish from Astronomy', Chapter 9 in Marie Boas, *The Scientific Renaissance 1450–1630* (London, 1970), is largely devoted to Kepler.

11. The enormity of undertaking a historical charting of Aristotle's influence is well appreciated by Jonathan Barnes when he says, 'An account of Aristotle's intellectual afterlife would be little less than a history of European thought' (Jonathan Barnes, *Aristotle* (Oxford, 1982)). My own view is that the history of Western thought could be rewritten as a dialogue between Plato and Aristotle. Despite Hobbes's repudiation of neo-Aristotelianism, more Aristotelian than Platonic tenets would be apparent in British empiricism in this large picture. Clearly, I cannot locate British empiricism in the whole of Western thought in the present work.

For Aristotle, see Barnes, op. cit.; J. L. Ackrill, *Aristotle the Philosopher* (Oxford, 1981); and the four volumes edited by J. Barnes, M. Schofield and R. Sorabji, *Articles on Aristotle* (London, 1975–9). Barnes has a brief but pointed final chapter, 'Afterlife', in Barnes, op. cit., pp. 85–8. Ackrill has edited a number of translations of Aristotle's works for the Clarendon Aristotle series. These are recommended for Greekless philosophers.

12. On Bacon, see Quinton, op. cit., and H. C. Dick, *Selected Writings of Francis Bacon* (New York, 1955).

13. Most of what is generally believed about Hobbes's life is gleaned from Aubrey's *Brief Lives* (many editions). I know of no historical work which systematically checks Aubrey's accuracy as a biographer of Hobbes.

14. Thucydides (460–400 B.C.), the Athenian general and political commentator, was in a sense the first empirical historian because he tried to replace myth and hearsay with meticulous reporting of events and their causes. Thucydides also witnessed many of the events he described, so there is a clear sense in which his history is grounded in experience. There is no reason to suppose this empiricism would have appealed to Hobbes any less than Thucydides' fear of political instability. See Thucydides, *The Peloponnesian War*, translated by R. Warner with an introduction and notes by M. I. Finley (Harmondsworth, 1972).

15. Hobbes was by no means alone in adopting a 'geometrical' method. It was a part of Cartesianism and so a growing seventeenth-century philosophical orthodoxy. Notably, the Dutch philosopher Benedictus Spinoza (1632–77) derived his monist ontology from quasi-geometrical axioms using putatively logical deductions. The Latin title of his major work, *Ethics*, is *Ethica Ordine Geometrico Demonstrata* ('Ethics Demonstrated in Geometrical Order', or, perhaps, 'Ethics demonstrated in the Geometrical Manner'). The sub-title is frequently omitted from English translations. See, for example, Spinoza, *Ethics*, translated by A. Boyle with an introduction by George Santayana (London, 1948).

16. Marin Mersenne (1588–1648) had published his *La Vérité des Sciences Contre les Sceptiques* in 1625, and Pierre Gassendi (1592–1655) had argued for a break with Aristotle in his *Exercitationes Paradoxicae Adversus Aristotelicos* (1624). Both philosophers are best known in English-speaking circles as the authors of *Objections to Descartes*. They seem to me worthy of philosophical study in their own right.

17. On the search for a settlement during the Interregnum, see Ivan Roots, *The Great Rebellion 1642–1660* (London, 1971), Part 3, pp. 137–280. Intellectual influences are notoriously difficult historical connections to trace because the empirical evidence that A read or listened to B and was thereby motivated to do *x* is often lost, as is the evidence for intermediaries in the causal chain. Affinities are easier to establish. Hobbes's prescriptions for political stability are likely to have found an attentive audience amongst those who did not regard them as subversive. Roots finds at least one affinity between the views of Hobbes and Cromwell which is symptomatic of wider political motivations: '. . . duelling was forbidden. Like Richelieu and Hobbes, Cromwell looked at it through unromantic spectacles, making it out a form of private warfare – a mocking contempt of the right of the organized State to settle by the forms of law disputes between subject and subject' (Roots, op. cit., p. 174).

18. For three important and distinct versions of materialism, see U. T. Place, 'Is Consciousness a Brain Process?', in Clive Borst (ed.), *The Mind/*

Brain Identity Theory (London, 1979); David Armstrong, *A Materialist Theory of the Mind* (London, 1968); and Colin McGinn, 'Philosophical Materialism', *Synthese*, 44 (1980). For a materialist account of the mental by a neuroscientist, see Jean-Pierre Changeux, *Neuronal Man: The Biology of the Mind* (Oxford, 1986). Edgar Wilson sees in Hobbes's materialism a partial anticipation of his own version of the mind–brain identity theory. See Edgar Wilson, *The Mental as Physical* (London, 1979), pp. 30, 39, 47.

19. On mental representation, see the papers collected by Andrew Woodfield in *Thought and Object, Essays on Intentionality* (Oxford, 1982), and 'Mental Representation' by Hartry Field, in N. Block (ed.), *Readings in Philosophy of Psychology* (London, 1981), vol. 2, pp. 78–114.

20. For this distinction as pursued by Locke, see the chapter 'Locke' in the present work, sections 3 and 4.

21. As part of his quest for epistemological foundations, Descartes entertains the sceptical logical possibility that the whole of one's experience could be a dream: 'Well, suppose I am dreaming, and these particulars, that I open my eyes, shake my head, put out my hand, are incorrect, suppose even that I have no such hand, no such body' (Descartes, op. cit., pp. 62–3). Norman Malcolm argues that Descartes's attempt to escape his own scepticism is unsatisfactory, in 'Dreaming and Scepticism', *Philosophical Review*, LXV, 1 (January 1956), pp. 14–37; but see A. J. Ayer, 'Professor Malcolm on Dreams', *Journal of Philosophy*, LVII, 16 (August 1960). Malcolm replied in 'Professor Ayer on Dreaming', *Journal of Philosophy*, LVIII, 11 (May 1961), pp. 294–7, and Ayer responded in turn in 'Rejoinder to Professor Malcolm' in the same issue, pp. 297–9. Tom Sorell argues that Hobbes's attempts to draw a clear distinction between memory, imagination and dreaming is vitiated by his using as a model differences he has drawn between the senses (Tom Sorell, *Hobbes* (London, 1986), p. 84). It does not logically follow from Sorell's account that Hobbes's argument for a distinction between dreams and sense experience fails.

22. For reservations about the thesis that the mental could turn out to be nothing over and above the physical, see Tom Nagel's 'Panpsychism' in his *Mortal Questions* (Cambridge, 1980). Nagel writes: 'No properties of the organism or its constituents discovered solely by physics will be the familiar mental properties with their conscious or preconscious aspects, nor will they be the more basic proto-mental properties that imply these; for it will never be legitimate to infer, as a theoretical explanation of physical phenomena alone, a property that includes or implies the consciousness of its subject' (p. 183). I would put the problem for Hobbes in this way: from no true physical description of the world can we logically derive any true mental description of the world, and from no true mental description of the

world can we logically derive any true physical description of the world. ('Physical' here means 'only physical' and 'mental', 'only mental'.) Nagel is right, Hobbes is wrong, and the mind–body problem has not been solved.

23. Hobbes's thesis that propositional thought is necessarily linguistic anticipates similar claims by Kant and Frege. Kant says 'we can reduce all acts of the understanding to judgements' and 'thought is knowledge by means of concepts', but 'concepts' are 'predicates of possible judgements' (Kant, op. cit., p. 106). Frege says, 'What is improperly called the truth of pictures and ideas is reduced to the truth of sentences' (Gottlob Frege, 'The Thought: A Logical Inquiry', translated by A. M. and Marcelle Quinton, in P. F. Strawson (ed.), *Philosophical Logic* (Oxford, 1967), p. 19). If we agree with Hobbes, Kant and Frege, then a problem arises about whether and in what sense a non-human or non-linguistic animal may think something is or is not the case. On this topic, see Jonathan Bennett, *Rationality: An Essay Towards Analysis* (London, 1964), and Colin McGinn, *The Character of Mind* (Oxford, 1982), especially pp. 59ff.

24. I have in mind here the claim made by Ayer and the logical positivists that metaphysical language is meaningless (see the chapter 'Ayer' in the present work).

25. Within Hobbes's philosophy of language every meaningful name names something physical, and, paradigmatically, something with which we may be acquainted empirically. 'God' is construed as the name of a physical but not empirical object. There is here a partial anticipation of the theory of Moritz Schlick, the chairman of the Vienna Circle, that linguistic definition depends on ostensive definition, so all meaning is ultimately empirical. See his 'Meaning and Verification', in H. Feigl and W. Sellars (eds.), *Readings in Philosophical Analysis* (New York, 1949), especially p. 148. For the Vienna Circle, see the chapter 'Ayer', section 1, in the present work.

26. Renford Bambrough argues that Wittgenstein solved the problem of universals in a way that overcomes the shortcomings of Hobbes's account in 'Universals and Family Resemblances', *Proceedings of the Aristotelian Society*, LXI (1960–61), pp. 207–22, reprinted in George Pitcher (ed.), *Wittgenstein: The Philosophical Investigations* (London, 1970), pp. 186–204. For a materialist theory of universals, see David Armstrong, *Universals and Scientific Realism* (2 vols., Cambridge, 1978).

27. Therefore I cannot agree with Richard Peters when he writes: 'In Hobbes' view every man has his own private world of phantasms and words stand for these phantasms of things, not for the things themselves' (Richard Peters, *Hobbes* (Harmondsworth, 1956), p. 123). Hobbes has a materialist theory of meaning in which language paradigmatically refers to

mind-independent physical objects, and our psychological concepts depend on this material meaning. Peters reverses the Hobbesian order of logical priorities.

28. So Hobbes's theory of meaning is not only materialist but radically empiricist. Compare Schlick: 'There is no way of understanding any meaning without ultimate reference to ostensive definitions, and this means, in an obvious sense, reference to "experience" or "possibility of verification"' (Schlick, in Feigl and Sellars, op. cit., p. 148).

29. Hobbes would thus have sympathized with Frege's claim that 'one might come to believe that logic deals with the mental process of thinking and the psychological laws in accordance with which it takes place. This would be a misunderstanding of the task of logic' (Frege, in Strawson, op. cit., p. 17). For Russell, see the chapter 'Russell' in the present work, especially sections 7 and 8, below.

30. For a practical introduction to notions of validity and soundness in argument, see Peter Geach, *Reason and Argument* (Oxford, 1976).

31. Kant argues that the non-empirical and putatively metaphysical use of reason generates contradictions, but if a putative claim is in fact contradictory that is a sufficient condition of that claim's meaninglessness. Hobbes and Kant therefore have it in common that metaphysical uses of language are meaningless. See Kant, op. cit., especially pp. 384ff.

32. Hobbes therefore has a holistic and accumulative, rather than a historically relativistic or falsificationist, concept of science. For historical relativism, see T. S. Kuhn, *The Structure of Scientific Revolutions* (Chicago, 1970), and, more radically, Paul Feyerabend, *Against Method* (London, 1975). For falsificationism, see Karl Popper, *The Logic of Scientific Discovery* (London, 1968). Kuhn and Feyerabend underestimate the accumulative nature of scientific knowledge in a way that Hobbes does not.

33. Hobbes has no notion of the 'theory ladenness' of scientific observation. The underestimation of the roles of preconception and selectiveness in scientific method is a constant in empiricist theories of science. See, for example, Arthur Pap, *An Introduction to the Philosophy of Science* (London, 1963). Also Hobbes shares Pap's positivist view that science and philosophy are continuous (see Pap, op. cit., pp. 3–4).

34. It is possible that Hobbes's concept of the will initiates a peculiarly modern concern with the moral and political status of the individual. Timothy O'Hagan claims that 'Just as modern epistemology is inaugurated by the Cartesian cogito, so modern moral and political theory is inaugurated by the Hobbesian conception of the individual human being's "endeavour", transformed by deliberation into his will, as the source of all social

practice' (Timothy O'Hagan, 'On Hegel's Critique of Kant's Moral and Political Philosophy', in Stephen Priest (ed.), *Hegel's Critique of Kant* (Oxford, 1987), p. 135). Williams allocates to Hobbes an equally important historical role, but for a different reason: '[The] naturalistic conception of society, expressed by Hobbes and Spinoza at the beginning of the modern world, represents one of the ways in which the world has become "entzaubert", in Max Weber's famous phrase: the magic has gone from it' (Bernard Williams, *Ethics and the Limits of Philosophy* (London, 1985), p. 165).

35. For Descartes's view that non-human animals are mindless complex physical objects in motion, see *Discourse on the Method*, Part 5, in Anscombe and Geach, op. cit. For arguments against Descartes on animals, see Mary Midgeley, *Animals and Why They Matter: A journey around the species barrier* (Harmondsworth, 1983), especially pp. 11ff.

36. Hobbes's theory of the emotions is less vulnerable than those of Descartes and Hume to the criticisms adduced by Anthony Kenny in his *Action, Emotion, and Will* (London, 1963). For example, love and hate are essentially not merely causally related to their intentional objects for Hobbes.

37. For Marx on God, see Lucio Colletti (ed.), *Marx: Early Writings* (Harmondsworth, 1974), pp. 70, 99, 224, 245, 260–61, 324, 357, 395–6. Marx's atheism was heavily influenced by Feuerbach's. Feuerbach published *Das Wesen Christentums* in 1841. See Feuerbach, *Philosophical Fragments*, translated by D. F. Swenson (Princeton, 1936), especially pp. 31–5, reprinted in John Hick (ed.), *The Existence of God* (London, 1964), pp. 191–204.

38. Compare Hobbes with Nietzsche, who says: 'In Christianity neither morality nor religion come into contact with reality at any point. Nothing but imaginary causes ("God", "soul", "ego", "spirit", "free will" – or "unfree will"): nothing but imaginary effects ("sin", "redemption", "grace", "punishment", "forgiveness of sins")' (Friedrich Nietzsche, *Twilight of the Idols/The Anti-Christ*, translated by R. J. Hollingdale (Harmondsworth, 1968), p. 125.

39. The opposition I have in mind is between Hobbes's Leviathan and the communist ideal of the withering away of the state. For Marx's materialism, see Colletti, op. cit., pp. 173–5, 381, 389, 421–3.

Maurice Cranston draws interesting parallels between Hobbes's political theory and Sartre's as advocated in *Critique de la Raison Dialectique* (Paris, 1960) in his 'Sartre: Solitary Man in a Hostile Universe', in A. de Crespigny and Kenneth Minogue (eds.), *Contemporary Philosophers* (London, 1976). Cranston writes:

> Sartre is putting forward a doctrine of social covenant which is virtually identical with that of the seventeenth-century English philosopher,

Thomas Hobbes. Sartre then adds to Hobbes's doctrine something which comes directly from one of Hobbes's critics – that is, the theory of scarcity put forward by the eighteenth-century Scotsman David Hume.

Hobbes's word is not 'Violence', it is 'War'; he does not speak of a 'Pledge', but a 'Covenant'; he does not speak of 'Terror', but of a sovereign who keeps peace between men by 'holding them in awe'. The words are slightly different, but the theory is uncannily the same. Neither Hobbes nor Sartre offers what is, strictly speaking, a social contract theory of the kind one finds in Locke or Rousseau, but both Hobbes and Sartre hold promise-and-force theories. And although Sartre's theory of sovereignty is a little more elaborate, perhaps, than Hobbes's, Sartre says exactly what Hobbes says about fear being the basis of political society and about the sovereign being authorized by the people to do whatever he decides to do, and so giving them back their freedom when he commands them to act as he wills. And just as Hobbes is haunted by fear of political society relapsing into the intolerable condition of the state of nature where no man is safe, Sartre goes on and on about the danger of the group's relapsing into an intolerable condition of seriality. (Cranston, op. cit., p. 224)

40. Hobbes's emotivism is therefore to be distinguished from that of Ayer, for whom value judgements are expressions of, and excitants of, emotion (see the chapter 'Ayer' in the present work, section 10).

41. See W. D. Hudson, *Modern Moral Philosophy* (London, 1970).

42. There is an enormous literature on Hobbes's political theory, and on his idea of the state of nature in particular. See, for example, H. Warrender, *The Political Philosophy of Hobbes* (Oxford, 1957). Warrender's reading of Hobbes is subject to cogent criticism by Tom Nagel in his 'Hobbes' Concept of Obligation', *Philosophical Review*, LXVIII, 1 (January 1959), pp. 68–83, reprinted in Ted Honderich (ed.), *Philosophy Through Its Past* (Harmondsworth, 1984), pp. 100–115. See Honderich's introduction to the debate between Warrender and Nagel (Honderich, op. cit., pp. 97–9). See also D. D. Raphael, *Hobbes: Morals and Politics* (London, 1977); Peters, op. cit., Chapters 7, 8 and 9; Sorell, op. cit., Chapters 8 and 9; and M. Oakeshott, *Hobbes on Civil Association* (Oxford, 1975). For a historical treatment by a historian with the excellent ability imaginatively to reconstruct past mentalities, see Keith Thomas, 'The Social Origins of Hobbes' Political Thought', in K. C. Brown (ed.), *Hobbes Studies* (Oxford, 1965).

Locke

1. The best short introduction to Locke is John Dunn's *Locke* (Oxford, 1984). Dunn covers both political theory and epistemology and places them

in their historical context. See also Dunn's 'John Locke: The Politics of Trust', in Redhead, op. cit., pp. 108–19. The most historically accurate and thoughtful biographical piece on Locke is Peter Laslett's introduction to Locke's *Two Treatises*. See John Locke, *Two Treatises of Government* edited by Peter Laslett (New York, 1963), pp. 15–168. See also Maurice Cranston, *John Locke: A Biography* (London, 1957). For the historical influences which moulded Locke's thinking, see John Dunn's 'Individuality and Clientage in the Formation of Locke's Social Imagination', in R. Brandt (ed.), *John Locke* (Berlin and New York, 1981).

2. For British history during this period, see Christopher Hill, *The Century of Revolution 1603–1714*, op. cit. George Clark's volume of the Oxford History of England, *The Later Stuarts 1660–1714* (Oxford, 1964), is rather dated but useful for an overview of English history from the Restoration to the death of Queen Anne. Clark claims that Locke 'succeeded in making a synthesis of the English thought of that active and creative period' (p. 385), but does not develop this interesting idea.

3. For Shaftesbury's life, see K. H. D. Haley, *The First Earl of Shaftesbury* (Oxford, 1968).

4. 'Preamble to The Declaration of Independence, in Congress, July 4, 1776' in *The United States of America: A Government by the People*, by the United States Information Service (London, 1957), p. 101.

5. Locke's most sustained critic is the German philosopher and mathematician G. W. Leibniz (1646–1716), who wrote his *New Essays Concerning Human Understanding* expressly to refute Locke's empiricism. This work is well translated and edited by Peter Remnant and Jonathan Bennett (Cambridge, 1981). For Leibniz's defence of innate ideas against Locke, see Book I of the *New Essays*. It is important to pit Leibniz against Locke in deciding whether there are any innate ideas, but no good reason to confine the debate to this historical one. See N. Block, 'What is Innateness?'; Jerrold J. Katz, 'Innate Ideas'; Hilary Putnam, 'The "Innateness Hypothesis" and Explanatory Models in Linguistics'; Noam Chomsky, 'Reply to Putnam' and 'On Cognitive Capacity'; J. A. Fodor, T. G. Bever and M. F. Garrett, 'The Specificity of Language Skills'; Hilary Putnam, 'What is Innate and Why'; Noam Chomsky, 'Discussion of Putnam's Comments'; and Hilary Putnam, 'Comments on Chomsky's Reply', all in N. Block, op. cit., Vol. 2.

The refutation of Locke is a logical requirement for two important tendencies in late twentieth-century thought: Chomsky's thesis that there is an innate 'depth grammar' and Fodor's 'language of thought' hypothesis. If Locke's argument that there are no innate ideas is sound, then the central tenet of Chomsky's linguistics and Fodorian cognitive psychology is refuted.

6. Ludwig Wittgenstein, *Philosophical Investigations*, translated by G. E. M. Anscombe (Oxford, 1958), para. 243ff. Saul Kripke maintains that 'the real "private language argument" is to be found in the sections preceding para. 243' ('Wittgenstein on Rules and Private Language: An Elementary Exposition', in I. Block (ed.), *Perspectives on the Philosophy of Wittgenstein* (Oxford, 1981), p. 239). However, Kripke's reading of Wittgenstein is contentious. See Colin McGinn, *Wittgenstein on Meaning* (Oxford, 1984). Kripke and McGinn are – rightly – primarily concerned with trying to solve philosophical problems and secondarily with Wittgensteinian exegesis.

7. See Wittgenstein, op. cit., para. 258ff. However, note McGinn's criticisms of Kripke's ideas on rules and community in McGinn, op. cit., *passim*, especially pp. 190–200.

8. I mean that knowledge of the third-person behavioural criteria for the ascription of a concept, and the ability to use that concept in a rule-governed way, are each singularly necessary but not even jointly sufficient for the possession of that concept if it is psychological. Unless I know what pain is I do not understand 'pain', and I cannot know what pain is unless I know what pain is like – what it is like to feel pain – and this I can learn only from my own case. Wittgenstein fails to recognize the essentially first-person, so in one sense private, component in the meaning of experiential concepts.

9. In what follows we have to bear in mind that Locke uses 'idea' to denote both intellectual and perceptual contents. Jonathan Bennett calls this 'the double use of "idea"' and says: 'His double use of "idea" . . . is not a mere terminological nuisance: it embodies his substantive mistake, shared with Berkeley and Hume and others in the empiricist tradition, of assimilating the sensory far too closely to the intellectual' (Jonathan Bennett, *Locke, Berkeley, Hume: Central Themes* (Oxford, 1977), p. 25). Bennett's view is consistent with that of Kant who also criticized the rationalists for making the opposite assimilation: 'Leibniz intellectualized appearances, just as Locke . . . sensualized all concepts of the understanding' (Kant, op. cit., p. 283).

10. For Locke, the meaning of a word is an idea, so Bennett is clearly right to claim that 'Locke was an empiricist about meanings' (Bennett, op. cit., p. 26).

11. Locke can be understood as addressing two logically related problems: the problem of reconciling the truth of a scientific world-picture with facts about our experience, and the problem of deciding what is mind-independent and what mind-dependent. P. M. S. Hacker argues that 'The scientist's story, properly understood, is not in conflict with our ordinary

descriptions of the world around us, i.e. our ordinary characterizations of things as red or green, solid or gaseous . . .' ('Are Secondary Qualities Relative?' *Mind*, XCV, 378 (April 1986), p. 196). Hacker concludes it is not. For McGinn, secondary qualities and indexical thoughts are jointly constitutive of what he calls 'the subjective view' and this is relative in the sense that it exists only in relation to some conscious perceiver. See Colin McGinn, *The Subjective View* (Oxford, 1983), especially Chapter 7.

12. Jonathan Bennett is right to deny that the claim that a physical object has primary qualities is empirical, and right to say, 'it is a point about the meaning of the word "body", or about the concept of a body or physical thing' (Bennett, op. cit., p. 90).

13. On Locke's representational theory of perception see J. L. Mackie, *Problems from Locke* (Oxford, 1976), Chapter 2, pp. 37ff.

14. Thus the phenomenological content of a visual perception of a red object as red would be called by Locke an 'idea' of red. Even if 'idea' denotes experiential as well as intellectual contents in Locke's theory, there remains the philosophical problem of distinguishing between phenomenological red and our experience of it.

15. If *A* grounds *B*, then *A* makes *B* possible. For example, the molecular structure of wood allows it to burn, and to say that wood may burn is to ascribe a disposition to wood – to say that it is combustible. Clearly, to say that wood is combustible is not identical with saying that wood has a certain molecular structure, even though the truth of the description of the disposition depends on the truth of the description of the ground.

16. Galileo draws the primary/secondary quality distinction in this way: 'I say that whenever I conceive any material or corporeal substance, I immediately feel the need to think of it as bounded, and as having this or that shape; as being large or small in relation to other things, and in some specific place at any given time; as being in motion or at rest; as touching or as not touching some other body and as being one in number, or few, or many'; but he is able to conceive of physical objects lacking the properties of being 'white or red, bitter or sweet, noisy or silent, and of sweet or foul odor', and so concludes: 'Tastes, odors, colours, and so on are no more than mere names so far as the object in which we place them is concerned, and . . . they reside only in consciousness. Hence if the living creature were removed, all these qualities would be wiped away and annihilated' (*Discoveries and Opinions of Galileo*, translated by Stillman Drake (New York, 1957).

See also Robert Boyle, 'The Origin of Forms and Qualities According to the Corpuscular Philosophy', in M. A. Stewart (ed.), *Selected Philosophical Papers of Robert Boyle* (Manchester, 1979), especially pp. 32ff.

17. Examples are legion, but I have in mind the logical behaviourism of Carl Hempel and Gilbert Ryle; the exponents of the mind–brain identity theory, including J. J. C. Smart and David Armstrong; and the North American functionalists and eliminative materialists, including the Churchlands. These, in many ways very different, philosophies have a common project in devising an ontology which excludes the individual conscious subject.

18. See Jonathan Bennett, 'Substance, Reality and Primary Qualities', *American Philosophical Quarterly*, 2 (1965), reprinted in C. B. Martin and David Armstrong (eds.), *Locke and Berkeley* (London, 1969), and Bennett, op. cit., pp. 59ff. See also M. R. Ayers, 'The Ideas of Power and Substance in Locke's Philosophy', *Philosophical Quarterly*, 25 (1975), pp. 1–27.

19. The various schools of twentieth-century philosophy are united in their attack on mental substance but have been reluctant to similarly criticize matter. Metaphysical progress in the twenty-first century may well depend on jettisoning the assumption that the universe is made of matter, material substance, or any kind of 'stuff' at all.

20. See Descartes, op. cit., especially pp. 66ff.

21. Descartes says: '"I am" precisely taken refers only to a conscious being; that is a mind, a soul (animus), an intellect, a reason – words whose meaning I did not previously know. I am a real being, and really exist; but what sort of being? As I said, a conscious being', and, a little later: 'I am not that set of limbs called the human body' (Descartes, op. cit., p. 69).

22. Some of the most cogent thinking in modern philosophy has been concerned with the problems surrounding personal identity. See, for example, Bernard Williams, *Problems of the Self* (Cambridge, 1973); Derek Parfit, *Reasons and Persons* (Oxford, 1984); and Sydney Shoemaker and Richard Swinburne, *Personal Identity* (Oxford, 1984). See also Swinburne's 'Personal Identity', *Proceedings of the Aristotelian Society*, 74 (1973–4), pp. 231–48; Shoemaker's *Self-Knowledge and Self-Identity* (Ithaca, N.Y., 1963); and David Wiggins, *Sameness and Substance* (Oxford, 1980). Wiggins, like Locke, locates his account of personal identity in a discussion of the identity of a variety of sorts of entity.

23. In the case of most mental states, if a person believes they are in a mental state it does not logically follow that they are in that mental state. This is because it is logically possible that a person should be caused to believe they are in a mental state by something other than being in that mental state.

24. Nevertheless, Locke may have adduced some of the conditions for possessing the concept of oneself as enduring over time. See Mackie, op. cit., pp. 176–7.

25. The logical possibility I entertain here is the opposite of that imagined by P. F. Strawson in *Individuals: An Essay in Descriptive Metaphysics* (London, 1959), pp. 90–91. In Strawson's case one subject is contingently related to three bodies at the same time.

26. Clearly, however, 'I was Napoleon' is incoherent unless 'person' is used ambiguously.

27. On the possibility that one is one's brain, see Thomas Nagel, *The View from Nowhere* (Oxford, 1986), pp. 49ff. Shoemaker adduces functionalist arguments to support his materialist theory of personal identity in Shoemaker and Swinburne, op. cit., pp. 92ff.

28. 'Leibniz's Law' states that (x,y) $\{(x=y) \equiv (Fx \equiv Fy)\}$; that is, consider any objects x and y, x is identical with y if, and only if, every property of x is a property of y and every property of y is a property of x. For the concept of identity, see Wiggins, op. cit.

29. See Isaac Newton, 'Absolute Space and Time', in J. J. C. Smart (ed.), *Problems of Space and Time* (London, 1964). Descartes's thesis that there is no empty space is discussed by D. M. Clarke in his *Descartes' Philosophy of Science* (Manchester, 1982), pp. 88–9, 155, and by Kenny, *Descartes*, p. 204.

30. This is argued by Leibniz in 'The Relational Theory of Space and Time' in Smart, op. cit., pp. 89–98.

31. Aristotle's concept of time is examined by G. E. L. Owen in 'Aristotle on Time' and by Richard Sorabji in 'Aristotle on the Instant of Change', both in Barnes, Schofield and Sorabji, op. cit., pp. 140–58, 159–77. Aristotle argues the dependence of time on motion in W. D. Ross (ed.), *Aristotle's Physics* (Oxford, 1936). For modern discussions of space and time, see D. H. Mellor, *Real Time* (Cambridge, 1981), and J. R. Lucas, *Space, Time and Causality* (Oxford, 1984).

32. Mackie (op. cit., pp. 121ff.) is dismissive of Locke's account of numbers. However, it could be that Locke has identified some of the conditions for any capacity to count.

33. Wittgenstein's target in the Private Language Argument is a putative language which could only be understood by one speaker. Clearly, such a putative language could not be used to communicate: 'The individual words of this language are to refer to what can only be known to the person speaking; to his immediate private sensations. So another person cannot understand this language' (Wittgenstein, op. cit., para. 243). A public language is precisely one in which communication is possible, and for Wittgenstein only a public language is meaningful or, to put it another way, language is necessarily public.

34. For Berkeley's criticisms of Locke's theory of abstraction, see section

3 of 'Locke' in the present work. Peter Geach argues that the theory of abstraction is muddled, that there is therefore no such process as abstraction and therefore no concept acquired by abstraction. See Peter Geach, *Mental Acts* (London, 1971), especially pp. 18ff.

35. It is this putative process which Berkeley finds incoherent. See pp. 116–19 above.

36. The tension is between the view that it is possible to specify a subject's mental state without thereby mentioning facts about the subject's environment, and the view that this is impossible because some of those states *qua* those states have environmental objects as intentional objects. See T. Burge, 'Belief *De Re*', *Journal of Philosophy*, LXXV (1977), and 'Individualism and the Mental', Midwest Studies in Philosophy, Vol. IV: *Studies in Metaphysics*, ed. P. A. French, T. E. Uehling and H. K. Wettstein (Minneapolis, 1979); also Woodfield, *Thought and Object* (Oxford, 1982). Locke is ambivalent because he holds that all anyone is directly acquainted with is their own mental state (idea) so it seems logically possible that ideas should persist yet the physical environment change (or not exist). However, ideas are representations causally dependent upon the mind-independent objects they represent. Once we accept that fact it is hard to see that a subject could have just those ideas but not be representing just that environment.

37. See the chapter 'Hume' in the present work, section 6. For Locke on causation, see Bennett, op. cit., pp. 70, 127, 205ff., 260–62, 286, and Mackie, op. cit., pp. 51–4, 62, 64–9. For an examination of what it is for a relation to be causal, see J. L. Mackie, *The Cement of the Universe* (Oxford, 1974).

38. As Hobbes thought. See the chapter 'Hobbes' in the present work, section 8.

39. For Locke's political theory, see John Dunn, *The Political Thought of John Locke* (Cambridge, 1969), and Geraint Parry, *Locke* (London, 1978); also Dunn's *Political Obligation in its Historical Context* (Cambridge, 1980).

40. Peter Laslett thinks the number of references to primitive societies in the *Two Treatises* and the *Essay* are sufficient to make Locke the foremost founder of comparative anthropology. However, Laslett also says, 'he was well aware that the evidence did not demonstrate a "state of nature" of the sort he described in his political theory' (Introduction, *Two Treatises of Government* (New York, 1963), p. 112).

41. The *Two Treatises* may be read as principally directed against Filmer's justification of monarchy by divine right. Filmer had published his *Patriarchia* in 1680. On Filmer's political theory, see J. Daly, *Sir Robert Filmer and English Political Thought* (Toronto, 1979), and G. J. Schochet, *Patriarchalism in Political Thought* (Oxford, 1975).

42. For Marx on surplus value, see G. A. Cohen, *Karl Marx's Theory of History: A Defence* (Oxford, 1978), pp. 82–3, 104, 117–18, 123, 197, 327–8.

43. The influence of Locke is partially traced in John Dunn, 'The Politics of Locke in England and America in the Eighteenth Century', in I. Hont and M. Ignatieff (eds.), *Wealth and Virtue* (Cambridge, 1983). For Locke and the American Revolution, see Bernard Bailyn, *The Ideological Origins of the American Revolution* (Cambridge, Mass., 1976), pp. 8, 22, 27–30, 36, 38, 40–54, 83, 132, 150, 168, 173, 235, 242–3. Bailyn writes: 'Franklin, Adams, Jefferson . . . In pamphlet after pamphlet the American writers cited Locke on natural rights and on the social and governmental contract' (p. 27).

Berkeley

1. The fourth volume of A. C. Fraser's edition of Berkeley's works is largely biographical. Fraser includes much documentary evidence for his account of Berkeley's life, and this is useful for locating Berkeley's thought in its historical context. See A. C. Fraser, *The Works of George Berkeley* (4 vols., Oxford, 1871). Fraser's *Berkeley* (London and Edinburgh, 1903) is largely historical in approach and contains much biographical information. For a brief but excellent recent treatment which locates Berkeley's philosophy in the history of seventeenth- and eighteenth-century ideas, see J. O. Urmson, *Berkeley* (Oxford, 1982), especially pp. 2–11.

2. John Foster is right to claim that 'The existence of God and his relation to us is, arguably, the central theme of Berkeley's theory' in that 'it was as a defence of Christian theism that he offered the theory to his readers' (*The Case for Idealism* (London, 1982), p. 19). Nevertheless, idealism and theism are logically independent because from the fact that only minds and their ideas exist it does not logically follow that God exists, and from the fact that God exists it does not logically follow that only minds and their ideas exist. This is true even though theism and idealism are mutually consistent: the truth of one does not logically preclude the truth of the other.

3. For an introduction to the central positions in the philosophy of mind, see Stephen Priest, *Theories of the Mind* (Penguin Books, forthcoming). The most sophisticated contemporary exponent of idealism is John Foster (see Foster, op. cit.), and modern materialists have yet to come to terms with his claim that 'ultimate contingent reality is wholly non-physical' (p. 5). Foster devotes Chapter 3 to an exposition of Berkeleyan idealism (pp. 17–32).

4. If Berkeley's argument that primary qualities logically depend upon secondary qualities were sound, then that would be a reason for accepting

what McGinn calls the 'ineliminability of the subjective view' (McGinn, op. cit., especially pp. 73–110).

Even if Berkeley misses the mark in so far as his criticisms are directed against Locke on secondary qualities, if cogent they are damaging against Descartes, who writes:

> I observed that nothing at all belonged to the nature or essence of body except that it was a thing with length and breadth and depth, admitting of various shapes and various motions ... and on the other hand that colours, odours, savours and the rest of such things, were merely sensations existing in my thought, and differing no less from bodies than pain differs from the shape and motion of the instrument which inflicts it. (Reply to the Sixth Objection, quoted by Anthony Kenny in *Descartes*, op. cit., p. 204)

Kenny is correct to point out that 'Descartes anticipates Locke's distinction between primary qualities, secondary qualities, and powers' (Kenny, op. cit., p. 204), even though Locke construes secondary qualities as primary quality grounded objective capacities and Descartes does not.

For Berkeley on the primary/secondary quality distinction, see Bennett, op. cit., Chapters 24 and 25; also pp. 71, 89–91, 95, 196ff. On the exegetical problem, see M. D. Wilson, 'Did Berkeley Completely Misunderstand the Basis of the Primary–Secondary Quality Distinction in Locke?', in C. Turbayne (ed.), *Berkeley: Critical and Interpretative Essays* (Manchester, 1982), pp. 108–23.

5. The role of metaphor in philosophical thinking, especially spatial metaphor in metaphysical thinking, has never been systematically explored despite, for example, Gilbert Ryle's chastisement of Descartes in *The Concept of Mind* (London, 1949), Chapter 1.

6. See, for example, Kant, op. cit., pp. 501ff., and that brilliant monumental failure, M. Heidegger's *Being and Time*, translated by J. Macquarrie and Edward Robinson (Oxford, 1973). Hegel has a reason why it is so difficult to say what it consists in to be. He thinks the concept of being is presupposed by all our other concepts, so there just are no concepts more primitive than 'being' to use in its analysis. See Hegel's *Logic*, translated by W. Wallace (Oxford, 1975), especially pp. 123ff., 127.

7. For Berkeley on material substance, see Bennett, op. cit., Chapter 14, and pp. 75–9, 81, 86ff., 117, 124, 129, 139, 213ff., 217ff., 347ff.; also Urmson, op. cit., Chapters 2 and 3; I. C. Tipton, *Berkeley: The Philosophy of Immaterialism* (London, 1974), pp. 41–7, 176–7, 256ff.; C. D. Broad, 'Berkeley's Denial of Material Substance', *Philosophical Review* 63 (1954), reprinted in Armstrong and Martin, op. cit., pp. 255–83; and G. J. Warnock, *Berkeley* (Harmondsworth, 1953), especially Chapter 5.

Karl Popper is one of the few contemporary philosophers to recognize the affinity between Berkeley's idealism and certain tendencies in modern physics. Twenty-one theses common to Berkeley's philosophy and physics since Ernst Mach and Heinrich Herz are listed by Popper in his paper, 'A Note on Berkeley as Precursor of Mach and Einstein', *British Journal for the Philosophy of Science*, 4 (1953), reprinted in Karl Popper, *Conjectures and Refutations* (London, 1974), Chapter 6, pp. 166–74.

8. Locke says, 'leave out of the complex idea . . . that which is peculiar to each, and retain only what is common to them all' (*An Essay Concerning Human Understanding*, III. 3. 8).

9. Berkeley's repudiation of abstraction is consistent with that of Geach, op. cit. For Berkeley on abstraction, see Bennett, op. cit., Chapters 6 and 8, and pp. 22ff., 57, 155, 201, 223; Urmson, op. cit., pp. 23–31; and Warnock, op. cit., pp. 60–69, 71–3, 80–85, 192–4, 232–3.

10. Berkeley's use of the term 'notion' is analysed by Daniel E. Flage in *Berkeley's Doctrine of Notions: A Reconstruction based on his Theory of Meaning* (London, 1987). Geach thinks it possible Berkeley inherited the concept of a notion from St Augustine's 'notiones' (op. cit., p. 108).

11. Bennett argues that Berkeley's postulation of a mental substance is vulnerable to the objections Berkeley brings against Locke's material substance. See Bennett, op. cit., pp. 213ff. See also I. C. Tipton, 'Berkeley's View of Spirit', in W. E. Steinkraus (ed.), *New Studies in Berkeley's Philosophy* (New York, 1966), and Tipton, op. cit., Chapter 7.

12. For Berkeley on God, see Urmson, op. cit., Chapter 5; Bennett, op. cit., Chapters 35–41; and Tipton, op. cit., Chapter 8.

13. Berkeley's position is consistent with that adopted by Alvin Plantinga in *God and Other Minds* (New York, 1967).

14. See note 7 above.

15. See 'Newton' in J. J. C. Smart, op. cit. Berkeley is broadly accurate in his reporting of Newton's position.

16. Newton's follower Samuel Clarke and Leibniz corresponded about the nature of space and time, Clarke advocating the Newtonian absolutist view, Leibniz his own relational view. See H. G. Alexander (ed.), *The Leibniz–Clarke Correspondence* (Manchester, 1984). Alexander adduces criticisms of Berkeley's attack on Newton but accepts that Berkeley's discussion of Newton 'is in some respects more important than that of either Leibniz or Clarke' (op. cit., xli). For Berkeley on space and time, his *De Motu* should be consulted as well as the *Principles*.

17. Despite this, Kant misunderstands Berkeley when he refers to 'the dogmatic idealism of Berkeley' and says, 'He maintains that space, with all the things of which it is the inseparable condition, is something which is in

itself impossible; and he therefore regards the things in space as merely imaginary entities' (op. cit., p. 244).

18. This is argued by W. H. Newton-Smith in 'Space, Time and Space-Time: A Philosopher's View', in Raymond Flood and Michael Lockwood (eds.), *The Nature of Time* (Oxford, 1986).

19. Wittgenstein asks us to give up the attempt to explain what meaning is and notice instead that language has a vast plurality of uses, and that many of these are very different from one another. See Wittgenstein, op. cit., *passim*.

For a clear introduction to Wittgenstein which emphasizes the continuity of his thinking, see Anthony Kenny, *Wittgenstein* (Harmondsworth, 1973).

20. William P. Alston seems to me to assimilate Berkeley's view of meaning too closely to Locke's. See his *Philosophy of Language* (New Jersey, 1964), pp. 63ff. Alston does not see the proto-Wittgensteinian tendencies; nor does Flage (op. cit.).

21. Unless the word denotes a notion.

22. For Berkeley on meaning, see Flage, op. cit., Chapter 3, and Bennett, op. cit., Chapters 5–10.

Hume

1. Descartes, *Second and Sixth Meditations*, in Anscombe and Geach, op. cit., pp. 66–75 and 109–124. *A Treatise of Human Nature*, I, IV, sections V and VI, pp. 232–62. Section V is called 'Of the Immateriality of the Soul' and section VI, 'Of Personal Identity'.

2. For Hume's biography, see Ernest Campbell Mossner, *The Life of David Hume* (Oxford, 1970). Mossner argues that biography is of philosophical importance in his 'Philosophy and Biography: The Case of David Hume', in V. C. Chappell (ed.), *Hume: A Collection of Critical Essays* (London, 1966). In the present work I assume that understanding a philosopher's biography is always and everywhere irrelevant to reading his work as philosophy, and include biographical remarks only for their historical interest.

3. The impressions–ideas distinction is discussed in A. J. Ayer, *Hume* (Oxford, 1980), pp. 17, 25–9, 31–2, 34–6, 51, 54–5, 63, 65; John Passmore, *Hume's Intentions* (London, 1968), pp. 8, 18, 61–2, 67–8, 71, 74–5, 84–96, 98, 100, 117, 129, 158; Barry Stroud, *Hume* (London, 1977), pp. 18–19, 27–33, 70.

4. The problem of understanding the mentality or world-view of a culture that is not our own is a version of the problem of other minds: a social version of the questions whether and how we may understand if and

what persons from other cultures think. See Peter Winch, 'Understanding a Primitive Society', in his *Ethics and Action* (London, 1972), pp. 8–49, and Bernard Williams, 'The Truth in Relativism', in his *Moral Luck* (Cambridge, 1981), pp. 132–43.

5. Ayer, op. cit., pp. 15, 16, 28, 35, 40–46, 50, 54, 57, 61, 95, and Stroud, op. cit., Chapter 5, 'The Continued and Distinct Existence of Bodies', pp. 96–117.

6. For Hume on space and time, see C. D. Broad, 'Hume's Doctrine of Space', *Proceedings of the British Academy*, XLVII (1962), pp. 161–76; Ayer, op. cit., pp. 6, 27, 33, 42–3, 47–8, 61–5; J. R. Lucas, *A Treatise on Time and Space* (London, 1973), especially pp. 27, 29, 193. Hugh Mellor thinks that Hume's problem of induction arises essentially because of a problem about time: future events may be predicted but they cannot be perceived (D. H. Mellor, *Real Time* (Cambridge, 1981), pp. 165–6).

7. There is a close and important anticipation here of the logical positivist's thesis that all and only sentences expressing propositions which are either analytic, *a priori* and necessary, or synthetic, *a posteriori* and contingent, are meaningful. Also, as Ayer points out, 'it is astonishing to find how much of what is thought to be distinctive in modern analytical philosophy was already foreshadowed in Hume's work' (Editorial Foreword to A. H. Basson, *David Hume* (Harmondsworth, 1958), p. 7. See also the chapter 'Ayer' in the present work, section 2.

8. If beliefs are dispositions to behave, then it could be that my disposition to flee in terror is partly constitutive of my belief that a bomb is about to fall where I stand, and not a causal consequence of it. Even if this is right, it cannot answer the question of how I know the difference between my beliefs in particular and my thoughts in general. This is because I must already be in a position to make this distinction in order to know how to behave appropriately. Beliefs are explained as dispositions to behave by Gilbert Ryle in *The Concept of Mind*, op. cit., Chapter 5, Section (3), especially pp. 133–5. For discussion of the behavioural, functional, cognitive and semantic properties of beliefs, see the papers collected by Radu J. Bogdan in his *Belief: Form, Content, and Function* (Oxford, 1986), and by Andrew Woodfield in *Thought and Object: Essays on Intentionality* (Oxford, 1982). For Hume on belief, see Stroud, op. cit., Chapter 4, 'Belief and the Idea of Necessary Connection: The Positive Phase', especially pp. 69–76, and Anthony Flew, *Hume's Philosophy of Belief* (London, 1961).

9. The idea that a person may be regarded as a generator of beliefs and that we ought to find ways to maximize the number of our true beliefs is developed by David Papineau in an unpublished paper, 'Naturalised Epistemology'.

10. Hume's account of causation is critically discussed by J. L. Mackie in *The Cement of the Universe: A Study of Causation*, op. cit., especially Chapter 1, 'Hume's Account of Causation', pp. 3–28, but see also pp. 54–60, 76–7, 86–91, 118, 121, 132–6, 140, 143, 167, 193–5, 215, 221, 224–5, 229, 234, 287, 295–6; also the debate between J. A. Robinson and T. J. Richards called 'Hume's Two Definitions of "Cause"', in *Philosophical Quarterly*, XII (1962) and XV (1965), reprinted with Robinson's 'Hume's Two Definitions of "Cause" Reconsidered', in Chappell, op. cit. J. R. Lucas's discussion in his *Space, Time and Causality* is informed by both Hume scholarship and philosophy of physics. See especially pp. 28–44 *passim*, 67, 69, 75, 82, 105–7, 157–8, 163, 165, 175–6, 185. Jonathan Bennett devotes Chapters 11 and 12 of *Locke, Berkeley, Hume: Central Themes* (Oxford, 1971) to Hume on causation, as does Stroud, op. cit., Chapters 3 and 4, pp. 42–95. The realist defence of natural necessity by Rom Harré and E. H. Madden in *Causal Powers* (Oxford, 1975) is radically anti-Humean. For other sophisticated alternatives to Hume, see the papers collected by Ernest Sosa in *Causation and Conditionals* (Oxford, 1975).

11. Whether he did or not is of historical but not philosophical interest. However, it is philosophically illuminating to contrast Hume here with Descartes, *Second Meditation*, in Anscombe and Geach, op. cit., and with Leibniz in G. H. R. Parkinson, *Leibniz: Philosophical Writings* (London, 1973), pp. 42–3, 59–60, 80, 90–91, 121–4, 127, 173, 175, 177, 192, 196.

12. Sophisticated recent approaches to personal identity are Derek Parfit, *Reasons and Persons* (Oxford, 1984), Part 3, pp. 199–347; Bernard Williams, *Problems of the Self* (Cambridge, 1973); and Richard Swinburne, 'Personal Identity', *Proceedings of the Aristotelian Society*, 74, pp. 231–48. See also Sidney Shoemaker and Richard Swinburne, *Personal Identity* (Oxford, 1984), and Kathleen V. Wilkes, *Real People: Personal Identity Without Thought Experiments* (Oxford, 1988). On Hume on personal identity, see Stroud, op. cit., Chapter 6, 'The Idea of Personal Identity', pp. 118–40, and Terence Penelhum, 'Hume on Personal Identity', in Chappell, op. cit., pp. 213–39.

13. 'Russell', section 6, and 'Ayer', section 7, in the present work.

14. On competing ontologies in the philosophy of mind, see Stephen Priest, *Theories of the Mind* (Penguin Books, forthcoming). For Hume on minds, see Ayer, op. cit., pp. 16, 25, 27, 39, 51–2, 76.

15. See Stroud, op. cit., pp. 141–54; Ayer, op. cit., pp. 76–8, 88; and Passmore, op. cit., pp. 53–4, 73. On the problem of freedom and determinism, see B. Berofsky (ed.), *Free Will and Determinism* (New York, 1966); Gary Watson (ed.), *Free Will* (Oxford, 1982); and Daniel C. Dennett, *Elbow Room: The Varieties of Free Will Worth Wanting* (Oxford, 1984). However, all

future work on the topic will have to take account of Ted Honderich's monumental and original *A Theory of Determinism: The Mind, Neuroscience, and Life-Hopes* (Oxford, 1988).

16. On the problem of induction, see Richard Swinburne (ed.), *The Justification of Induction* (Oxford, 1974) and the same author's *An Introduction to Confirmation Theory* (London, 1973); Simon Blackburn, *Reason and Prediction* (Cambridge, 1973); and Karl Popper, *Objective Knowledge* (Oxford, 1972). See also the chapter 'Mill', section 4, and 'Russell' section 4, of the present work. The problem of induction, like many other genuine philosophical problems, has not been solved. Hume himself does not use the expression 'problem of induction' but that seems to me philosophically unimportant.

17. See Ayer, op. cit., pp. 26, 29, 30–31, 43–51, and Stroud, op. cit., pp. 34–5, 40, 53, 68–70, 72, 90, 97, 99, 102–4, 108, 112, 114–15, 120–23, 129–30, 196, 226, 228, 234, 247, 261. On what imagination is, see Mary Warnock, *Imagination* (London, 1976). Hume is discussed in Parts I and II of the latter, see especially pp. 35–41.

18. Richard Swinburne defends the rationality of belief in miracles in *The Concept of Miracle* (London, 1971).

19. Richard Swinburne argues that it is more probable than not that God exists in *The Existence of God* (Oxford, 1979). For Hume on God, see Stroud, op. cit., pp. 12, 31–2, 69, 75, 110, 152, 153, 187, and Ayer, op. cit., pp. 16, 21, 79, 93–5.

20. W. D. Hudson (ed.), *The Is/Ought Question* (London, 1969).

21. This is clear in, for example, R. M. Hare, *The Language of Morals* (Oxford, 1952), Chapter 3, pp. 32–55, and the same author's *Practical Inferences* (London, 1971).

22. On Hume's moral philosophy, see D. G. C. Macnabb, *David Hume: His Theory of Knowledge and Morality* (Oxford, 1966); Philippa Foot, 'Hume on Moral Judgement', in David Pears (ed.), *David Hume: A Symposium* (London, 1963); P. S. Ardal, *Passion and Value in Hume's Treatise* (Edinburgh, 1966); Ayer, op. cit., pp. 51, 75, 77, 80–82, 84–6, 89; Stroud, op. cit., Chapter 8, 'Reason, Passion and Morality', pp. 171–92; and Jonathan Harrison, *Hume's Moral Epistemology* (Oxford, 1976).

23. See Jonathan Harrison, *Hume's Theory of Justice* (Oxford, 1981).

Mill

1. The best source for Mill's life is his own celebrated autobiography. See *Autobiography* of John Stuart Mill, with a Foreword by Asa Briggs (New York, 1964). Bertrand Russell assesses Mill's philosophical significance in 'John Stuart Mill', in his *Portraits from Memory* (London, 1951), reprinted in J. B. Schneewind (ed.), *Mill: A Collection of Critical Essays* (London, 1968),

pp. 1–21. (Asa Briggs is also the author of the most satisfactory history of England during the first two-thirds of the nineteenth century: *The Age of Improvement* (London, 1959).) Mill is located in the context of nineteenth-century English Benthamism and utilitarianism by Elie Halévy in *The Growth of Philosophic Radicalism* (London, 1928), and by Leslie Stephen in *The English Utilitarians* (3 vols., London, 1900). See also J. Plamenatz, *The English Utilitarians* (Oxford, 1949), and Basil Willey, *Nineteenth-Century Studies* (London, 1949). An excellent recent treatment is Alan Ryan, *John Stuart Mill* (London, 1975).

2. See 'Hobbes', section 3, in the present work.

3. Mill's theory of causation is discussed by John Mackie in *The Cement of the Universe: A Study of Causation*, op. cit., pp. 25, 30, 56, 60–63, 68–75, 81–6, 90, 117–21, 136, 146–9, 152, 167, 203–7, 234–5, 297–321. See also Robert McRae, 'Phenomenalism and J. S. Mill's Theory of Causation', *Philosophy and Phenomenological Research*, 9 (1948), and J. R. Lucas, *Space, Time and Causality* (Oxford, 1984), Chapter 4, pp. 44–68.

4. Mill's philosophical logic is located in the chronological development of his thought by R. P. Anschutz in 'The Logic of J. S. Mill', *Mind*, 58 (July 1949), reprinted in Schneewind, op. cit., pp. 46–83. See also Oskar A. Kubitz, *The Development of J. S. Mill's System of Logic* (Illinois, 1932).

5. Mill's claim that so-called necessary truths are contingent is implied by his thesis that no claim is in principle immune to revision of truth-value. It seems to me that Mill's position here is at least logically consistent with, and may be logically equivalent to, Quine's pragmatic critique of the analytic–synthetic distinction when he writes:

> . . . it becomes folly to seek a boundary between synthetic statements, which hold contingently on experience, and analytic statements, which hold true come what may. Any statement can be held true come what may if we make drastic enough adjustments elsewhere in the system. Even a statement very close to the periphery can be held true in the face of recalcitrant experience by pleading hallucination or by amending certain statements of the kind called logical laws. Conversely, by the same token, no statement is immune to revision. (W. V. O. Quine, 'Two Dogmas of Empiricism', in *From a Logical Point of View* (New York, 1961), p. 43)

6. For Mill on mathematics, see Karl Britton, 'The Nature of Arithmetic, A Reconsideration of Mill's Views', *Proceedings of the Aristotelian Society*, 48 (1947–8); Reginald Jackson, 'Mill's Treatment of Geometry', in Schneewind, op. cit.; and Karl Britton, *John Stuart Mill* (Harmondsworth, 1953), pp. 130–40.

7. See J. P. Day, 'Mill on Matter', *Philosophy*, 38 (1963), and G. Vesey, 'Sensations of Colour', both in Schneewind, op. cit. Mill's phenomenalism is discussed in Britton, op. cit. (1953), Chapter 6, pp. 186–218.

8. Bentham's systematic presentation of utilitarianism is in his *An Introduction to the Principles of Morals and Legislation* (New York, 1959) which was first published in 1789. The best study of Bentham is Ross Harrison's *Bentham* (London, 1983).

9. It is sometimes argued that rule utilitarianism collapses into act utilitarianism, for example by David Lyons in *The Forms and Limits of Utilitarianism* (Oxford, 1965).

10. On utilitarianism, see Lyons, op. cit. See also M. D. Bayles (ed.), *Contemporary Utilitarianism* (New York, 1968); T. K. Hearn, Jnr (ed.), *Studies in Utilitarianism* (New York, 1971); and Anthony Quinton, *Utilitarian Ethics* (London, 1974). Utilitarianism is defended by J. J. C. Smart and criticized by Bernard Williams in their *Utilitarianism For and Against* (Cambridge, 1978). Williams brings additional criticism in his *Moral Luck*, op. cit., especially Chapter 3, 'Utilitarianism and Moral Self-Indulgence', pp. 40–53. For a historical and philosophical introduction to Bentham, Mill and utilitarianism, see Mary Warnock's Introduction to Mill's *Utilitarianism* (London, 1973), pp. 7–32.

11. On Mill's political theory, see Ryan, op. cit.; J. Gray, *Mill on Liberty: A Defence* (London, 1983); R. J. Halliday, *John Stuart Mill* (London, 1976); C. L. Ten, *Mill on Liberty* (Oxford, 1980); and Sir Isaiah Berlin, 'Two Concepts of Liberty', in Anthony Quinton (ed.), *Political Philosophy* (Oxford, 1977), especially pp. 143–8. 'Two Concepts of Liberty' is also printed in Berlin's *Four Essays on Liberty* (Oxford, 1969). In the final paper of this book, 'John Stuart Mill and the Ends of Life', Berlin presents a liberal defence of human rights and civil liberties, and argues that Mill was the founder of modern liberalism.

Utilitarianism has been the subject of much debate in modern political theory since the publication of John Rawls's massive and brilliant contractarian alternative, *A Theory of Justice* (Oxford, 1972). Utilitarianism is also inconsistent with the highly libertarian political theory of Robert Nozick in *Anarchy, State and Utopia* (Oxford, 1974). The tensions between Rawls, Nozick and utilitarianism are well brought out in Philip Pettit's introduction to contemporary political theory, *Judging Justice* (London, 1980).

Russell

1. The most fruitful source of information about Russell's life are his own autobiographical writings: *The Autobiography of Bertrand Russell* (3 vols.,

London, 1967, 1968, 1969), *My Philosophical Development* (London, 1959), *Portraits from Memory* (London, 1956), and *The Amberley Papers*, with Patricia Russell (2 vols., London, 1937).

R. Crawshay-Williams, *Russell Remembered* (Oxford, 1970), G. H. Hardy, *Bertrand Russell and Trinity* (Cambridge, 1970) and Alan Wood, *Bertrand Russell, the Passionate Sceptic* (London, 1970) are biographical. See also Wood's 'Russell's Philosophy', in *Russell* (London, 1959), pp. 189–205. David Pears locates the ideas of the early Russell (1905–19) in their philosophical context in his excellent *Bertrand Russell and the British Tradition in Philosophy* (London, 1972).

2. I mean that once we have described phenomenological red there does not seem conceptual room to mention the sensation of phenomenological red, any more than once one has described what a pain feels like there is conceptual room to describe the sensation of it. If we describe colour or pain (only) physiologically, then clearly this conceptual room remains.

3. Sense data are unfashionable postulates in the theory of perception at the time of writing. It is usually thought, on quasi-Kantian grounds, that any perceptual input to the subject is conceptually ordered by that subject in such a way as to preclude the input being truly characterized as a 'datum' ('given'). The content of perception – what is perceived – is determined by the sense organs, neurology and perhaps the language of the subject, and so not simply and passively received. If the quasi-Kantian view is true it still seems to me that the rejection of sense data is too hasty. Something is given in perception as its content, even if this is partly made what it is by facts about the subject. We may then use 'sense data' to denote what appears to the subject just as it appears to the subject. For more by Russell on sense data, see 'The Relation of Sense-Data to Physics' in his *Mysticism and Logic* (Harmondsworth, 1953), pp. 139–71, and his 'Reply to Criticisms' in P. A. Schilpp (ed.), *The Philosophy of Bertrand Russell* (Chicago, 1944). On the sense-data debate, see W. P. Alston, 'Is a Sense-Datum Language Necessary?', *Philosophy of Science*, 24 (1957), pp. 41–5; J. L. Austin, *Sense and Sensibilia* (Oxford, 1962); A. J. Ayer, 'Has Austin Refuted the Sense-Datum Theory?', *Synthese*, 17 (1967), pp. 117–40; Max Black, 'The Language of Sense-Data' in his *Problems of Analysis* (New York, 1946); Ludwig Wittgenstein, 'Notes for Lectures on "Private Experience" and "Sense-Data"', *Philosophical Review*, 77 (1968), pp. 275, 320; Charles Taylor, 'Sense Data Revisited', in G. F. Macdonald (ed.), *Perception and Identity: Essays Presented to A. J. Ayer* (New York, 1979), pp. 99–112.

4. On acquaintance, see also Russell's 'On the Nature of Acquaintance' in his *Logic and Knowledge* (London, 1971), pp. 125–74, and his 'Knowledge by Acquaintance and Knowledge by Description', in Russell, op. cit.

(1953), pp. 197–218. For Russell's epistemology, see A. J. Ayer, *Russell* (London, 1972), Chapter 3, 'Russell's Theory of Knowledge', pp. 72–102; also Russell's *An Inquiry into Meaning and Truth* (Harmondsworth, 1973), pp. 9, 18, 45ff., 110ff., 116ff., 132, 135–6, 223ff., 270ff., 281, 296, 322ff. On propositions, see Russell's 'On Propositions: what they are and how they mean', in Russell, op. cit. (1971), pp. 283–320, and Russell, op. cit. (1973), pp. 10, 15ff., 32–3, 38, 43–4, 48ff., 54ff., 61, 77, 81ff., 85ff., 130–41, 144ff., 158ff., 228–38, 244–52, 259–64, 283–308. On Russell's early epistemology, see Pears, op. cit. (1972), *passim*, but especially Chapters 3, 6 and 11 (pp. 32–42, 71–96 and 174–96).

5. See 'Hume', section 7, in the present work.

6. On Russell on induction, see Paul Edwards, 'Russell's Doubts About Induction', in Richard Swinburne (ed.), *The Justification of Induction* (Oxford, 1974), pp. 26–47; Pears, op. cit. (1972), pp. 259–63; Ayer, op. cit. (1972), pp. 93–102; Russell, op. cit. (1973), pp. 72, 76ff., 84ff., 220–21, 236ff., 270–71, 285ff., 297–8; and Russell, *An Outline of Philosophy* (London, 1970), pp. 83ff., 279ff., 280ff.

7. Plato, *The Republic*, translated by Desmond Lee (Harmondsworth, 1977), Part VII, pp. 260–325.

8. See also 'On the Relations of Universals and Particulars', in Russell, op. cit. (1971), pp. 103–24, and Russell, op. cit. (1973), pp. 22, 34, 90, 296, 324, 327ff. A thoroughly anti-Platonic theory of universals is developed by David Armstrong in his *Universals and Scientific Realism* (2 vols., Cambridge, 1978), and *What is a Law of Nature?* (Cambridge, 1983), especially Part II, pp. 78ff. Renford Bambrough thinks that Wittgenstein solved the problem of universals. See his 'Universals and Family Resemblances', *Proceedings of the Aristotelian Society*, LX (1960–61), reprinted in G. Pitcher, *Wittgenstein: A Collection of Critical Essays* (London, 1968), pp. 186–204. See also M. J. Loux (ed.), *Universals and Particulars* (New York, 1970); a useful collection.

9. Russell's sustained treatments of this problem are *The Analysis of Mind* (London, 1921) and *The Analysis of Matter* (London, 1927). For an introduction to Russell on mind and matter, see Ayer, op. cit. (1972), pp. 111–15, and Stephen Priest, *Theories of the Mind* (Penguin Books, forthcoming).

10. Russell probably has in mind his idealist opponents F. H. Bradley (1846–1924) and Bernard Bosanquet (1848–1923). See Bradley's *Appearance and Reality: A Metaphysical Essay* (London, 1902) and Bosanquet's *The Principle of Individuality and Value* (London, 1912). Both idealists are profoundly influenced by Hegel's holism. For Hegel, see *Hegel's Phenomenology of Spirit*, translated by A. V. Miller (Oxford, 1979), especially 'Absolute Knowing', pp. 479–94. The best introduction to Hegel is Richard Norman's *Hegel's Phenomenology* (Sussex, 1976).

11. Russell's logical atomism should be studied in conjunction with that of Wittgenstein for the light they shed on one another. See L. Wittgenstein, *Tractatus Logico-Philosophicus*, translated by D. F. Pears and B. F. McGuiness (London, 1961). On Russell's logical atomism, see David Pears's Introduction to *Russell's Logical Atomism*, pp. 7–30; also Pears, op. cit. (1972), pp. 16–17, 48, 59, 119, 160, 173, and Ayer, op. cit. (1972), Chapter 4, pp. 103–111. On Wittgenstein's logical atomism, and its relation to Russell's, see Anthony Kenny, *Wittgenstein* (Harmondsworth, 1979), especially Chapters 5 and 6, pp. 72–119; David Pears, *Wittgenstein* (London, 1974), pp. 55ff.; and Pears, op. cit. (1972), pp. 59, 141, 144–5, 147–58.

12. William P. Alston, *Philosophy of Language* (N.J., 1964), contains introductions to the referential and other theories of meaning (see p. 10ff.).

13. On the theory of descriptions, see Ayer, op. cit. (1972), pp. 52–62, and Pears, op. cit. (1972), pp. 14, 17, 23–4, 49–52, 68–70, 101–15, 121–6, 221, 243.

14. See Russell, *An Inquiry into Meaning and Truth*, Chapters 16, 17 and 21, and Pears, op. cit. (1972), pp. 32, 97, 174ff., 179–93. See also Russell, *The Problems of Philosophy*, pp. 119–30.

15. On the philosophy of mathematics, see Jean van Heijenoort (ed.), *From Frege to Gödel: A Source Book in Mathematical Logic 1879–1931* (Harvard, 1967), and Paul Benacerraf and Hilary Putnam (eds.), *Philosophy of Mathematics: Selected Readings* (N.J., 1964).

16. See Kurt Gödel, *On Formally Undecidable Propositions* (New York, 1962), which is a translation of Gödel's 1931 paper 'Über Formal Unentscheidbare Sätze der "Principia Mathematica" und Verwandter Systeme, I', *Monatshefte für Mathematik und Physik*, 38 (1931), pp. 173–98. For a non-mathematical introduction to Gödel, see Raymond Smullyan, *Forever Undecided* (Oxford, 1988).

17. Introductions to mathematical logic are legion. W. H. Newton-Smith, *Logic: An Introductory Course* (London, 1985) is more elementary than E. J. Lemmon, *Beginning Logic* (London, 1971).

18. See also 'On the Notion of Cause' in Russell, op. cit. (1953), pp. 171–96, and Russell, op. cit. (1927), especially Chapters 30, 31 and 35.

19. 'Ayer', section 2, in the present work.

20. Russell confronts the Catholic philosopher Frederick Copleston over the existence of God in 'A Debate on the Existence of God', in John Hick (ed.), *The Existence of God* (London, 1964); also in Russell's *Why I am not a Christian*, pp. 133–53. Hick's volume is a useful anthology of arguments for and against God's existence.

Ayer

1. See A. J. Ayer, *Language, Truth and Logic* (2nd ed., Harmondsworth, 1976). Ayer added an Introduction to the second edition, which appeared ten years after the first edition, in 1946. I strongly advise the reader to read this introduction only after reading the main body of the text, because 'introduction' is something of a misnomer here. It is Ayer's defence against criticism and is largely unintelligible without prior acquaintance with the book.

2. The most useful survey of the movement is Leszek Kolakowski's *Logical Positivism* (Harmondsworth, 1972). For a forceful summary of its central tenets, see Herbert Feigl, 'Logical Empiricism', in D. D. Runes (ed.), *Twentieth-Century Philosophy* (Philosophical Library, New York, 1943), reprinted in H. Feigl and W. Sellars (eds.), *Readings in Philosophical Analysis* (New York, 1949), pp. 3–26.

3. See Plato, *The Republic*, translated by Desmond Lee (Harmondsworth, 1977), Books VI–VII, especially pp. 299–325; Hegel's *Phenomenology of Spirit*, translated by A. V. Miller (Oxford, 1979), Chapter 8, 'Absolute Knowing', pp. 479–93; G. H. R. Parkinson (ed.), *Leibniz: Philosophical Writings*, translated by Mary Morris and G. H. R. Parkinson (London, 1984), 'Monadology', pp. 179–94. Plato, Leibniz and Hegel are ably discussed by Father Frederick Copleston in his *A History of Western Philosophy* (New York, 1963), in Vols. 1, 4 and 7 respectively. On materialist and idealist metaphysics, see Stephen Priest, *Theories of the Mind* (Penguin Books, forthcoming).

4. According to Ayer, 'Heidegger ... bases his metaphysics on the assumption that "Nothing" is a name which is used to denote something peculiarly mysterious' (*Language, Truth and Logic*, p. 59). This assumption involves two kinds of mistake: the error of assuming that all nouns denote entities or 'things', and the error of using a vocabulary in a fashion which precludes its translation into a set of primitive empirical concepts. The claim that nouns, or pronouns, may mislead the thinker into the postulation of illusory metaphysical objects is a leitmotif of empiricist and critical philosophy. It is to be discerned, for example, in Berkeley's critique of Locke's doctrine of abstract ideas, Kant's attack on the Cartesian theory of the soul, Wittgenstein's Private Language Argument, and Ryle's notion of a category mistake. See Berkeley, *The Principles of Human Knowledge* (London, 1977), pp. 57–9, and pp. 116–19 of the present work. See also Kant's *Critique of Pure Reason*, op. cit., 'Transcendental Dialectic', Chapter 1, 'paralogisms', pp. 328–83; Wittgenstein, *Philosophical Investigations*, op. cit., paras. 243ff.; Gilbert Ryle, *The Concept of Mind*, op. cit., Chapter 1,

'Descartes' Myth', section 3, 'The Absurdity of the Official Doctrine', pp. 15–18, and 'The Origin of the Category Mistake', pp. 18–23. The idea that any meaningful term must ultimately and in principle be translatable into some empirical term or terms is discussed on pp. 30–31 of the present work. It is anticipated by Hobbes.

In his criticism of Heidegger, Ayer is influenced by Rudolf Carnap in his 'Überwindung der Metaphysik durch logische Analyse der Sprache', *Erkenntnis*, II (1932). It seems to me that Heidegger is at pains *not* to reify 'nothingness', at least in *Being and Time*, and Heidegger was of course steeped in pre-Socratic writings and would have been fully apprised of the Parmenidean view that nothingness does not exist. I have in mind Heidegger's claim that nothing ('Nichts') is the object of anxiety, but that 'That in the face of which one has anxiety is not an entity within-the-world' (Martin Heidegger, *Being and Time*, translated by J. Macquarrie and E. Robinson (Oxford, 1973), p. 231). Ayer and Carnap, however, have in mind the use of 'nothing' in Heidegger's essay 'What is Metaphysics?'. (See D. F. Krell (ed.), *Martin Heidegger: Basic Writings* (London, 1978), pp. 91–112.) For Heidegger's use of 'nothing', see *Being and Time*, op. cit., pp. 43, 128, 186–9, 266, 273, 276f., 279, 308, 341, 343, 352; for 'not-Being' ('Nichtsein'), see pp. 170, 243, 431, 434; for 'notness' ('Nichtheit'), see pp. 285ff.; and for 'the "not"' ('das Nicht'), see pp. 29, 283–6. References are to Macquarrie and Robinson's marginal numbers taken from the later German editions of *Sein und Zeit*.

5. Philosophers who, according to Ayer, were largely engaged in philosophical analysis rather than metaphysics include Plato, Aristotle, Hobbes, Locke, Berkeley, Hume, Kant, Mill and Bentham (*Language, Truth and Logic*, op. cit., pp. 70–75). A clear-cut case of a philosopher whose utterances are neither empirically verifiable nor analytic is the British neo-Hegelian idealist philosopher, F. H. Bradley. Quoting 'at random' from Bradley's *Appearance and Reality*, Ayer says: 'Such a metaphysical pseudo-proposition as "the Absolute enters into, but is itself incapable of, evolution and progress" is not even in principle verifiable' (ibid., p. 49). For Bradley's use of the term 'Absolute', see his *Appearance and Reality: A Metaphysical Essay* (London, 1902), pp. 144, 159, 172, 182, 195, 204, 411–12, 487–9, 519ff., 536ff., 556.

6. The best introduction to Wittgenstein's philosophy is Anthony Kenny's *Wittgenstein* (Harmondsworth, 1973). For Ryle, see note 4, above.

7. My biographical remarks on Ayer are based on the two volumes of his autobiography, *Part of My Life* (Oxford, 1977) and *More of My Life* (Oxford, 1985).

8. See notes 3 and 4 above. Spinoza's thesis that only one substance

exists, and that it has two attributes, thought and extension, is argued for in his *Ethics*, translated by A. Boyle (London, 1948), especially pp. 38–40.

9. Clearly, then, logical positivism is a kind of radical empiricism. Ayer's claim that a sentence is meaningful only if the proposition it expresses is either analytic and *a priori* or synthetic and *a posteriori* is semantically similar to Hume's distinction between 'relations of ideas' and 'matters of fact' (*Hume's Enquiries*, ed. L. A. Selby-Bigge and P. H. Nidditch (Oxford, 1975), IV, 1, p. 25). Notice too that relations of ideas for Hume and *a priori* truths for Ayer are necessary, and that matters of fact for Hume and *a posteriori* claims for Ayer are contingent. For Hume as well as Ayer, the consequences for some putative claim which falls into neither logical category are devastating. Hume invites us to inspect the sentences of any book of 'divinity' or 'metaphysics' and decide whether it contains 'any abstract reasoning concerning quantity or number' or 'any experimental reasoning concerning matter of fact and existence'. If the answer is 'no', then Hume's advice is 'Commit it to the flames: for it can contain nothing but sophistry and illusion' (E XII, III, 165). Notice that Hume is so confident of his empiricism that he recommends book-burning – something characteristic of the associates of Heidegger rather than Mill and Ayer. Hume's intolerance is misplaced on at least three counts: he might be wrong and the views he burns might be true. If he is right and the views he burns are false or meaningless, it is not clearly morally right to deny people the right to hold views which are mistaken or meaningless. Finally, it is educative to understand empathetically views which are not one's own, irrespective of their truth value or meaningfulness. At worst, one's own truths are tested against falsity and nonsense. Notice that Ayer cannot consistently share Hume's practical intolerance. This is not just because of Ayer's liberal politics but also because Ayer thinks it is always in principle possible that we could be mistaken (except, maybe, about logical truths).

10. Moritz Schlick says: 'Stating the meaning of a sentence amounts to stating the rules according to which the sentence is to be used, and this is the same as stating the way in which it can be verified (or falsified). The meaning of a proposition is the method of its verification' ('Meaning and Verification', in H. Feigl and W. Sellars (eds.), *Readings in Philosophical Analysis* (New York, 1949), p. 148).

11. The merits of the verification principle are debated critically by Sir Isaiah Berlin in 'Verification', and the verification principle is defended by Friedrich Waismann in 'Verifiability', both in G. H. R. Parkinson (ed.), *The Theory of Meaning* (Oxford, 1976), pp. 15–34 and 35–60 respectively. Berlin brings three broad objections to verificationism. He suggests that it must be possible to understand a sentence in order to decide whether it is

the sort of sentence that could be verified or falsified. Hence, meaning is prior to, and so not the same as, possibility of verification. Secondly, he doubts that sentences about the past or future may be wholly translated into sentences about the present (in particular because this generates two senses of 'present'). Thirdly, he claims there are meaningful sentences which are not verifiable even in principle: universal generalizations, unfulfilled singular hypothetical statements, and statements about physical objects and other minds. Ayer defends verificationism against its critics in the Introduction to the second edition of *Language, Truth and Logic*, op. cit., pp. 7–35.

12. *Language, Truth and Logic*, op. cit., p. 70.

13. Ayer's phenomenalism is in the tradition of that of Mill and Russell. See the chapters 'Mill' and 'Russell' in the present work, pp. 189 and 211–13 respectively. Ayer devotes Chapter 3 of *The Problem of Knowledge* (Harmondsworth, 1956) to the philosophy of perception (pp. 84–133). This chapter is an improvement on the more rudimentary epistemological discussion in his *The Foundations of Empirical Knowledge* (London, 1940).

14. See the chapter 'Hume' in the present work, pp. 146–9.

15. The papers in Richard Swinburne (ed.), *The Justification of Induction* (Oxford, 1974), largely treat the problem as genuine. Ayer emphasizes the centrality of induction to our commonsensical and scientific conceptual schemes in Chapter 7, section A, of *The Central Questions of Philosophy* (London, 1973), pp. 137–9.

16. It follows that the commonsensical distinction between mental and physical is meaningful, even if, say, Descartes's metaphysical distinction between mental and physical substance is meaningless. It is not quite right then to say, as Jacques Bouveresse does, that 'La démarcation entre la science et la métaphysique est la même que celle qui existe entre le sens et le non-sens (cognitifs)' (Jacques Bouveresse, 'Le Positivisme Logique', in François Chatelet (ed.), *La Philosophie au XXe Siècle* (Paris, 1979), p. 82). To suggest that the science–metaphysics distinction is identical with the meaningful–meaningless distinction misleadingly conceals the meaningfulness of commonsense, even though the world of commonsense is not numerically distinct from the objects of science for the logical positivists. Bouveresse is clearly right to imply that the sentences of science are meaningful and the sentences of metaphysics meaningless on the logical positivists' account.

17. Descartes, 'Meditations on First Philosophy', in Anscombe and Geach (eds.), *Descartes: Philosophical Writings*, op. cit., especially the Second and Sixth Meditations (pp. 61–5 and 109–24).

18. See *The Problem of Knowledge*, op. cit., Chapter 5, pp. 176ff., and *The*

Central Questions of Philosophy, op. cit., Chapter 6, especially pp. 112–32. For a materialist and a dualist alternative to Ayer's phenomenalist theory of the self, see respectively the papers by Sydney Shoemaker and Richard Swinburne in their *Personal Identity* (Oxford, 1984).

19. Here it looks as though Ayer is a materialist about personal identity, i.e. subscribes to the view that B at t_2 is numerically identical with A at t_1 if, and only if, B is a body which is spatio-temporally continuous with a body A at t_1. Ayer does hold something like this, but it should be remembered that physical objects are logical constructions out of sense contents for Ayer. There is a *prima facie* problem of circularity here. To establish what the identity of the person over time consists in, we need good criteria for the identity of physical objects. But to obtain criteria for the identity of physical objects we need good criteria for a set of sense contents being logical constituents of one and the same physical object, and that in turn may require good criteria for distinguishing the sense contents of more than one subject. If that is right, then criteria for personal identity are needed to establish the identity of physical objects, and criteria for the identity of physical objects are needed to establish personal identity. So far as I can see, Ayer offers us no escape from this difficulty. I am not saying one could not be devised.

20. For a lucid and philosophically sophisticated defence of the existence of God, see Richard Swinburne's trilogy *The Coherence of Theism* (Oxford, 1977), *The Existence of God* (Oxford, 1979) and *Faith and Reason* (Oxford, 1981). In *The Coherence of Theism* Swinburne is particularly concerned to defend theism against the charge that religious language is nonsensical.

FURTHER READING

In the case of each philosopher I mention first a standard edition of his works, then some readily available editions of his most influential writings, and finally secondary literature.

Hobbes

STANDARD EDITION

William Molesworth (ed.), *The English Works of Thomas Hobbes* (London, 1839), and *Opera Latina* (London, 1845)

READILY AVAILABLE EDITION

C. B. Macpherson (ed.), *Leviathan* by Thomas Hobbes (Harmondsworth, 1985)

SECONDARY LITERATURE

M. Oakeshott, *Hobbes on Civil Association* (Oxford, 1975)

Richard Peters, *Hobbes* (Harmondsworth, 1956)

D. D. Raphael, *Hobbes: Morals and Politics* (London, 1977)

G. A. J. Rogers and Alan Ryan (eds.), *Perspectives on Thomas Hobbes* (Oxford, 1988)

Quentin Skinner, 'The Ideological Context of Hobbes' Political Thought', *Historical Journal*, 9 (1966)

T. Sorell, *Hobbes* (London, 1986)

Keith Thomas, 'The Social Origins of Hobbes' Political Thought', in K. C. Brown (ed.), *Hobbes Studies* (Oxford, 1965)

H. Warrender, *The Political Philosophy of Hobbes* (Oxford, 1957)

Locke

STANDARD EDITION
Peter Nidditch and E. S. de Beer (eds.), *The Clarendon Edition of the Works of John Locke* (Oxford 1976–)

READILY AVAILABLE EDITIONS
Peter Laslett (ed.), *Two Treatises of Government* by John Locke (Cambridge, 1960)
A. S. Pringle-Pattison (ed.), *An Essay Concerning Human Understanding* by John Locke (Oxford, 1950)

SECONDARY LITERATURE
Richard I. Aaron, *John Locke* (Oxford, 1971)
Jonathan Bennett, *Locke, Berkeley, Hume: Central Themes* (Oxford, 1977), especially Chapters 1–5
John Dunn, *The Political Thought of John Locke* (Cambridge, 1982)
John Dunn, *Locke* (Oxford, 1984)
J. L. Mackie, *Problems from Locke* (Oxford, 1976)
C. B. Martin and D. M. Armstrong (eds.), *Locke and Berkeley: A Collection of Critical Essays* (London, 1968)
Geraint Parry, *John Locke* (London, 1978)
I. C. Tipton (ed.), *Locke on Human Understanding* (Oxford, 1977)
John W. Yolton (ed.), *John Locke: Problems and Perspectives* (Cambridge, 1969)
John W. Yolton, *Locke and the Compass of Human Understanding* (Cambridge, 1970)

Berkeley

STANDARD EDITION
A. A. Luce and T. E. Jessop (eds.), *The Works of George Berkeley* (9 vols., Edinburgh, 1948–57)

READILY AVAILABLE EDITION
G. J. Warnock (ed.), *The Principles of Human Knowledge with Other Writings* by George Berkeley (London, 1977)

SECONDARY LITERATURE
Jonathan Bennett, *Locke, Berkeley, Hume: Central Themes* (Oxford, 1977), especially Chapters 5–8

John Foster and Howard Robinson (eds.), *Essays on Berkeley: A Tercentennial Celebration* (Oxford, 1988)

C. B. Martin and D. M. Armstrong (eds.), *Locke and Berkeley: A Collection of Critical Essays* (London, 1968)

George Pitcher, *Berkeley* (London, 1977)

I. C. Tipton, *Berkeley: The Philosophy of Immaterialism* (London, 1976)

J. O. Urmson, *Berkeley* (Oxford, 1982)

G. J. Warnock, *Berkeley* (Harmondsworth, 1953)

Hume

STANDARD EDITION

T. H. Green and T. H. Grose (eds.), *The Philosophical Works of David Hume* (4 vols., London, 1964)

READILY AVAILABLE EDITIONS

Norman Kemp-Smith (ed.), *Hume's Dialogues Concerning Natural Religion* (Indianapolis, 1962)

L. A. Selby-Bigge (ed.), *A Treatise of Human Nature* (Oxford, 1955)

L. A. Selby-Bigge (ed.), *Enquiries Concerning Human Understanding and Concerning the Principles of Morals* (Oxford, 1955)

SECONDARY LITERATURE

A. J. Ayer, *Hume* (Oxford, 1980)

Jonathan Bennett, *Locke, Berkeley, Hume: Central Themes* (Oxford, 1977), especially Chapters 9–13

V. C. Chappell (ed.), *Hume: A Collection of Critical Essays* (London, 1968)

A. G. N. Flew, *Hume's Philosophy of Belief* (London, 1961)

Jonathan Harrison, *Hume's Moral Epistemology* (Oxford, 1976)

Jonathan Harrison, *Hume's Theory of Justice* (Oxford, 1981)

Norman Kemp-Smith, *The Philosophy of David Hume* (London, 1949)

D. F. Pears (ed.), *David Hume: A Symposium* (London, 1963)

H. H. Price, *Hume's Theory of the External World* (Oxford, 1940)

Barry Stroud, *Hume* (London, 1977)

Mill

STANDARD EDITION

The Collected Works of John Stuart Mill (Toronto, 1965–)

READILY AVAILABLE EDITIONS

D. Winch (ed.), *Principles of Political Economy* by John Stuart Mill (Harmondsworth, 1970)

M. Warnock (ed.), *Utilitarianism, On Liberty, Essay on Bentham* by John Stuart Mill (London, 1973)

SECONDARY LITERATURE

Karl Britton, *John Stuart Mill* (Harmondsworth, 1953)

J. Gray, *Mill on Liberty: A Defence* (London, 1983)

R. J. Halliday, *John Stuart Mill* (London, 1976)

John Plamenatz, *Mill's Utilitarianism* (Oxford, 1949)

Alan Ryan, *John Stuart Mill* (London, 1975)

J. B. Schneewind, *Mill: A Collection of Critical Essays* (London, 1969)

C. L. Ten, *Mill on Liberty* (Oxford, 1980)

Russell

NO STANDARD EDITION

READILY AVAILABLE EDITIONS

Bertrand Russell, *The Principles of Mathematics* (London, 1937)

Bertrand Russell and A. N. Whitehead, *Principia Mathematica* (3 vols., Cambridge, 1910, 1912, 1913)

Bertrand Russell, *The Problems of Philosophy* (London, 1946)

Bertrand Russell, *An Outline of Philosophy* (London, 1970)

Bertrand Russell, *Our Knowledge of the External World* (London, 1926)

Bertrand Russell, *Mysticism and Logic* (London, 1929)

Bertrand Russell, *The Analysis of Mind* (London, 1921)

Bertrand Russell, *The Analysis of Matter* (London, 1927)

Bertrand Russell, *An Inquiry into Meaning and Truth* (Harmondsworth, 1973)

Bertrand Russell, *A History of Western Philosophy* (London, 1945)

Bertrand Russell, *Human Knowledge: Its Scope and Limits* (London, 1948)

SECONDARY LITERATURE

A. J. Ayer, *Russell and Moore: The Analytical Heritage* (London, 1971)

A. J. Ayer, *Russell* (London, 1972)

D. F. Pears, *Bertrand Russell and the British Tradition in Philosophy* (London, 1967)

Mark Sainsbury, *Russell* (London, 1979)

P. Schilpp (ed.), *The Philosophy of Bertrand Russell* (Cambridge, 1944)

Ayer

NO STANDARD EDITION

READILY AVAILABLE EDITIONS
A. J. Ayer, *Language, Truth and Logic*, 2nd ed. (Harmondsworth, 1976)
A. J. Ayer, *The Foundations of Empirical Knowledge* (London, 1961)
A. J. Ayer, *The Problem of Knowledge* (Harmondsworth, 1956)
A. J. Ayer, *The Concept of a Person and Other Essays* (London, 1963)
A. J. Ayer, *Metaphysics and Common Sense* (London, 1969)
A. J. Ayer, *The Central Questions of Philosophy* (London, 1973)

SECONDARY LITERATURE
John Foster, *Ayer* (London, 1985)

INDEX

St Augustine, 265n
St Clair, General, 134
Steinberg, S. H., 249n
Steinkraus, W. E., 265n
Stephen, Leslie, 270n
Stewart, M. A., 259n
Strawson, Sir Peter, 253n, 261n
Stroud, Barry, 266n, 268n, 269n
structure, 85, 86
Stuart, house of, 51
subject, grammatical, 177
subjective view, the, 259n, 263–4n
subjectivity, 44–5; of consciousness,
  68; definition of 'subjective', 109;
  and meaning, 65, 97; and
  numbers, 127–8; of secondary
  qualities, 108–10; of self, *119–22*.
  151; of space and time, 127
subsistence, 211
substance, 70, 73, 78, 79, 80, 84, 99,
  120, 132, 178–9, 189, 233, 260n,
  276–7n; and causation, 99, 179;
  cause of sensation, 179; single
  and collective, 70, 73; Locke on,
  78–80, 84; Mill on, 178
substance: immaterial, 32, 39, 40,
  41, 73, 79, 81, 82; cause of ideas,
  122; God as, *122–5*; soul as, 121;
  Berkeley on, *119–22*
substance, material, 120, 152, 264n;
  meaningless, 110; and causation,
  113–14
substantives, 210
succession, 68, 91, 92, 141, 148,
  152, 179; and motion, 92;
  Berkeley on, 126
superstition, 39, 53
Swenson, D. F., 255n
Swift, Jonathan, 106
Swinburne, Richard, 260n, 268n,
  269n, 273n, 278n, 279n

symbols, 214, 215, 238
'synthetic', definition of, 234

taste, 24, 58, 64, 66, 110, 263–4n;
  in the mind, 109; and other
  cultures, 136; a secondary
  quality, 76
tautology, 58, 143, 216, 217–18,
  234, 240
Taylor, Charles, 272n
telescope, 20
terror, 256n
Test Acts, 51
theatre, mind as a, 152
theism, 27; and empiricism, 123–4;
  and idealism, 263n; meaningless,
  244ff., Berkeley's, *122–5*; Hume
  on, 132, *161–6*
theocentrism, 17
Theocritus, 173
theology, Ayer on, *244–5*
theory ladenness, 254n
Thirty Years War, 18, 45, 249n
Thomas, Keith, 256n
Thomson, David, 249n
thought, 63, 67, 143, 165; free,
  154ff.; freedom of, 194ff.; as
  motion, 34; propositional, 28,
  253n; *de re*, 97; and universals,
  210; Hobbes on, 23–4, 27; Mill
  on, 178
Thucydides, 21, 173, 251n
time, 108, 125; absolute, 92, 125;
  and identity, 83–4; and laws,
  158; mind-dependent, 125–6;
  and temporal things, 92; and
  succession, 68; Locke on, *91–2*;
  Berkeley on, *125–7*; Hume on,
  141–2
timelessness, 211
Tipton, I. C., 264n, 265n